W9-BMB-795

Internet Texas Hold'em

Winning Strategies from an Internet Pro

Revised First Edition

By

Matthew Hilger

Dimat Enterprises, Inc.
www.InternetTexasHoldem.com

Internet Texas Hold'em: Winning Strategies from an Internet Pro.
Copyright © 2003 by Matthew Hilger.
Dimat Enterprises, Inc.

Cover Illustration: Eva Kuczynski
Book Design: Andrew Kuczynski

ISBN 0-9741502-0-7

Dedication

To my amazing wife who displayed incredible patience and gave me tremendous support in my career change from business executive to poker professional.

Acknowledgement

This book could not have been possible without the tremendous help I received from family and friends. I first want to thank my friends and poker buddies Andrew Dimock, Peter Field, and Albert Sands. They each spent countless hours helping me to develop many of the ideas in the book, challenged my thinking, and helped me focus the writing towards the reader.

My family also helped a lot with the book. Dad provided a lot of ideas in how to present some of the material. My stepfather, Monroe, provided many of the low-limit hand examples and gave me ideas on how to improve the structure of the starting hand tables. My mother and sister, Laura, had the glamorous job of proofreading the book for grammar and sentence structure, which is quite a challenge when you don't even play poker.

Finally, I would like to thank all of the poker authors who taught me and challenged me to look at this game from many different perspectives.

Table of Contents

Introduction

"If you can't spot the sucker in your first half-hour at the table, then you are the sucker." This is a common poker saying spoken by Matt Damon in the classic poker movie *Rounders*. I used to play in a tournament every Sunday night in Costa Rica with some of the best players in the world. Unfortunately, I had no idea at the time who those players were! Hopefully this book will help you spot the sucker rather than be the sucker.

It takes a lot of experience and study of the game before one realizes what it takes to play at an advanced level. Everyone needs to start somewhere. This book should increase your learning curve, but there is no substitute for experience. The Internet is an excellent vehicle to develop your game, no matter if you just play low limits a few hours a week or strive to develop into a world-class player. The following story gives you a glimpse into my poker life and the struggles I went through before I started playing on the Internet.

My first memory of poker is sneaking out into the woods when I was about eight or nine years old to play penny poker with my friends. In middle school, I remember getting sent to the principal's office for playing craps in the bathroom. In high school, I was assistant manager at a local movie theater and one night my buddies and I played poker in the projectionist booth while the movies were playing. To my dismay, the manager decided to show up that night to check up on things. Fortunately, the concession girl quickly alerted us. My friends were going down one staircase as my boss was going up the other one! I had no idea that someday this passion would become my profession.

I played very little poker during college except the occasional game with my old high school buddies. During my first real job with Andersen Consulting, I worked on projects that lasted months at a time, and we soon found a way to get a weekly poker game going playing the typical wild home games.

After a few years with Andersen, I decided to move to Phoenix to get a Master's degree in International Business. I soon discovered the local Indian reservations where I first played Texas Hold'em. I would go and play $4-$8 Hold'em every few weeks and managed a small profit. After graduating, I went to work for Chiquita Brands International at their headquarters in Cincinnati and my poker life was again put on hold.

After a year and a half, Chiquita transferred me to Costa Rica. This is where I discovered the thrill of poker tournaments and no-limit Hold'em. They had small poker tournaments every Tuesday and Thursday night. I had no idea how to play tournaments and especially no idea how to play no-limit Hold'em but I soon learned! I then discovered a Hold'em club that had a tournament every Sunday night. These players were a little more serious and the tournament was a little more expensive. The buy-in was cheap, but Costa Rica has made a name for itself in the poker community with its crazy *rebuy* tournaments (some players would rebuy over 20 times).

I slowly improved each and every month. Fortunately, I didn't lose so much the first six months to make me want to quit. Suddenly, I got on a nice streak and won three of the small Tuesday/Thursday night tournaments in a row! These tournaments only had between 16 and 24 players, but winning three in a row gave me a lot of confidence.

I was still struggling however at the Hold'em Club on Sunday nights. These tournaments had up to 40 entrants and typically paid a couple grand to the winner. A lot of the players seemed to have a lot of experience, so it was difficult to compete. But about eight months after I first started playing tournaments, I posted my first big win. Then the next week I finished second! Finally, I felt like I was starting to understand the game.

This story about the Hold'em Club shows just how little I knew about poker, but also how I was able to gain some great experience to develop my game. I thought these players at the Hold'em Club were just a bunch of rich Ticos (Costa Ricans) who enjoyed a nice game of poker on Sunday nights. It wasn't until *after* I moved from Costa Rica when I found out that I was playing against some of the top poker players in the world.

Some of the players included Humberto Brenes, who has won more than $1.0 million in prize money at the World Series of Poker (WSOP) and was the 2002 World Poker Open champion, which paid a $500,000 top prize. His brother Alex Brenes is also a successful player in U.S. tourneys. Another top player was Dr. Max Stern who has won the WSOP 7-Card Stud championship and is the author of a poker book. Jose Rosenkrantz won a World Poker Tour title televised on the Travel channel and has placed in several events at the World Series of Poker. My Spanish wasn't very good at the time, so I guess I missed them talking about all of their poker successes in the states. Talk about a sucker! I probably never would have walked into that club if I had known whom I was up against.

Although those tournaments were a struggle for me starting out, they gave me a tremendous amount of experience. The smaller tournaments during the week prepared me for the larger tournaments on Sunday, which gave me invaluable experience playing with some of the best players in the world. I finished the year posting a small win, so it was a great learning experience, a lot of fun, and a little profitable.

In early 2000, Bristol-Myers Squibb transferred me to Argentina. Unfortunately, Argentina does not have any live poker, so I thought my poker game was again on hold until I heard about Internet poker. At first I was skeptical, since I had always thought of poker as more of a game inter-acting with other people; however, I downloaded a site and was impressed by the graphics, chat feature, and overall feel of the game.

I decided that I needed to get a piece of the action, so I took the plunge and made my first deposit of $600 at an Internet poker site. Within a few weeks I had won over $5000! I was officially hooked and soon poker would be changing my life in a big way.

However, I was fortunate that I got a good run of cards the first few months I played. I realize now that I was playing at limits too high in relation to my bankroll (more about this in the "Bankroll Management" chapter). I easily could have lost the small bankroll I had if I had run into some poor cards. But even though I was winning, I knew I had a great deal to learn. I started reading every book I could find and studied the game as much as I could. The quality of my play really improved a lot in those first six months.

I soon found myself bored in my day job, and couldn't wait to get home to my newfound passion. Eventually, I decided to give up my six-figure income job, hang my two master's degrees on the wall, and was on my way to New Zealand to become an Internet poker pro!

Everyone needs to start somewhere. My story took me around the world before this "successful" home player really began to understand the game. Whether you are going to be playing this game just a few hours a week, or whether you strive to make poker a second or main income, it makes sense to study the game. Combining study with experience should make poker more enjoyable by making it that much more profitable.

About this Book

This book is a comprehensive tool for players at all levels to be *successful* at limit Texas Hold'em on the Internet. Hopefully the material in this book will help beginners to not make some of the same mistakes I did when starting out. There is also a lot of discussion of advanced concepts and strategies for those wanting to take their game to another level.

A comprehensive overview of Texas Hold'em is presented including general poker concepts such as probability and odds, bluffing, raising and check-raising. Various deceptive tactics are also discussed such as free cards, slow-playing, and inducing bluffs and calls. You'll learn the correct strategies for starting hand play as well as playing on the flop, turn, and river. You'll learn the intricacies of playing on the Internet and the differences in strategies between Internet and live play. Finally, you'll be able to practice all of these strategies on over 200 actual Internet hands.

I have proven that these strategies work through more than 7000 hours of actual play on the Internet. Practically all of the strategies presented in the book regarding Hold'em should also be suitable for the live poker game; however, differences are noted throughout the text between online and live games that require adjustments to your play.

In reading any poker book, you should realize that there are many different strategies and styles of poker. Most good players play a *tight* game, which means they do not play very many hands. Some good players, although much less common, are able to play a *loose* game, which means they play a decent amount of hands. My approach is "tight aggressive," which basically means being conservative with how many hands I play and playing aggressively once I find a hand I like. I believe this is the best approach for the majority of players and especially beginners.

"Test Your Skills"

At the end of each chapter is a chapter summary and a section "Test Your Skills" where you can practice the strategies you have learned with actual hands from the Internet. The basic format is that you will be presented with a sequence of events that have occurred during a hand and then you must decide what you would do next.

Most of the examples come from the higher limits, although you will see some hands from the lower limits. The strategies at both the limits are similar once you have a good understanding of how the number and type of players in a hand relate to strategy and strength of hand. I have played in some $3-$6 games tougher than some of the $20-$40 games I have played. There are some really good players who only play at the lower limits, while at the same time there are plenty of really poor players who play at $20-$40. Sometimes it is more difficult to "read" your opponents at the lower levels since they generally make more mistakes. Nevertheless, I believe all of the examples are relevant and helpful no matter what limit you are playing as long as you keep in mind the number and type of players you are playing against.

When reading through the problems, it is important to realize that the play of the particular player is not always correct but usually reasonable. Nevertheless, the question will guide you through the hand and then ask what you would do next given the sequence of events, even though you may not agree with all of the player's moves up to that point.

For each question, I give my recommended "answer" to the problem. To best improve your game, answer the problems yourself before reading my answer and explanation. My answers are meant to demonstrate the best strategy to use *most* of the time against *typical* opponents. The typical opponent in these examples is neither a **shark** nor a **fish** unless otherwise indicated. Sometimes there are situations where I would raise about 60% of the time and call 40% of the time. For example, raising in a certain situation might have a profit expectation of $10 on average while calling only $5; therefore, raising would be my "answer," but sometimes I might call to mix up my play depending on the type of opponent and particular situation of the flow of the game. In either situation, raising or calling are both profitable, but my answer would be to raise since this is more profitable.

Hold'em is a complex game and there are many situations that don't have clear-cut answers. For example, you could present a certain situation to 100 poker professionals and 1/3 might fold, 1/3 might call, and 1/3 might raise. Most of the questions in the book are pretty clear, but there are some that have answers that are very close. I present these types of problems mainly to guide you in your thinking process. I will usually indicate if two answers are very close to show and explain the different alternatives.

Some Definitions

In almost all Hold'em decisions, your position and the position of your opponents can have a big impact on the strategies you decide to use. *Position* refers to the order in which a player has to act. Your position will change each hand as the "button" is moved around the table. In a ten-handed Hold'em game, early position is defined as the first three players to the left of the big blind, middle position is the next three players, and late position consists of the last two players. The first player to act in early position is said to be *under the gun*. The player in seat 10 is often referred to as the *button* or *dealer*. The player before the button is often called the *cutoff*.

Note the order of seats and position below:
- Seat 1   Small Blind
- Seat 2   Big Blind
- Seat 3   Early Position - Also known as *under the gun*
- Seat 4   Early Position
- Seat 5   Early Position
- Seat 6   Middle Position
- Seat 7   Middle Position
- Seat 8   Middle Position
- Seat 9   Late Position - Also know as the *cutoff*
- Seat 10   Late position - Also known as the *button* or *dealer*

Learn these positions well as they will be referred to throughout the text. Once the flop is dealt, position is used as a relative term to describe when you have to act. For example, if you are in the small blind, you are acting in "early" position after the flop since you must act first. A player sitting in seat 5 could be acting in "late" position if he is the last player who has to act.

There is a glossary in the back of the text if you come across a term that you do not understand.

One note about the use of the pronoun "he." For simplicity, I use "he" throughout the text to refer to all players of both sexes.

This book is meant to be read and studied many times. You will find that as you gain more experience, you will be able to better understand some of the concepts with each new reading of the book. Hopefully it will serve as a reference to your play for many years to come.

The Skill of Poker

Poker is a game of skill. This is not easy to explain to people who do not understand the game, but good poker players will win the money.

Good Poker Players = The MONEY

However, there is one huge caveat in this equation. That caveat is *time*. Good poker players will win the money given enough time.

Good Poker Players = The MONEY...given TIME

In any one hand, the odds are pretty even for everybody. Over an hour, the better poker players have a little advantage, but could easily lose a lot. In a session of eight hours, a good poker player will win the majority of the time, but not all the time. If a good poker player plays 100 hours of $20-$40 limit Hold'em, he could win as much as $20,000, but once in a blue moon he might lose $10,000. A good poker player could only *break even* after 1400 hours of play. Given any time below that, he could possibly lose.

As you can see, a good poker player will win given enough time, but it may not be as easy as it seems in a short time period. Granted, these are extreme cases, but they can happen. What happens in between the extremes is a lot of short-term fluctuations, which can frequently last several days, sometimes several weeks, and even several months. We will talk more about these fluctuations in the "Bankroll Management" chapter.

It is important to realize that there are subtle differences between a good poker player and a bad one that take effect over time. The beauty of poker is that the bad players always remember the times they had some good short-term luck, so they keep coming back for more until they eventually go broke.

However, understanding how to play good poker is not enough to win the money. You must APPLY this knowledge at all times. Poker is a fun and exhilarating game, but there is nothing more frustrating than outplaying an opponent only to lose money to him.

MANY players begin to play badly when things do not go their way. This is commonly referred to as *tilt*. However, I don't think tilt fully explains the range of emotions. Of course, the first step is preventing yourself from going on tilt, but there is a big difference between playing your "A" game and going on tilt. Many players may not go on full tilt, but they begin to play just a few more hands or make a few more calls than they should. This often happens late at night when a player is trying to get back to even before going to bed. *Good players realize that they can always get back to even the next day.*

I expect that the difference between the expert players and the good players is their emotional control. You must have discipline to be successful playing poker.

So remember:
   Good Disciplined Poker Players = The MONEY...given TIME

Introduction to Internet Poker

Real money poker was first introduced to the Internet in 1999. Since then, Internet poker has grown to degrees few could imagine. On any given night, you can find thousands of players from all over the world playing poker for real money on the Internet.

The dimension of the Internet is bringing the game to thousands of players who never had access to the game before. Many beginning players are able to play online for play money or at micro limits that are not offered in live casinos. Of course, many players do not live in areas that have a live casino, so the Internet now gives them a way to find a game.

Many of these new players born on the Internet are finding their way to the live casino. The tremendous growth of live tournaments around the world is an excellent example. Many of the players going to these tournaments are honing their skills on the Internet. For example, the 2003 World Series of Poker main event featured over 30 entrants who won their $10K entry at Internet poker sites. The winner, Chris Moneymaker, had never played a live tournament before and was able to outplay over 800 of the best players in the world to take home the $2.5 million top prize at the World Series of Poker!

Online vs. Live Play

Many poker players now prefer online play compared to live play. Some of the benefits to playing online include:
- No commute
- No tipping
- Quicker action/More hands per hour
- Deposit bonuses and other promotions
- 24-hour action
- Tremendous selection of games
- No second-hand smoke
- Ability to play multiple tables at the same time
- Availability of play money and micro-limit games

A common theme throughout this book is *strategy* differences between online and live play. Most of the strategies described in this book could be used successfully whether you play live poker or on the Internet; however, subtle strategy differences between the Internet and live games are important to understand. These strategy differences arise from several characteristics unique to the Internet:

- **Short playing sessions:** Players move in and out of games a lot more than they do in a live game, so you are rarely playing the same opponents for a very long time.
- **A virtual environment:** Players tend to be more deceptive and tricky on the Internet where there is no face-to-face interaction, and betting or raising is just a mouse click away.
- **Internet distractions:** Opponents are not as observant playing on the Internet as they are in live games since they sometimes play two tables, read e-mail, watch television, talk on the phone, and many other things that might distract them from the game.

Let's discuss these unique characteristics in a little more detail and the impact they may have on your strategy.

Short Playing Sessions

One big difference between the Internet and live play is that players are constantly moving in and out of games. The accessibility of the Internet allows players to sit down and play just a few hands, a few minutes, or maybe only an hour.

In a live game, you generally are playing with the same opponents for at least a few hours and maybe even up to seven or eight hours. Most people don't bother to drive to a casino unless they plan on staying for at least a few hours. Once there, it even takes a little effort to switch tables. You must notify the floor person to list your name and then you must physically get up and move yourself along with all of your belongings. Some poker rooms even manage the tables to keep an even number of players at each table, so you might have to wait a long time before you are even able to move.

Compare this to the Internet where games are running 24 hours a day in your home or office. Switching poker sites or switching tables is just a mouse click away, so it is very easy to move in and out of games.

The end result is that in a live game you might be playing with the same opponents for several hours. This rarely occurs on the Internet. How does this affect strategy?

Your opponents will not have a very long time to evaluate your play. This means that you should play more straightforward and less deceptively than you would in a live game. One of the benefits of playing deceptively or try-ing a bluff is the advertising value you receive on future hands when your opponents think you are a loose wild player. A loose *table image* can help you earn more chips later when you hold strong hands that your opponents call because they think you might be bluffing. On the Internet, you may not be sitting with the same opponents long enough to benefit from this image.

Against regular opponents, you need to mix up your play even on the Internet, as you cannot be too predictable. But overall, you should mix it up less than you would in a live game. Against new opponents, the best strate-gy is to simply play a straightforward tight game without worrying too much about how your table image might affect future hands.

A Virtual Environment

On the Internet, you are dealing with names, not faces. You cannot stare your opponents in the eyes to see what they tell you. This psychological part of poker makes for a different type of game on the Internet versus live games. For example, although I don't advise it, there seems to be more bluff-ing and tricky play on the Internet compared to live games. I suspect this to be the case because players don't have to "show" their face when making ter-rible plays or terrible bluffs. They can simply wilt away at home in front of their computer screens. In live play, many players find it difficult to make crazy bluffs when they have to look their opponents in the eye.

Another reason why players may tend to bluff more online than in a casino is the ease in which you can bluff. Online you just have to click your mouse. In a live game, you have to physically move your chips into the center of the table. I believe that some players on the Internet forget that they are dealing with "real" money and may tend to get careless at times by simply hitting the bet or raise button for that slim chance at a win.

Of course, these are generalizations, but players tend to be more deceptive and tricky on the Internet than in a live game. This impacts strategies in two ways. First, you can't assume your opponents are bluffing all the time, but you will need to call and raise a little more often against those opponents who are trying to win every pot. On the other hand, you should probably bluff a little less often than in a live game since your opponents will tend to call you a little more. They also realize that players online bluff a lot, so they will tend to call more even with weak hands. They will also find it easier to just click the mouse to call compared to physically moving their chips in a live game.

Internet Distractions

Many players play two tables, read e-mail, watch television, talk on the telephone, and many other things that might distract them from the game. Since there are so many distractions, some of your opponents may not be aware of all the action that is taking place. This is yet another reason to use less deception in your game, since some of your opponents will not even see some of your plays so that you can gain some future value out of them.

One final point about play on the Internet. Since players move in and out of games a lot, can't see your face, and are distracted by many other things, they tend to notice less that you are playing a tight game. In a live game, if you sit there a couple of hours without playing a hand, don't expect a lot of action when you decide to bet or raise. On the Internet, you can play a straightforward tight game for a long time and still get good action when you bet since opponents either do not notice or have not had enough time to realize that you are such a tight player.

On the other hand, if you don't play many hands in a live game, your chances for pulling off a successful bluff are high, while on the Internet I doubt this gives you much of an advantage. A bluff on the Internet is usually only profitable by the merits of the play of the particular hand, not by table image.

Advanced Concept: Table image is not as important online as in a live poker game since players are easily distracted and move in and out of games a lot; therefore, generally play a more straightforward tight game online than you would in a live game.

This section ought to give you a good idea of some of the things you ought to think about when playing online versus live. We will be coming back to a lot of these themes throughout the book as I will repeat and elaborate on each of these concepts more as we discuss in more detail specific strategies for playing Hold'em.

Internet Poker Jargon

One of the enjoyable things about poker is the social aspect of the game. Although the Internet is very different than live play in this aspect, the chat feature adds a unique dimension to Internet poker. Of course, you can chat in live games, but if people said the same things in a live game that they sometimes say on the Internet, there would be a lot of bloody noses sitting at the table! Although some players abuse the chat feature, in general it adds a great dimension that allows you to talk to players from all over the world.

Internet chat has created a lot of jargon to shorten the amount of typing required. One of the most popular is *lol* or Laugh Out Loud. Most players use this to laugh at how a hand developed usually in a bad beat situation, but it can also be used as a laugh in general. *Arg* is another common term used when someone is not happy with something. Some other common terms you will see include:

- :)   Smiling face
- :(Frown
- vnh   Very nice hand
- brb   Be right back
- tx or ty Thanks
- woohoo   Celebration
- zzzz   Going to sleep from the slow play
- t   Testing or time

One site even has sound effects for some of these shorthand expressions, including *loo* where you will hear a toilet flushing, and *tyvm* (thank you very much) spoken by Elvis himself!

You will see a few of these terms in the book. I only hope that no one will want to add "zzzz" to the text, lol.

The Internet has created a whole new poker community. Internet poker is exciting, it is fun, and can be very profitable. Hopefully this book will put you one step ahead of your opponents to help you win more money and have even more fun. Best of luck!

Poker Concepts

Introduction

The first section of the book covers poker concepts such as odds and probability, bluffing, raising/check-raising, and deceptive tactics such as free cards, slowplaying, and inducing bluffs and calls. Why do you raise? When should you bluff? When should you slowplay? How do you apply odds and probability in a poker game? A good understanding of these concepts and tactics is essential before we proceed to specific strategies on the flop, turn, and river.

At the end of each chapter in the "Test Your Skills" section, there are hand examples to practice the concepts you have learned. For those players who are relatively new to Hold'em, you may not fully understand all of the examples given until you have read the chapters about the flop, turn, and river. For example, to apply odds at the poker table, it is important to be able to read your opponents' possible hands. Your ability to read your opponents' hands should improve once you have completed the book and gain more experience.

My advice for beginning players is to read each chapter in this section now with the goal of gaining a *basic* understanding of the concepts and the thought processes you go through in evaluating strategies. Don't get discouraged if you don't fully understand some of the hand examples given. Once you have finished the book, come back to these chapters and you should be able to do better with the "Test Your Skills" sections. This applies to the four chapters in this section on poker concepts: "Probability and Odds," "Bluffing," "Raising/Check-Raising," and "Deceptive Tactics."

Once again, I would like to stress that the hands in the "Test Your Skills" sections come from actual play. I do not necessarily agree with all the moves the various players made in the hands. Nevertheless, read the question as if you were the player and decide what you would do next, even though you might not agree with everything the player had done up to that point.

As almost every poker decision eventually relates to odds, we start out by discussing how to calculate and apply odds and probability in Hold'em.

Probability and Odds

Applying odds at the poker table is essential to making good poker decisions. Some experienced players can do this simply by their excellent feel and judgment for the game, but most of us need to rely on mathematics to help guide us with close decisions. Players who understand how to apply odds in a poker game will have a significant advantage over most of their opponents.

Let's look at an example to demonstrate how to apply odds to make good poker decisions. You are playing in a $1-$2 game and are seated on the button. You hold K♥ T♥ and the board shows 9♥ 2♣ 4♦ A♥. An opponent bets $2 for a total pot of $10. To simplify the example, we assume your opponent is betting a pair of aces but will fold if another heart comes on the river. Should you call to try and improve to a flush?

We will show later that the odds against improving to a flush are 4 to 1. In other words, you will improve to a flush once every five tries. If you played this hand five times, you should expect to lose $2 four times and win $10 once for a total profit of $2; therefore, calling has a positive expectation. What if the pot is only $7? In this case, you would expect to lose $2.00 four times and win $7 once for a loss of $1, so you should fold.

To better understand this process, we begin the chapter with some definitions and then discuss how to calculate various odds and probabilities for the most typical situations in Hold'em. The actual calculation however is not as important as how you *apply* odds to make better decisions, so we will discuss this process in detail.

Definitions

Odds and probabilities are two ways to express the same thing. *Probability* tells you how many times an event *will* happen. For example, you will be dealt a pocket pair once every 17 hands or 5.88% of the time. *Odds* tell you how many times an event *will not* happen. For example, the odds are 16 to 1 against being dealt a pocket pair.

Pot odds is the relationship between the current pot to the current bet. For example, if the pot is $100 and you must bet $10, the pot odds are 10 to 1. *Implied pot odds* is the relationship between the current pot and the bets you expect to win, to the current bet.

Let's look at an example of implied pot odds. You are playing in a $1-$2 game and your lone opponent bets out $2 on the turn. There is $10 in the pot, so your pot odds are 5 to 1; however, if you improve your hand on the river, you expect to earn at least one more bet from your opponent. You are risking $2 on the turn to win a total of $12, the $10 in the current pot plus your opponent's $2 bet on the river; therefore, your implied odds are 6 to 1. If you expect that your opponent will bet out on the river and call a raise should you improve, you would earn two more bets, so your implied odds would be 7 to 1.

Advanced Concept: When calculating pot odds and implied pot odds, always be aware of the possibility of a raise behind you.

If your bet doesn't close the betting, you may not be getting the pot odds you expect. For example, an opponent bets $1 and there is $9 in the pot. Your pot odds are 9 to 1; however, if a player behind you raises, you now must pay an additional $1. A raise lowers your pot odds to only 6 to 1 since you will have to pay a total of $2 to win $12 (assuming the original bettor calls the raise). Note that the total pot would be $14, but this includes your $2 bet, so you don't include this in the calculation. There are many situations in Hold'em that require folding when there is a possibility that a raise will decrease the pot odds you are receiving.

An *out* is an important concept when discussing probability and odds. An out is a card that improves your hand. For example, when you hold two hearts and there are two hearts on the board, you need one more heart for a flush. There are nine remaining hearts or "outs" to improve your hand. If you have A♥ T♥ and you think another ace would also win the hand, you now have 12 outs: the nine hearts and the three remaining aces.

An out is *counterfeited* when a card that improves your hand gives an opponent an even better hand. One of the most common mistakes made by many players is assuming that they will win when a particular card improves their hand; however, it does you no good to draw to a hand that will only lose. For example, you could be hoping for a flush card only to lose to a higher flush or maybe even a full house. You could hit an *overcard*, a card higher than any card on the board, only to lose to two pair, three of a kind, a straight, or a flush.

When applying odds, you should *discount* an out whenever there is a chance that you could improve but still lose the hand. *Once you know the number of discounted outs that can win the hand, you can calculate the odds against improving to the winning hand to determine your best strategy.* How much you discount an out is dependent on how many players you are against and your read on your opponents' possible holdings given the betting sequences in the hand.

For example, you have three outs to an overcard ace and feel that you might win about 2/3 of the time against a lone opponent if you hit the ace; therefore, you would discount your three outs to two outs. However, against two opponents you might feel you will only win about 1/3 of the time, so you discount your three outs to one out. If you are against three or more opponents, you might feel that even with another ace, there is a high chance that you will not be able to win the pot. In this case, you should **disregard** the outs to the ace since you are drawing dead.

Drawing dead is when you cannot improve to the winning hand. This occurs when your opponents counterfeit all of your outs or already have a hand better than the one you are drawing to. For example, you might be drawing dead to two overcards if an opponent already has three of a kind, two pair, or your outs would give your opponent an even better hand.

We will go through several examples to look at how you should determine the number of *discounted* outs you have in a hand based on the probability that your outs are counterfeited or that you are drawing dead. First let's look at how to calculate odds.

Calculating Odds

To determine the odds against improving your hand on the next card, compare the total number of cards that will not help you to the number of cards or "outs" that will. For example, you hold 7♥ 6♥ with a flop of A♣ T♥ 5♥. On the flop there are 47 unseen cards. Out of these 47, there are nine hearts remaining that will improve your hand to a flush and 38 cards that won't; therefore, the odds against improving to a flush are 4.2 to 1 (38/9). An open-ended straight draw has eight outs, which is 4.9 to 1 against improving (39/8). An inside straight draw, a.k.a. **gut-shot** draw, has four outs, which is 10.75 to 1 (43/4).

If you don't improve on the turn and want to know the odds that the river card will improve your hand, the odds will improve just slightly as one more card has been seen. There are only 46 unseen cards on the turn; therefore, a flush draw is now 4.1 to 1 (37/9), which is just slightly better than the 4.2 to 1 odds you had when drawing on the flop.

To determine the *probability* of improving on the next card, simply divide your outs by the total number of cards left in the deck. For example, the probability of improving to a flush on the next card is 19% (9/47). You will improve to an open-ended straight 17% of the time (8/47), and a gut-shot straight 8.5% of the time (4/47). I prefer to know the odds are 11 to 1 rather than the probability is 8.5%, because it is easier to compare to the pot odds you are receiving.

This section looked briefly at how to calculate simple odds and probabilities; however, calculating odds in your head during a poker game can be quite cumbersome. In reality, all you need to do is memorize the following chart.

Number of Outs	One card*
20	1.3 to 1
19	1.5
18	1.6
17	1.8
16	1.9
15 (Flush draw with two overcards)	2.1
14	2.4
13	2.6
12 (Flush draw with overcard)	3
11	3.3
10	3.7
9 (Flush draw)	4
8 (Open-ended straight draw)	5
7	6
6 (Two Overcards)	7
5	8
4 (Gut-shot draw)	11
3	15
2 (Trying to hit a pocket pair)	23
1	46

* *The one card column looks at drawing on the flop. When drawing one card on the turn, the odds are slightly better since one more card has been exposed.*

Internet Tip

In a live game you need to memorize this chart. On the Internet, you can simply post the chart next to your computer for easy reference.

Determining the Number of Discounted Outs

When calculating odds, you need to use the number of discounted outs that will help you *win* the hand. As discussed before, it does you no good to improve your hand only to lose to a better hand. Let's look at some examples to see better how you determine the number of discounted outs.

You have K♦ Q♣ and the board is J♦ T♣ 5♥ 2♠. You have eight strong outs to the *nut* straight with any ace or 9 and six weak outs to the king or queen. The six outs to the king or queen are weak since your opponent could already have two pair or a *set* or is counterfeiting your outs.

In this example, a king would give you a pair but might also give an opponent a straight, two pair, or a pair with a better kicker. Note all the hands you would lose to if a king comes: KK, JJ, TT, 55, 22, AK, AQ, KJ, KT, K5, K2, Q9, JT, J5, J2, T5, T2 and 52. If a queen comes you would lose to QQ, JJ, TT, 55, 22, AK, AQ, K9, QJ, QT, Q5, Q2, JT, J5, J2, T5, T2, 52 and 98.

How much you should discount your weak outs often depends on how many opponents you are against. In the example above, you have six weak outs. Against a lone opponent, if you feel that 50% of the time a king or queen will help you win, you should discount the six weak outs to three. In this case, you would play the hand as if you had an equivalent of 11 outs to win the hand, the three discounted outs and the eight strong outs to the nut straight. If you are against two opponents, you might estimate that a king or queen would win only once every six times; therefore, you would play as if you had nine outs, eight nut outs to the straight plus the one discounted out. Against three opponents, you should probably disregard the weak outs since it is unlikely a king or queen will win. In this case, you would play only if your draw to your eight nut outs is justified. Let's look at some more examples.

You have A♣ T♥ and the flop is K♦ T♣ 5♠. You have two strong outs to the ten, unless an opponent holds KT or T5. Another ace would give you two pair, but your out is counterfeited if an opponent holds AA, AK, or QJ, so you should discount the out to the ace. All your outs should be discounted slightly for the possibility that an opponent holds a set. Depending on the number of opponents and the betting sequences, you should play this hand as if you had between two and four outs.

You have A♣ 9♥ and the flop is J♦ 9♦ 4♣ with several callers on the flop. You probably are against a flush draw, so the A♦ is counterfeited. You could also lose to another ace if someone has AA or AJ. Always account for the possibility of a set.

Advanced Concept: Whenever the flop is two-suited, you should discount a suited out against a lone opponent and probably disregard the out against several opponents for the risk that one of them holds a flush draw.

A common mistake made by many players is drawing to weak hands when flush draws are likely. As a general rule, most draws are not profitable with a two-suited flop and several callers in the hand. The only exception to this is when the pot is exceptionally large. This is a key concept since you will be playing with a two- or three-suited flop about 60% of the time! This concept is discussed further in the flop chapters. For now, simply understand that you need to discount or disregard your outs based on the likelihood that they are counterfeited.

Another consideration when determining your outs on the flop is the possibility that you could improve on the turn only to see an opponent improve to an even better hand on the river.

Advanced Concept: When drawing on the flop, you should discount your outs a little, and maybe a lot, for the probability that your opponents could draw to an even better hand on the river.

There are very few hands that are a lock to win on the turn. Nut flushes can lose to a full house if the board pairs on the river. The nut straight can lose to a flush on the river. Your two pair could lose to an opponent hitting a set. When the flop is two-suited, these types of situations occur often since there are a lot of river cards that could hurt your hand.

Most players complain about their bad luck when they improve on the turn only to lose on the river. Good players recognize that these types of situations occur a lot and include this possibility in their decision-making process. With weak borderline draws on the flop, the possibility that you could improve on the turn only to be beaten on the river is often reason to fold.

Now that we know how to determine the number of discounted outs and calculate the odds against improving to the best hand, we can look at how to apply odds at the poker table.

Application of Odds

The basic steps in applying odds at the poker table are as follows:

1. Determine the number of discounted outs.
2. Calculate the pot odds. This is the size of the pot in relation to the bet.
3. Calculate the implied pot odds. This is the current pot plus the bets you expect to win in relation to the current bet.
4. Compare the implied pot odds to the odds against improving your hand.
5. Determine your best strategy.

When applying odds at the poker table, always make decisions one street at a time. In other words, apply these steps on the flop to determine your best move on the flop. Once the turn comes you will need to go through the steps one more time to make your next decision. In evaluating odds, it is often correct to call the flop and fold on the turn when the bets are bigger. Sometimes you might even call on the flop and then be faced with two raises behind you forcing you to now fold. Let's look at a few examples to show how to apply these steps.

A middle player calls and you raise from the cutoff with K♣ Q♥ in a $10-$20 game. The big blind calls and three players see the flop of T♣ 7♦ 5♠. The big blind, a tight rock who never bluffs, bets out and the middle player folds. What should you do?

⇨ **Determine the number of discounted outs.** We assume your opponent has at least a pair since he never bluffs; therefore, you need a king or queen to improve, which is six outs. You would be drawing dead against TT, 77, or 55, unless you hit a *runner-runner* straight. Other likely holdings of your opponent include AT, KT, QT, and JT. In this case, a king or queen would not help against either KT or QT. It is doubtful that your opponent would call a raise preflop with K7, K5, Q7, Q5, T7, 75, or T5; therefore, you only need to discount your outs for the probability that your opponent holds KT, QT, TT, 77, or 55.

One other consideration is what could happen if you hit the king or queen on the turn. Your opponent could possibly win on the river by hitting two pair or better. You should discount your outs a little more for this possibility.

To determine how much you should discount your outs, it is helpful to evaluate the probable hands of your opponent. Probable hands that you could beat if you improve include JJ, AT, A7, A5, JTs, and 99. Discounting outs is always a matter of judgment, but you might expect to win this hand 50% of the time when you improve, considering the possibility that your opponent might have a set, KT, QT, or improve on the river. Therefore, you should discount your six outs and play as if you had three outs.

⇨ **Calculate the pot odds.** The total pot at this point is $75 (three players paid $20 to see the flop + $5 small blind + $10 bet on flop by the big blind); therefore, your pot odds are 7.5 to 1 for a $10 bet.

⇨ **Calculate the implied pot odds.** Do you expect to win more bets when the king or queen comes? You should win bets 50% of the time when you improve, but you will lose more bets the other 50% when your opponent has a better hand. A simplified assumption would be that all future bets break even.

⇨ **Compare the implied pot odds to the odds against improving your hand.** In this case, we look at the pot odds since the implied odds are the same. The pot odds of 7.5 to 1 are compared to the odds against improving with three outs of 15 to 1 (see out chart).

⇨ **Determine your best strategy.** The odds against improving are 15 to 1; therefore, we should fold since the pot odds are only offering 7.5 to 1.

Let's discuss this hand a little further to show the importance of discounting outs. Many players draw to overcards on the flop hoping to pair up, and this example shows that this often is a big mistake. If we played our hand thinking we have six outs to the king or queen, our odds are 7 to 1 against improving. This compares favorably to the 7.5 to 1 pot odds; therefore, we would call expecting to make a small profit. However, this assumes we would *always* win when the king or queen comes. As we discussed before, our opponent could very well have KT, QT, TT, 77, 55 or beat us on the river.

Some players also justify calling by saying that they have implied odds of winning more bets should they improve. This is true if your hand wins, although sometimes you won't even collect more bets when your opponent folds on the turn to a bet or raise. The problem is that sometimes you will lose additional bets. If your king or queen comes on the turn, you will probably raise and then be faced with a reraise if your opponent has a set or two pair.

Let's look at another example of $10-$20. An early and middle position player call. You call on the button with A♣ 5♣. The small blind calls, and five players see the flop of K♣ 9♣ 4♦. The small blind bets and the big blind folds. A strong player in early position raises. The middle position player folds. What should you do?

⇨ **Determine the number of discounted outs.** The early position player most likely has a pair of kings and might have 99. The small blind most likely has a pair of kings, K9, 99, 44, or possibly a flush draw. You have nine outs to the nut flush and three outs to the ace.

If one of your opponents has a set or two pair, you could hit your flush and possibly lose to a full house; therefore, a small discount is needed. An estimate might be to discount your flush draw from nine outs to eight outs.

Your three outs to the ace need to be discounted since you would lose to AA, KK, 99, 44, AK, A9, A4, K9, K4, 94, and for the possibility that someone hits a better hand on the river. Again, this is a matter of judgment, but you might estimate that a pair of aces would win about 33% of the time; therefore, you could discount your three outs to one out. As a result, I would discount my 12 total outs and play as if I had nine outs.

⇨ **Calculate the pot odds.** The total pot at this point is $80 (five players paid $10 to see the flop + $10 bet on flop by the small blind + $20 raise by the early position player). You face a bet of $20, so your pot odds are 4 to 1.

⇨ **Calculate the implied pot odds.** If you hit the flush on the turn or river, you can expect to gain some extra bets, especially if one of the players has a set. Since there are two opponents in this hand, you might expect to gain at least one big bet on the turn and one big bet on the river for a total of $120 ($80 +$20 +$20). Your implied odds are 6 to 1 faced with a $20 bet. Note: A *big bet* is the amount of a bet on the turn and river, compared to *small bets* on the first two rounds of betting.

⇨ **Compare the implied pot odds to the odds against improving your hand.** Nine outs are 4 to 1 against improving, which is equal to the pot odds of 4 to 1; however, your odds compare favorably to the implied pot odds of 6 to 1.

⇨ **Determine your best strategy.** Calling is profitable. Raising is a consideration to try to buy a *free card* (see "Deceptive Tactics" chapter).

Let's look at one more example of $10-$20. You raise in early position with J♥ J♠. Two middle players, the button, small blind, and big blind all call for a total of six players. The flop is T♣ 8♦ 8♥. It is checked to you, and you bet. One middle player, the button, and small blind call.

Four players see the turn card of Q♦. The small blind checks and you bet. The middle position player raises and everybody folds to you. There is $220 in the pot. What do you do?

⇨ **Determine the number of discounted outs.** Assuming the middle player is not a tricky opponent, your opponent has at least a pair of queens with a hand like AQ or KQ. He might also have TT, 88, or A8. QQ is unlikely since he probably would have reraised preflop. Q8, J9, and T8 are unlikely since he probably would have folded to a raise before the flop. You have four outs to a straight and two outs to a full house (the two eights to a full house are disregarded since it would give your opponent a better full house). Your two outs to a jack and a full house are strong since the only two hands that would beat you are QQ and 88. Your four outs to the straight are relatively strong unless your opponent has QQ, TT, 88, or 98. QQ and 88 are unlikely, but TT is a decent possibility. Only a weak player would call a raise preflop with 98s. One other small possibility is that your opponent has QJ, in which case you would split the pot if a 9 comes. Therefore, I would only discount your six outs by one out to account for QQ, TT, 88, and QJ, and play the hand as if you had five outs.

⇨ **Calculate the pot odds.** The total pot is $220 and the bet is $20, so your pot odds are 11 to 1.

⇨ **Calculate the implied pot odds.** You should expect to earn another bet on the river if you improve. You might lose two bets on the river if you come out betting with the straight and lose to a full house. You might estimate that you would win $15 on average when improving; therefore, the implied odds are $235/20, which are 11.75 to 1.

⇨ **Compare the implied pot odds to the odds against improving your hand.** 11.75 to 1 implied pot odds compares favorably to the 8 to 1 odds against improving with five outs.

⇨ **Determine your best strategy.** Given the large pot, calling is correct.

Advanced Concept: In many cases, it is the size of the pot that determines if drawing to a particular hand is profitable. Given the same exact hand and scenario, your hand could either be folded or played depending on the size of the pot.

The above advanced concept sounds rather simple and obvious, but many weak players play their hands the same way no matter how big the pot is. Weak draws can sometimes be profitable, but you usually need a large pot.

These examples should give you an idea in how to apply odds during a poker game. For beginning players, it will take time and experience before you are comfortable applying these concepts.

Internet Tip

Unfortunately, on the Internet you have a very short time to calculate these decisions in your head. Try memorizing the outs for the most common types of draws. For example, you should automatically know that a flush draw has nine outs, an open-ended straight draw eight outs, and a gut-shot draw is four outs. Quickly discount your outs for the possible holdings of your opponents. Once you know your outs, simply look at the chart posted next to your computer to determine the odds against improving. You can then easily compare these odds to the pot odds you are getting.

Fortunately, it is easy to calculate pot odds on the Internet since the sites always show the total amount in the pot. In a live game, this becomes more difficult since there is just a big stack of chips in the middle of the table. Keep following these simple steps every time you have a draw, and pretty soon you will find yourself going through the steps quite quickly.

Once a hand is over, ask the site for a hand history so that you can go back after your session and evaluate your play when you have more time. Look at the actual number of outs you could have won with based on your opponents' hands and see if calling was correct. Keep a log of your mistakes so that you can keep reviewing them to ensure that you don't make the same mistakes in the future.

One other way to practice using these concepts is to study hand examples and recommended plays by top players. Read books that give lots of hand examples to see how the authors explain the scenarios. The Forum at my website, www.InternetTexasHoldem.com, is a great place to post hands and see how other players determine outs and probabilities. There is also a specific Forum to discuss questions about odds and probabilities. The "Study of the Game" chapter at the end of the book gives more references to help improve your game.

Some helpful statistics and probabilities

Besides learning the "Out" chart, here are some common odds that can be helpful or just interesting to know:

• Dealt a pocket pair	16 to 1
• AA	220 to 1
• Any AK (suited or unsuited)	82 to 1
• Three-suited flops	18 to 1 or 5%
• Two-suited flops	55%
• An A will flop (and no K) when you hold KK	3.3 to 1 or 23%
• An A or K flops (and no Q) when you hold QQ	1.3 to 1 or 43%
• An A, K, or Q flops (and no J) when you hold JJ	.7 to 1 or 59%
• Flopping at least a pair with any two cards	2.2 to 1 or 32%
• Flopping at least a set when you hold a pair	7.5 to 1
• Flopping a flush when holding two suited cards	118 to 1
• Completing a flush when starting with two suited cards	15 to 1 or 6%
• Flopping a flush draw when holding two suited cards	8 to 1
• Completing the flush draw by the river	1.8 to 1
• Backdoor flush	23 to 1 or 4.2%
• KK loses to QQ if played to river	4.4 to 1
• Set on flop completing to a full house or better	2 to 1 or 33%
• 2♥ 2♦ beats A♠ K♣	53%

Chapter Review

❑ *Probability* tells you how many times an event *will* happen while *odds* tell you how many times an event *will not* happen. For example, the odds are 3 to 1 against improving your hand while the probability of improving your hand is 25% or 1 in 4.

❑ *Pot odds* is the relationship between the current pot and the current bet. *Implied pot odds* is the relationship between the current pot and the bets you expect to win, to the current bet.

❑ An *out* is a card that improves your hand. An out is *counterfeited* when a card that improves your hand improves your opponent's hand to an even better hand. Outs that are potentially counterfeited should be *discounted* when calculating odds, and *disregarded* if you are probably drawing dead.

❑ On the Internet, you can simply post a chart next to your computer showing you the odds against improving your hand for each number of outs.

❑ One of the most common mistakes made by many players is assuming that they will win when a particular card improves their hand. When determining your outs, you must look at those outs that will improve your hand to the *winning* hand.

❑ Whenever the flop is two-suited, you should discount a suited out against a lone opponent and probably disregard the out against several opponents for the risk that one of them holds a flush draw.

❑ When drawing on the flop, you should discount your outs a little, and maybe a lot, for the probability that your opponents could draw to an even better hand on the river.

❑ The basic steps in applying odds at the poker table are as follows:
  1. Determine the number of discounted outs.
  2. Calculate the pot odds.
  3. Calculate the implied pot odds.
  4. Compare the implied pot odds to the odds against improving your hand.
  5. Determine your best strategy.

❑ In many cases, it is the size of the pot that determines if drawing to a particular hand is profitable. Given the same exact hand and scenario, your hand could either be folded or played depending on the size of the pot.

Test Your Skills

Refer to the "About this Book" chapter and the intro to "Poker Concepts" for more information and explanations on the format of the "Test Your Skills" sections of the book.

1/ $20-$40. You hold 9♦ 6♦ in the small blind. A middle player and the button calls. You call and four players see the flop of A♠ Q♥ 6♣. The middle player bets and the button calls. There is $120 in the pot. What do you do?

Answer: Fold. You have five outs to improve your hand, which is 8 to 1. The pot odds are only offering 6 to 1 so you should fold. Even with better pot odds, you would need to discount your outs for the possibility that you are drawing practically dead to AA, QQ, 99, 66, AQ, A9, A6, K6, Q9, Q6, J6, and T6. Rarely draw to two *small* pair unless the pot is exceptionally large, and preferably when an ace is not on the board since there is a better chance that your outs are counterfeited with someone holding Ax (any hand with an ace in it).

2/ **$20-$40.** You hold A♠ 9♦ in the small blind. A middle player and the cutoff call. You call and four players see the flop of Q♣ T♦ 9♥. You check, the big blind bets, and the middle player and cutoff both call. There is $140 in the pot. What do you do?

Answer: Fold. You have five outs to improve your hand; therefore, you are 8 to 1 against improving requiring a pot of $160. In addition, with so many callers, there is a good chance that one of your opponents flopped a straight, a set, or two pair with this type of flop. If an opponent has two pair, your outs are reduced to three if they hold a 9 also. If an opponent holds a pair, your ace is counterfeited against AQ or AT. Even in the best case scenario where you improve to the best hand on the turn, with so many opponents there will be many ways you could lose on the river. You need very good pot odds to draw with such a dangerous flop against so many opponents. In the actual hand, the player folded. One opponent showed Q9 and the other KJ.

3/ **$1-$2.** You hold A♣ T♣ on the button. An early player and middle player call. You raise and the small blind calls. Four players see the flop of Q♠ T♥ 9♦. The middle player bets. There is $10 in the pot. What do you do?

Answer: Raise. Note how your hand and the flop are almost identical to the previous problem; however, there are two main differences. First, the pot was raised preflop, giving you better pot odds. Second, two opponents have checked, indicating weakness. This differs from the previous hand where you already had three callers, making it difficult for you to have a winning hand. Your opponent could be betting a straight draw with a weak pair, in which case you may currently have the best hand.

In low-limits, most opponents slowplay straights, sets, or even two pair, so usually you do not have to worry about those hands. Even if your opponent has top pair, you have five outs, which is 8 to 1. The pot odds are 10 to 1, so calling is justified; however, I prefer raising in this situation. Raising will drive out the other opponents from weak gut-shot draws and may allow you to possibly take a free card on the turn. Raising will also give you information on the flop about your opponent's hand once you see how he responds. In the actual hand, the player just called and hit a full house when an ace fell on both the turn and river. The bettor folded and the early player showed A8.

4/ $1-$2. You hold Q♠ J♥ in the big blind. A middle player, the cutoff, and the small blind call. Four players see the flop of A♦ T♠ T♦. The middle player bets and the cutoff calls. There is $6 in the pot. What do you do?

Answer: Fold. You have four outs to the gut-shot straight, and this is reduced to three outs if one of your opponents has a flush draw. You also are drawing dead if one of your opponents holds AA, TT, AT, or KT. Three outs are 15 to 1 and the pot is only $6. In the actual hand, the player called both the flop and turn and got his straight when the K♦ fell on the river. Unfortunately, one of his opponents had 6♦ 5♦ and hit a flush. Straight draws go down in value when the flop is two-suited or paired, especially when they are only gut-shot draws.

5/ $.50-$1. You hold J♣ 9♣ in the big blind. An early player calls, the next early player raises, and the button, small blind, and you call. Five players see the flop of J♦ T♥ 9♥. You decide to check and the early position player bets into the preflop raiser who decides to raise. The small blind and you call. The early player reraises and the preflop raiser caps the betting. The small blind calls. There is $11.50 in the pot. What do you do?

Answer: Call. With so much action you are probably against a straight, so you will need to improve. You have four outs to a full house, which is 11 to 1 against improving, but you are getting 12 to 1 pot odds assuming the early position player calls. If you do hit one of your outs, you should win a lot more bets. In the actual hand, the player folded. An opponent with Q♣ 8♥ won the hand. Although this player saved some bets since a jack or 9 did not come, the actual result of the hand does not mean his play was correct. In the long run, he would make more money by calling with the implied pot odds he was receiving.

6/ $10-$20. You hold 6♣ 5♣ in the big blind. An early player calls, the button raises, the small blind calls, and you call. Four players see the flop of

9♠ 6♦ 3♦. You bet out. The early player calls and the button raises. The small blind calls and you call. All four players see the turn of 5♦. The small blind bets. You raise, the early player reraises, and the small blind calls. There is $320 in the pot. What do you do?

Answer: Call. You are most likely against a flush. There is also a chance you could be against a straight or a set. You have four strong outs to a full house unless an opponent has 99, or possibly 66 or 55. Four outs are 11 to 1 requiring only a $220 pot for calling to be correct. Note that your raise on the turn was questionable, as a flush was a high possibility given that three opponents paid two bets on the flop to see the turn. In the actual hand, the player called and lost to the early player who showed A♦ Q♦.

7/ $15-$30. You hold Q♥ J♥ in early position. An early player calls, the next early player raises, and you call. A middle player, the cutoff, the button, and the big blind all call. Seven players see the flop of 9♣ 8♠ 6♥. The cutoff bets and the button raises. The first early player calls and the preflop raiser folds. You call and four players see the turn card of K♦. The cutoff bets, the button calls, and the early player calls. There is $430 in the pot. What do you do?

Answer: Call. Calling bets on the turn for a gut-shot straight is rarely correct unless the pot is quite large. In this hand, the pot is large and your call will close the betting so that you don't risk a raise behind you. Your four outs are to the nuts since the board is not two-suited or paired. Four outs are 11 to 1 against improving requiring a pot of $330 to justify a call. In the actual hand, the player called and the T♥ fell on the river. He bet and one opponent showed T♠ 9♠.

8/ $15-$30. You hold A♠ 3♠ in middle position. A middle player limps in and you call. The cutoff, button, and small blind all call. A wild unpredictable player raises from the big blind and everyone calls. Six players see the flop K♠ Q♦ J♠. The big blind bets, you call, the cutoff raises, and you both call. The turn is the K♣. The cutoff bets and the big blind raises. There is $360 in the pot. What do you do?

Answer: Fold. You are 4 to 1 against hitting the flush and are getting sufficient pot odds of 6 to 1 on the flush *if* it would win. However, there are several problems with calling in this situation.

Assuming that your opponents don't already have a full house, a couple of your outs are probably counterfeited and should be disregarded since it is likely that at least one of your opponents holds a king. In this case, you will lose to the Q♠ or to another spade if it matches your opponent's kicker card. This reduces your outs to seven, which is 6 to 1 against improving and is even money with a pot of $360; however, this is your best case. With a pair on the board, you need to discount your outs for the decent chance that you are drawing dead to a full house. Possible hands of your opponents include KK, QQ, JJ, KQ, and KJ. Some players may add outs for the possible straight; however, you would lose to a full house or KT. Even if the straight won, you would probably only split the pot.

In the actual hand, the player called. The flush came on the river. The big blind folded and the cutoff showed K9. The player collected a large pot in this particular case, but his call has a long run negative expectation given the pot size and betting sequences that occurred in the hand.

9/ $20-$40. You raise in early position with A♣ K♣. A middle player calls and both blinds call. Four players see the flop of 9♠ 5♦ 3♥. The big blind bets, you raise, the big blind reraises, and you call. The turn is the 2♣. The big blind bets. There is $320 in the pot. What do you do?

Answer: Call. The worst case scenario is that your opponent has a set or two pair. A straight is doubtful based on the betting sequences in the hand. Even in the worst case scenario, you still have four good outs to a gut-shot straight. A gut-shot draw is 11 to 1 requiring a pot of $440; however, you also have additional outs if your opponent is betting a pair. These outs are counterfeited however if your opponent holds A9, A5, A3, K9, K5, K3, a set, or two pair. I would discount the six outs to the ace or king down to three outs; therefore, I would play the hand as if I had seven outs, which is 6 to 1. Odds of 6 to 1 require a $240 pot; therefore, calling is justified. In the actual hand, the 4♦ came on the river giving the player a straight while his opponent showed 5♥ 3♣.

10/ $20-$40. You hold A♣ K♣ on the button. A middle player calls and you raise. The big blind reraises and you both call. Three players see the flop of Q♠ J♥ 8♠. The big blind bets and you call. The turn is the 9♦. The big blind bets. There is $270 in the pot. What do you do?

Answer: Fold. You have 10 outs to improve your hand; however, an ace is counterfeited or already no good if your opponent holds AQ, AJ, AT, AA,

QQ, JJ, or TT. All of these hands are possibilities from a reraise in the big blind. In fact, the only reasonable hand that you could expect to beat if an ace comes is KK. If the river is a king, your situation is worse as you could not beat any reasonable hands, and will only split if your opponent holds AK also. You have four strong outs to the gut-shot straight, although there still is the possibility you might split. Four outs are 11 to 1 and require a pot of $440 to be profitable. In the actual hand, the player folded.

11/ $20-$40. You hold A♣ K♣ in the small blind. The cutoff calls and you raise. Two players see the flop of Q♦ Q♥ 8♥. You bet and your opponent raises. There is $160 in the pot. What do you do?

Answer: Fold. You are practically drawing dead if your opponent holds a queen or 88. You have six outs if your opponent is betting a pair. You have five outs if he holds A8 or K8. You currently have the best hand if your opponent is raising a flush draw, but he will improve to the winning hand over half the time if he doesn't hold an ace or king in his hand. Six good outs would be 7 to 1 and is slightly profitable with a pot of $160; however, you need to discount your outs for the scenarios where your opponent holds a queen, 88, A8, or K8. I would fold against a typical opponent who raises in this situation. If you suspect that a tricky player is possibly raising on a draw, one option is to call the flop hoping to improve your hand or see if your opponent takes a free card.

12/ $20-$40. You hold A♣ K♣ in the big blind. The button raises and you reraise. The flop is J♠ T♥ 6♥. You bet and the button calls. The turn is the 4♥. You bet and your opponent raises. There is $290 in the pot. What do you do?

Answer: Fold, with calling a very close second. Opponents will raise pre-flop on the button with many hands. You first must consider the possibility that your opponent is raising the turn as a semi-bluff with a flush draw or possibly a straight draw. In this case, it is possible that you currently have the best hand, but your opponent still has a lot of outs. There is also the possibility that he has a flush and you are drawing dead. He could have a set or two pair, in which case you only have four outs to the queen for a straight (only three outs if he holds a heart). If he only has a pair, you have ten outs or only seven if he holds a heart. These outs are counterfeited however if your opponent holds AJ, AT, A6, KJ, KT, or K6. If your opponent has KQ, the ace is counterfeited. If he holds AQ, the king is counterfeited.

This hand is complicated. There are many variables in trying to determine the probability that you will win. If your opponent raised from early or middle position, we could narrow down the possibilities somewhat, but it is always difficult to put a button raise on a particular hand.

Most opponents will not try a tricky raise on the turn as a semi-bluff against an opponent who has reraised from the big blind; therefore, let's start with the assumption that we must improve our hand. If this is the case, we have three good outs to the straight, unless our opponent already has a flush, or four outs if our opponent doesn't hold a heart. I would treat the straight draw as if I had three outs. We have six weak outs to a pair, which should be discounted due to the possibility of our opponent holding a flush, set, two pair, a heart, or one of the hands that might give our opponent two pair. I would estimate a discount down to two outs. This gives me five total outs, which is 8 to 1 requiring a pot of $320. This is slightly below break even since the pot is only $290.

Let's go back to the possibility that your opponent is raising as a semi-bluff and you currently have the best hand. Will you call a bet on the river with *ace high*, a hand with an ace but no pair? Although there is the possibility your hand is best, calling would be difficult with this board and situation.

The mathematics of the problem does not give us a very clear answer. My instinct tells me that folding is best, although I would not argue a lot against calling. In the actual hand, the player called and his opponent showed J♣ 7♦ when the 9♠ came on the river. In retrospect, the player made the right call as he had ten good outs; however, ten outs was the best case scenario. There were many possibilities where drawing could have been unprofitable.

Bluffing

Bluffing is one of the most famous of all poker concepts. A **bluff** is a bet or raise when you have little chance of winning the pot if you are called. For example, you hold 6♦ 5♦ with a Q♦ T♦ 8♥ A♠ board. A 2♥ falls on the river and you bet. This is a bluff, as you have no chance of winning the pot if someone calls. A **semi-bluff** is a bet or raise in which, if called, you probably do not have the best hand, but you could improve to the best hand. Let's look first at pure bluffs.

Bluffing is profitable when your pot odds are better than the odds that your opponents will fold. For example, if you feel there is a 20% chance that your opponents will fold, then a $2 bet is profitable if the pot is greater than $8. The key to bluffing successfully is your ability in determining the probability that your opponents will fold.

Let's discuss several factors when considering a bluff:
- **Number of opponents**: Bluffs are generally only successful against one or two opponents and sometimes against three. Bluffs are rarely successful against four or more opponents.
- **Type of opponent**: It is easier to bluff against strong players than maniacs or weak players. Strong players are capable of folding mediocre hands. Maniacs and poor players call too often with weak hands, so it is more difficult to get them to fold.
- **Size of pot:** The larger the pot, the harder it is to bluff successfully. Your opponents are getting better pot odds, so they are more likely to call even with weak hands. On the other hand, you get a larger reward when you are able to bluff successfully at a large pot.
- **Table image:** *Loose* players play a lot of hands and tend to bluff a lot, while *tight* players play few hands and generally only bet when they have a strong hand. Bluffs have a higher chance of success when you have a tight table image since your opponents will tend to back off when you bet. If you have a loose table image, more opponents will tend to call you with weak hands. If you recently were "caught" trying to bluff, this may also make it more difficult to bluff successfully.
- **Betting sequences:** Your ability to read your opponents' possible hands based on their betting sequences will allow you to better identify opportunities to bluff.
- **Representation of a particular hand:** Bluffs are more successful when you are able to represent a particular hand based on the board

and your betting sequences. This is especially true when a *scare card* comes. A scare card is a card that could be threatening to your opponents. For example, an ace comes on the turn and you bet or raise representing a pair of aces. This kind of play works especially well if you raised preflop, since your opponents will be even more worried that you hold the ace.

- **Position:** You can sometimes use your position to identify good bluffing opportunities. For example, a common bluffing opportunity is to bet in last position when everyone has checked. Another bluffing opportunity is to bet out from the blinds when all *rags*, cards lower than a 9, or a small pair flops.
- **Early versus late betting rounds:** Bluffing is more difficult on the river than it is on earlier betting rounds, although you get a larger reward when you are successful. On the river, your opponents only have to call one more bet, and they usually have some type of hand unless they missed a draw.

Bluffs on the flop, especially in tight games, are much more common. First, many flops do not help your opponents, so a bet can often win the pot. Second, to call your bluff, your opponents know that there are still two betting rounds remaining making it expensive to call down to the river. When your bluffs don't work on the flop, they still have a chance of working on the turn since your opponents must still call two big bets to call your bluff.

- **Type of Flop/Board:** It is more difficult to bluff with some types of boards since there is a good chance that your opponents either have a good hand or a good draw. For example, it is difficult to bluff with several high cards on the flop since it is likely that your opponents hold either a pair or a straight draw. Two or three cards that are connected or one-gapped also make straight draws more likely. Two-suited flops add dangers of flush draws.

Let's look at some examples. *Rainbow* flops, flops of three different suits, such as J♣ 6♦ 4♠ or A♥ 9♠ 3♣, are good flops to try bluffing against one or two opponents. If your opponents don't hit top pair, a bluff might be successful. A flop of T98 is a dangerous flop, especially against two or more opponents. It is very likely that your opponents have either a pair or a strong draw. In fact, the only hand an opponent could hold with two high cards that doesn't have either a pair or a draw to a straight is AK!

Advanced Concept: Bluffing with exactly one high card on the flop is sometimes easier than bluffing at an all rag flop since there is a scare card your opponents must worry about.

Sometimes it is difficult to bluff at an all rag flop since your opponents are more inclined to call with low to medium pairs or with two overcards; however, a flop with just one high card gives you an opportunity to get them to fold. For example, if the flop is Q86, some opponents will fold medium pairs, and your opponents can't have two overcards unless they specifically hold AK. A flop of 862 is less threatening to your opponents since they will often have two overcards and they may think a weak middle pair is good. If there are two high cards on the flop, bluffing again becomes more difficult since there is an increased chance that your opponents hold a decent hand.

Let's look at some of the more common bluffing situations:

- **A bet on the river when you have missed a draw** - Sometimes you are betting or calling with a flush or straight draw and do not hit on the river. If you suspect that your opponent does not have a strong hand or has missed a draw also, a bet on the river can sometimes win the pot.

- **A bet on the flop in late position when no opponent has demonstrated strength** - Whenever you are in late position and everyone has checked, a bluff should be considered since all of your opponents have indicated weakness. Success depends on the likelihood that an opponent is planning to check-raise or that an opponent might call with a medium holding or a drawing hand.

- **A bet on the turn in late position when the flop and turn have been checked** - Related to the above, if you are in late position and both the flop and turn have been checked, betting is sometimes obligatory as a bluff since no opponent has shown any strength, especially against one or two opponents.

- **Betting out of the blinds when all rags fall** - Whenever you are in the blinds and all rags flop, you have a bluffing situation if your opponents are unlikely to hold low cards. For example, a solid early position player is the only caller and you are in the big blind with an 863 flop. Betting out with any hand has a decent chance of winning.

- **Betting out the flop after raising preflop** - One of the reasons you raise preflop is to take control of the hand and put the burden on your opponents to improve on the flop. AK is a great starting hand, but will only improve on the flop about 33% of the time; therefore, much of your profit comes from raising preflop and representing a stronger hand on the flop. In many cases, especially against a lone opponent, betting is almost automatic on the flop to see how your opponent reacts.

> **Internet Tip**
>
> Some players give online *tells*, which might indicate if their hand is strong or weak by the speed at which they bet. If you find a tell from one of your opponents indicating a weak hand, you can bet hoping to win the pot as a bluff. On the other hand, if they are strong, you can either fold or check to take a free card. These types of tells are discussed in more detail in the "Online Tells" chapter of the book.

Semi-bluffs

You will find that pure bluffs are not too common, because the only way to win is for your opponents to fold. Semi-bluffs on the other hand give you two ways to win. A semi-bluff is a bet or raise in which, if called, you probably do not have the best hand, but you could improve to the best hand. For example, you hold A5 on a flop of QT5. If you bet and are called, you are probably beaten; however, you have five outs that could possibly improve your hand to the winning hand. Another example of a semi-bluff is to bet or raise a flush draw. You hope to win the pot immediately, but if you are called, you still have outs to improve your hand.

Semi-bluffs become profitable by the combination of the probability that your opponents will fold and the probability that you could improve to the best hand. In many cases, if you have enough outs for calling a bet anyway, it is best to go ahead and try to win the pot with a semi-bluff bet.

Let's look at a few examples of possible semi-bluffs:
- You are in the big blind with 6♣ 7♦. There is one early caller and one late caller. The flop is K♦ 5♠ 4♥. This is a good time to try a semi-bluff and bet out. If they call or raise, you still have eight outs to a straight.
- You open for a raise with K♣ Q♣ from early position. Two players in late position call as well as the big blind. Four players see the flop of A♣ T♦ 5♣. This flop is relatively scary as there are two high cards including an ace that many opponents will play. Usually it is difficult to

get three opponents to fold; however, you are going to play this hand to the river in any case with so many outs, so go ahead and bet to try and win the pot immediately. Strong opponents may fold their gut-shot draws and even a pair of aces with a weak kicker, so there is some chance of success. The only risk in betting out is the risk of a raise, especially if the raise drives out the remaining opponents. By betting, you either want everyone to fold or everyone to call.

- You call in early position with A♦ T♦ and the button and big blind call. The flop is Q♣ T♥ 4♠. The big blind checks. A semi-bluff bet is usually correct in this situation. You should bet hoping that your opponents fold, but if they call or raise, you still have five outs that could improve your hand. Note that even if one opponent calls, you still might have the best hand as they could have a straight draw or a pair of tens with a weak kicker.

- You call in early position with Q♦ J♦ and the next opponent raises. There are two late callers along with the big blind for five total players. The flop is A♦ 8♦ 5♣. The big blind checks. What should you do? You should just check in this case. It is very difficult to get four opponents to fold on the flop, especially in a large pot due to the raise preflop and the A♦ on the flop. The problem with betting here is that the preflop raiser acts next and could raise, driving out the remaining opponents. Checking keeps as many players in the hand as possible, which improves your implied odds. Check-raising becomes an option once three players have already called the flop bet.

One important note about bluffing. ***Bluffing is a strategy that is not very successful in loose low-limit games.*** First, you generally need a good hand to showdown since there are many players playing each hand. Second, a lot of weak players at the low limits call too often with poor hands, so it is difficult to get them to fold. At higher limits, there usually are better players who will sometimes fold their medium holdings when faced with a bet or raise. If you insist on bluffing a lot, low-limit Hold'em games are probably not the game for you.

Most of the money you earn at the lower limits against weak players comes from playing better starting cards than your opponents and understanding when to continue your hand on the flop. Be careful not to give away your chips to weak opponents on unsuccessful bluff attempts.

In tight high-limit games, bluffing becomes an essential arsenal against your opponents. If you never bluff, your opponents will take notice and back off on their hands when you bet or raise. Bluffing can increase your profits by winning pots when you don't have the best hand, and by the advertising value you get when your opponents call your good hands more often in the future. Balancing your bluffs with your strong hands is important to becoming an advanced player at the higher limits.

Bluffing on the Internet

There are some differences between online and live poker in regards to bluffing. As a general rule, players tend to bluff a little more often on the Internet than they do in a live game. The virtual environment of the Internet makes many players play a little more deceptively than they would against a live opponent. The virtual environment also makes it easier to commit your chips since you only have to click your mouse. Compare this to a live game where you have to physically move your chips into the center of the table while your opponents are watching you. Therefore, you may need to keep your opponents honest a little more online than you would in a live game.

On the other hand, your opponents will tend to call your bluffs a little more often than they would in a live game since they also recognize that players tend to bluff quite often on the Internet. Calling is also easier online since they only have to click their mouse. For these reasons, you need to choose your bluffing opportunities a little more carefully online than you would in a live game.

One final note about bluffing. As we discussed before, some of the value in bluffing comes from the advertising value of bluffs to get your opponents to call more often in the future when you have a good hand. Bluffs do not have the same advertising value online as they do in a live game. First, many players may not notice your bluffs since they might be playing two tables, watching television, or reading email. In addition, you rarely play with the same opponents as long as you would in a live game to take advantage of your "loose" image. These are a couple of other reasons why you should tend to bluff a little less often on the Internet. Of course, if you are playing in a game where the players don't move in and out of the game a lot or you are against regular opponents, your bluffs can still derive some future value when used in good situations.

Chapter Review

❑ A *bluff* is a bet or raise when you have little chance of winning the pot if called. A bluff is profitable when your pot odds are better than the odds that your opponents will fold.

❑ A *semi-bluff* is a bet or raise in which, if called, you probably do not have the best hand, but you could improve to the best hand. A semi-bluff is profitable by the combination of the probability that your opponents will fold and the probability that you could improve to the best hand.

❑ Bluffs are generally only successful against one or two opponents and sometimes against three. Bluffs are rarely successful against four or more opponents.

❑ Bluffs are more successful against strong opponents as they are more apt to fold a hand, whereas maniacs and poor players call too often with weak hands.

❑ A large pot gives you better pot odds to attempt a bluff but also increases the odds that your opponents will call.

❑ A tight table image allows you to bluff successfully more often than someone with a loose table image.

❑ Your ability to read your opponents' possible hands based on their betting sequences will allow you to better identify opportunities to bluff.

❑ Bluffs are more successful when you are able to represent a particular hand based on the board and your betting sequences.

❑ You can sometimes use your position to identify good bluffing opportunities.

❑ Bluffing is more difficult on the river than it is in earlier betting rounds since your opponents only have to call one more bet, and they usually have some type of hand unless they missed a draw. Bluffs on the flop have a higher chance of success since most flops do not help your opponents, and to call your bluff, your opponents know that there are still two betting rounds remaining.

❑ It is more difficult to bluff with some types of flops since there is a good chance that your opponents either have a good hand or a good draw. Generally, flops with two high cards, two-suited flops, or two or three connected cards make it more difficult to bluff successfully.

❑ Bluffing with exactly one high card on the flop is sometimes easier than bluffing at an all rag flop since there is a scare card your opponents must worry about.

❑ Some of the more common bluffing situations include:
- A bet on the river when you have missed a draw and you think your opponent has either a weak hand or missed a draw also
- A bet on the flop in late position when no opponent has demonstrated strength
- A bet on the turn in late position when the flop and turn have been checked
- Betting out of the blinds when all rags fall
- Betting out the flop after raising preflop

❑ Online tells can sometimes give you a good indication of the strength of your opponent's hand.

❑ Semi-bluffs are more common than pure bluffs, as a semi-bluff gives you two ways to win the hand: your opponents might fold or your hand might improve to the best hand.

❑ When you have sufficient outs to call a bet, the best option is usually to bet a semi-bluff and try to win the pot immediately.

❑ Bluffing is a strategy that is not very successful in loose low-limit games since there usually are many players in the hand and they tend to call too often with weak hands.

❑ Bluffing can increase your profits by winning pots when you don't have the best hand, and by getting your opponents to call you in the future when you do have good hands.

❑ Online versus live considerations:
- Players tend to bluff more on the Internet than in a live game.
- Players tend to call your bluffs a little more often online than in a live game.
- Bluffs do not have the same advertising value online as they do in a live game.

Test Your Skills

1/ $20-$40. You raise in middle position with A♣ T♦. Another middle player and the small blind calls. Three players see the flop of K♥ 6♣ 3♠. The small blind checks. There is $140 in the pot. What do you do?

Answer: Bet. You raised preflop representing strength. Since you are only against two opponents, there is a decent chance your opponents were not helped by this flop. Against three opponents you might check.

2/ $20-$40. You hold A♣ K♣ in early position. Two early players call and you raise. The button and both blinds call. Six players see the flop of T♥ 9♠ 3♣. It is checked to you. There is $240 in the pot. What do you do?

Answer: Check. There is practically no chance that you have the best hand against so many opponents with a T9 on the flop. They will be calling with pairs and straight draws. Check and hope for a free card. In the actual hand, the player checked, the button bet, the small blind called, and the big blind raised. AK is a great hand preflop, but when the flop doesn't help you, don't get married to the hand.

3/ $20-$40. You hold K♦ 6♦ in the small blind. A middle player limps in and you call. Three players see the flop of 8♦ 7♠ 5♠. There is $60 in the pot. What do you do?

Answer: Bet. You will call with your straight draw, so go ahead and bet to try and win the pot immediately against only two opponents.

4/ $15-$30. You hold A♣ K♥ in the small blind. An early player and a middle player call. You raise and the big blind calls. Four players see the flop of J♠ 8♠ 6♠. There is $120 in the pot. What do you do?

Answer: Check. You are against three opponents with a very dangerous flop. I would check this flop against three opponents even if it wasn't three-suited.

5/ $20-$40. A middle player posts $20 and you hold T♥ 9♥ in the big blind. The button raises, you call, and the middle player folds. Two players see the flop of 8♣ 7♥ 5♣. There is $110 in the pot. What do you do?

Answer: Bet. Go ahead and try to win the pot right away on the flop against your lone opponent. Check-raising is an option but most players tend to call a check-raise more often than a bet since there is more money in the pot and they feel committed once they have bet.

6/ $1-$2. You hold 9♣ 5♣ in the big blind. Two middle players limp in. You get a free play and three players see the flop of J♣ 3♣ 2♦. There is $3.50 in the pot. What do you do?

Answer: Bet. You will call with your flush draw, so go ahead and bet to try and win the pot immediately against only two opponents.

7/ $15-$30. You hold J♦ 9♦ in the small blind. A middle player and the cutoff call. You call and four players see the flop of K♦ 5♣ 5♦. There is $60 in the pot. What do you do?

Answer: Bet. Even though you are against three opponents, there is less of a chance that your opponents hit the flop since there is a pair on flop. Note that with a pair on the flop, there are five cards your opponents could have to hit something versus nine cards when there isn't a pair on the flop. You are going to play your draw, so you ought to bet to try and win the pot immediately. The risk of a raise by an opponent holding a king is also not too high since they may be worried that you hold *trips*.

8/ $20-$40. You hold A♠ K♦ in early position. A middle player and the cutoff both post $20. An early player calls and you raise. Both posters and the big blind call. Five players see the flop of T♥ 3♥ 2♠. It is checked to you. There is $200 in the pot. What do you do?

Answer: Check. This flop is relatively harmless with only one high card, but you are against four opponents. Bluffing rarely succeeds against three or more opponents. Check and hope for a free card. In the actual hand, the middle player bet, the big blind called, and the early player raised. The player folded his two overcards. The early player won the hand with K♥ T♣.

9/ $20-$40. You hold A♥ K♦ in the big blind. The button raises and you decide to just call. The flop is T♥ 2♥ 2♦. You check and the button bets. There is $110 in the pot. What do you do?

Answer: Raise. Since the button could be raising with a wide variety of hands, you probably have the best hand. Even if your opponent has a pair, you have six outs to improve. Be prepared to bet the turn no matter what card falls.

10/ $20-$40. You hold Q♥ T♥ on the button. An early player, a middle player, and the cutoff limp in and you call. Five players see the flop of 8♣ 5♥ 3♠. Everyone checks. The turn is the J♦. It is checked to you. There is $110 in the pot. What do you do?

Answer: Check. I would bet out against two opponents and maybe three in this situation, but usually it is difficult to steal a pot against four opponents even when they have all checked.

11/ $20-$40. You hold Q♠ 3♦ in the small blind. Everyone folds to you and you call. You and the big blind see the flop of K♣ T♦ 2♥. You bet out a bluff hoping your opponent holds rags. The big blind calls and the turn is the J♣. You bet and your opponent raises. There is $200 in the pot. What do you do?

Answer: Reraise. The quality of hands changes a lot in small blind versus big blind situations. His raise on the turn does not necessarily mean a premium hand in these kinds of situations. Your opponent did not raise preflop, so there is a decent chance he does not hold a king. You are going to at least call the turn with your open-ended straight draw and possibly three outs to the queen. Go ahead and reraise and try to get your opponent to fold a weak pair. In the actual hand, the player reraised and his opponent folded.

12/ $20-$40. You hold K♥ 4♣ in the big blind. An early player and the cut-off call. You get a free play and three players see the flop of Q♦ 7♥ 6♠. Everyone checks. The turn is the 5♣. There is $70 in the pot. What do you do?

Answer: Bet. The 5♣ is unlikely to help anyone. Two opponents indicated weakness on the flop, so a bet might win the pot. You have a lot of outs if an opponent calls. In the actual hand, the player bet and his opponents folded.

13/ $15-$30. You hold 3♣ 3♠ in the big blind. A loose aggressive player calls from the cutoff and the small blind limps in. You get a free play and three players see the flop of Q♥ J♦ J♥. The small blind checks, you bet, and only the cutoff calls. The turn is the 4♠. You bet and the cutoff calls. The river is the 4♦. There is $135 in the pot. What do you do?

Answer: Bet. An aggressive player probably would have raised the flop or turn with a queen or jack. Your opponent is probably on a draw. Bet to try and steal the pot. You only need to win once every five times for betting to be profitable. In the actual hand, the player bet and his opponent folded.

14/ $20-$40. You hold T♣ 8♣ in the small blind. An early player limps in and you call. Three players see the flop of 9♣ 6♥ 6♦. You bet, the big blind raises, and you decide to call. The turn is the 2♣. You check and the big blind checks. The river is the 9♦. There is $140 in the pot. What do you do?

Answer: Bet. Your opponent's check on the turn indicates weakness. He may have had a pair of 9's and was worried about trips, but he also might be holding a draw or a small pocket pair. The pot odds are sufficient for you to represent a full house and bet out a bluff. In the actual hand, the player bet and his opponent folded.

15/ $15-$30. You hold A♣ K♠ in the small blind. An early player raises and a middle player calls. You only call and the big blind calls. Four players see the flop of 9♦ 5♠ 2♦. The big blind bets and everyone calls. The turn is the 3♠. The big blind bets and everyone calls. The river is the 5♥. The big blind checks, the early player bets, and the middle player calls. There is $360 in the pot. What do you do?

Answer: Raise. Bluff raises on the river rarely are successful, especially on the Internet since many players tend to call once they have bet. However, sometimes you can spot opportunities such as in this example. The early player has limped along the entire hand and decides to bet out when a 5 comes on the river. It is possible he has a hand like A5 but doubtful since he raised preflop. The middle player obviously has a weak hand or he would have raised on one of the earlier betting rounds. Raising in this situation will represent trip 5's and make it very difficult for one of your opponents to call. Your bluff only has to work once every seven times to break even. In the actual hand, the player folded. The early player showed Q♠ T♠ and the middle player A♠ 2♠.

Raising/Check-raising

Many players raise in poker without really thinking about what they are trying to achieve. There are several reasons why you might raise:

⇨ **You feel you have the best chance at winning the pot.** If you have a strong hand or a very strong draw, you can raise to get more money in the pot.

⇨ **You want your opponents to fold their drawing hands, or make a mistake by calling.** When you have a good hand that is vulnerable to future cards, you might raise so that your opponents will either fold or make a mistake by calling when they are not getting good pot odds.

⇨ **You are getting good pot odds to try a bluff or semi-bluff.** You might raise as either a bluff or semi-bluff hoping that your opponents will fold a better hand.

⇨ **You want to try for a free card.** Free cards are discussed in the next chapter, but they are usually won after a raise on the flop. The idea is that you demonstrate strength on the flop, hoping that everybody will check to you on the turn. You can then elect to play the turn for "free."

⇨ **You want to determine the strength of your hand relative to your opponents.** Consider raising to gain information if you are unsure whether or not you have the best hand and you don't have a lot of outs. Many players simply call down to the river with mediocre hands only to lose 2 1/2 big bets on the hand, the two bets on the turn and river plus the call on the flop. A cheaper option is to raise and then fold if you gain good information that you are against a strong hand. For example, you call a raise with A3s in the big blind and the flop is A75. If you check-raise against a strong opponent and he reraises, you can usually fold your weak kicker against most opponents.

Let's discuss the second point in a little more detail, as it is an important concept.

Advanced Concept: One goal in poker is to give your opponents opportunities to make mistakes.

When your opponents are correct to call just a single bet, raising is sometimes a good strategy to decrease your opponents' pot odds and force them to either fold or make a mistake by calling. Let's look at a common example.

You hold A♥ Q♦ on the button and raise preflop. Five players see a flop of Q♣ T♦ 5♠. There is $100 in the pot in a $10-$20 game. What should you do if the cutoff bets? The best strategy is to raise. You probably have the best hand, which is one reason to raise. More importantly, raising will force some of the remaining opponents to either fold or make a mistake by calling. An opponent would be correct to draw to a gut-shot straight for only one bet with hands like AJ, K9, and J8. He is 11 to 1 against improving and would have 12 to 1 pot odds if you only call; however, if you raise to $20, his pot odds are now only 6.5 to 1 ($130 total pot divided by $20 bet). By raising, opponents with gut-shot draws should fold; otherwise, they are making a mistake by calling.

Note how you raise with the intention of driving out an opponent with a gut-shot draw, but you actually prefer that he calls since calling would be a mistake. You will lose to this opponent once every 12 hands, but you will more than make up for that one loss by all the extra bets you earn the other 11 hands. This is a perfect example of why *bad beat* hands are not so disastrous. When an opponent draws to a hand that he shouldn't, yet still wins, think of all the extra bets you are earning on the times when he doesn't hit his hand.

If one of your opponents has KQ, he has three outs to the king, which is 15 to 1 against improving. If you just call, your opponent is making a slight mistake since his pot odds are 12 to 1; however, calling a single bet is not too bad since he will probably earn some more bets if he hits his king. If you raise, your opponent should fold or he will make a big mistake by calling with pot odds of only 6.5 to 1.

An opponent holding JT has five outs to beat you, which is 8 to 1 against improving. He would be correct to call just one small bet on the flop; however, your raise again forces him to either fold or make a mistake by calling with pot odds of only 6.5 to 1.

It is very important to *protect* your hand, and raising is often a good weapon to do this. One of the biggest mistakes you can make in poker is giving your opponents a chance to beat you without charging him a price to do so. Players who make the fewest mistakes make the most money, so be sure to give your opponents opportunities to make more mistakes rather than making a mistake yourself.

Check-raising

A *check-raise* is when you check with the intention of raising on the same betting round. Check-raising is sometimes a better strategy than betting out or checking and calling for several reasons:

⇨ **To drive out opponents.** Sometimes betting out will not drive out many opponents since they only have to call one bet. If you are acting early, one option is to check hoping that a late position player bets. This will allow you to raise and force the remaining opponents to call two bets or fold.

For example, you hold A♣ 8♣ in the big blind and call a raise by the button. Five players see the flop of 8♦ 5♥ 3♠. If you bet out, most of your opponents will call with their overcards for only one bet. If you check and the preflop raiser bets, your check-raise forces the remaining opponents to either call two small bets or fold. By check-raising and driving out the remaining opponents, you increase your odds of winning the hand since only one opponent is drawing to overcards rather than three or four. Of course if your opponent holds a pair higher than your 8's, a.k.a. an *overpair*, you are the player who is drawing, but Hold'em is a game that requires you to take risks to increase your chances of winning the hand.

⇨ **To give your opponents a chance to make a mistake by calling.** As discussed in the raising section, your opponents are often correct paying one small bet to their draws, but are making a mistake by calling two small bets if they are not getting sufficient pot odds.

⇨ **To induce a bet by an opponent with a weak hand.** Most preflop raisers will come out betting on the flop. A check-raise uses their aggression to your advantage. Betting out is an acceptable strategy also, but check-raising may gain that extra bet on the flop that you wouldn't gain otherwise.

⇨ **To put more money in the pot with the best hand.** Again, this is simply the basic goal of getting more money into the pot when you feel you have the best chance of winning the pot.

⇨ **To increase your pot odds on your good drawing hands.** Check-raising is sometimes correct with good drawing hands. If an opponent to your left bets and several other opponents call, you can raise your good draws like flushes and open-ended straights. Since these draws are about 2 to 1 against improving by the river, you earn money on every bet when there are at least three opponents in the hand.

⇨ **To try and win the pot on a semi-bluff.** Sometimes check-raising is used as an effective semi-bluff. These are especially effective when you plan on calling with a good draw in any case. By check-raising, you might win the pot immediately. Let's look at an example. You raise in middle position with Q♦ J♦ and get called by the button and big blind. The flop is T♦ 6♥ 3♠. You bet out and get raised by the button and the big blind folds. You decide to call with your overcards and backdoor flush and straight draw (a *backdoor* draw is one that requires both the turn *and* river card to improve your hand). The turn is the K♥. Check-raising might be a good strategy against a strong opponent who would fold a pair of tens or other middle pair. If he calls, you still have a decent chance of winning the pot by hitting your straight or even the queen or jack.

In order for a check-raise to be successful, you need to be fairly confident that one of your opponents will bet. Giving a free card when you have the best hand can be disastrous. When you are not too sure that an opponent will bet, tend to bet out hands that are vulnerable to free cards and check-raise hands that are less vulnerable. For example, giving a free card with a pair of tens or jacks is much more risky than if you hold a high pair such as aces or kings.

Finally, let's discuss check-raising in terms of advanced play. What would happen if you never check-raised? If you always bet your strong hands and checked your weak hands, your observant opponents would have a great read on your play. They could simply fold if you bet and bet if you check.

If you check-raise a lot, your opponents will also be less inclined to bet behind you in fear that you might check-raise. This serves as two benefits. First, when everyone checks, you now have a good opportunity of winning the pot by betting out on the next card. They will know that you were possibly planning on check-raising a good hand on the previous betting round. Second, your opponents will be more reluctant to steal the pot since they are worried about you check-raising, and the free card could help you improve to the best hand.

Of course, you shouldn't always check-raise. The key to playing at an advanced level is to mix up your plays so that your opponents have a hard time reading your hands.

Raising on the Internet

On the Internet, you have the option of using the "in turn" buttons to select your move even before your opponents have acted. I do not recommend the use of these "in turn" buttons unless you are going to fold. However, some of your opponents will use them, so it is important to recognize when they have used them and what it might possibly indicate about the strength of their hand.

It is easy to recognize when someone has selected one of these buttons since their move will occur almost *instantaneously* after the player before them acts. The chips enter the pot at practically the same time. This is very different than someone just acting quickly, since in this case they are selecting their move *after* their opponent has acted. Let's discuss some of the reasons why a player might raise instantaneously.

The first reason someone might raise instantaneously is the obvious one. They have a strong hand and decide to raise no matter what happens before them. For example, if a middle player limps in preflop, the next player quickly raises, and the cutoff reraises instantaneously, the cutoff probably has a super premium hand since he was going to raise or reraise no matter what happened before him.

Sometimes players use reverse psychology to bully you into calling their strong hands. They want you to think, "He would never raise so fast with a good hand, so he might be bluffing." Opponents generally have a strong hand whenever they raise instantaneously on the *turn or river* and to some extent preflop. This is an online *tell* common with many opponents. This tell is even stronger on the river, where I find an instantaneous raise almost always means the nuts or close to it.

However, this tell is not nearly as useful on the *flop*. Many opponents will raise instantaneously on the flop as a semi-bluff with two overcards or some other type of draw; therefore, they could have a strong hand or are just trying for a free card. In these cases on the flop, it is important to observe your opponent's individual tendencies. These online tells and others are discussed further in the "Online Tells" chapter towards the end of the book.

One last comment about raising on the Internet. As we discussed before, players tend to play more deceptively online than they do in a live game. Many players believe check-raising is impolite in a home game, whereas players on the Internet check-raise all of the time. Maybe they check-raise more since they don't have to face their opponent. This causes a small adjustment in your strategy when compared to live play. On the Internet, you should be more careful betting in late position with weak hands than you would in a live game since there is a better chance one of your opponents might check-raise.

Chapter Review

❑ There are five main reasons to raise in Hold'em:
  - You feel you have the best chance at winning the pot.
  - You want your opponents to fold their drawing hands, or make a mistake by calling.
  - You are getting good pot odds to try a bluff or semi-bluff.
  - You want to try for a free card.
  - You want to determine the strength of your hand relative to your opponents.

❑ One goal in poker is to give your opponents opportunities to make mistakes. When your opponents are correct to call just a single bet, raising is sometimes a good strategy to decrease your opponents' pot odds and force them to either fold or make a mistake by calling.

❑ Bad beat hands are not nearly as disastrous as most poker players think. When an opponent draws to a hand that he shouldn't, yet still wins, think of all the extra bets you are earning on the times when he doesn't hit his hand.

❑ There are several reasons why check-raising is sometimes a better strategy than betting out or checking and calling:
  - To drive out opponents
  - To give your opponents a chance to make a mistake by calling
  - To induce a bet by an opponent with a weak hand
  - To put more money in the pot with the best hand
  - To increase your pot odds on your good drawing hands
  - To try and win the pot on a semi-bluff

❑ In order for a check-raise to be successful, you need to be fairly confident that one of your opponents will bet. Giving a free card when you have the best hand can be disastrous.

❑ There are several benefits to check-raising in terms of advanced play:
  - You prevent opponents from always stealing the pot after you have checked.
  - You will be able to steal more pots by betting out on the next card when all of your opponents have checked.
  - You might gain a free card to help you win the hand.

❑ Considerations on the Internet:
  - On the Internet, you have the option of using the "in turn" buttons to select your move even before your opponents have acted, so that your move occurs almost instantaneously after your opponent.
  - Opponents generally have a strong hand when they raise instantaneously on the turn or river and to some extent preflop.

- An instantaneous raise on the flop is not a very good tell as some opponents raise with strong hands or as a semi-bluff with two over-cards or some other type of draw.
- Players tend to play more deceptively than they do in a live game and check-raise more often; therefore, you should be more careful betting in late position than you would in a live game.

Test Your Skills

1/ $20-$40. You hold Q♦ J♦ in middle position. A middle player calls and you call. The small blind calls and four players see the flop of J♥ T♦ 6♠. The middle player bets. There is $100 in the pot. What should you do?

Answer: Raise. You have top pair and should raise to drive out the remaining opponents from weak draws. Your opponent could be betting middle or bottom pair or a straight draw. Be the aggressor until an opponent indicates he may have a better hand.

2/ $20-$40. You hold K♠ Q♣ in the small blind. An early and middle player limp in and you call. Four players see the flop of Q♥ 5♣ 4♦. There is $80 in the pot. Should you bet or check-raise?

Answer: Check-raise. This is one of those hands where you should mix up your play by betting out, check-raising, or even slowplaying to the turn depending on how the betting goes on the flop. However, I would usually check-raise in this situation to try and get an opponent or two to put some more money in the pot with weak hands. The pot is small and even if your opponents all check and take a free card, the flop is not too dangerous since there is only one overcard that can hurt you. In the actual hand, the player checked and the big blind bet. The player waited to check-raise the turn and the big blind folded.

3/ $20-$40. You hold 9♥ 3♥ in the small blind. Two middle players call and you call. Four players see the flop of 9♣ 4♠ 2♣. There is $80 in the pot. Should you bet or check-raise?

Answer: Bet. You probably have the best hand since no one raised preflop. Checking is risky since your opponents might take a free card and there are a lot of overcards that can hurt you. This hand is similar to the previous example, but your strategy is different due to the five overcards that can hurt your hand versus only one in the previous example.

4/ $20-$40. You hold A♥ K♥ in the small blind. A middle player raises and you decide just to call. The big blind folds. The flop is K♣ 6♣ 2♠. There is $100 in the pot. Should you bet, check-raise, or check and call?

Answer: Check-raise. Your opponent will almost always bet out in a heads-up situation allowing you to raise. I prefer check-raising the flop rather than slowplaying to the turn, because your opponent might check the turn with a pocket pair such as QQ worried that you hit the king. In the actual hand, the player check-raised and his opponent called to the river with A♠ 9♠.

5/ $20-$40. You raise with A♦ K♦ in early position. The button and big blind call. Three players see the flop of A♠ J♠ 9♠. You bet and the button raises. There is $190 in the pot. What do you do?

Answer: Reraise. There is a good chance that your opponent is betting a flush draw. The best way to punish your opponent on a draw when you are acting before him is to reraise the flop and bet out the turn. In the actual hand, the player reraised and his opponent folded to a river bet.

6/ $20-$40. You hold K♠ Q♠ in the big blind. An early player raises and a middle player calls. You call and three players see the flop of 5♠ 4♠ 3♠. You check, the early player checks, and the middle player bets. There is $150 in the pot. What do you do?

Answer: Raise. One option is to just call to lure the early player into calling; however, I prefer raising because you will earn at least one more small bet on the flop, assuming the middle player calls, which is the same as calling and the early player calls. If you only call and the early player folds, you do not gain anything. In addition, you could earn three more small bets if they both call the raise. Trying to slowplay and check-raise the turn is also risky since you are unsure if·your opponent will bet; therefore, raising the flop and betting out the turn is usually the best option.

7/ $1-$2. You hold T♦ 7♦ in the cutoff. An early and middle player limp in. You make a weak call, the button raises, and the big blind calls. Five players see the flop of 7♥ 4♦ 3♦. The big blind bets. There is $12 in the pot. What should you do?

Answer: Raise. You have top pair with a flush draw. Raising might drive out the button increasing your chances of winning the large pot if a high card should come. Even if the button calls or reraises, you probably are at least even money to win the hand with outs to the flush, T, and 7. In the actual hand, the player raised but lost to the big blind with 8♦ 8♠.

8/ $15-$30. You hold Q♣ Q♥ in the big blind. A middle player raises and the button reraises. You decide to just call and the middle player calls. The flop is 7♦ 7♣ 5♠. There is $145 in the pot. Should you bet or check-raise?

Answer. Check-raise. It is very likely the button will bet and you will be able to raise driving out the middle player. If you bet, both of your opponents will likely call, decreasing the chance that you can win the hand if an ace or king comes. In the actual hand, the player checked, the middle player bet, and the button raised. The player decided to just call and wait to check-raise the turn, but unfortunately both his opponents took a free card. Be careful in slowplaying vulnerable hands when a player holding AK might take a free card.

9/ $20-$40. You hold K♦ T♦ on the button. The cutoff posts $20. A strong early player raises, the cutoff calls, and you make a weak call. The big blind calls and four players see the flop of T♣ 8♣ 6♥. The cutoff bets and you raise. Everyone calls. The turn is the 3♦. The cutoff bets out again. There is $370 in the pot. What do you do?

Answer: Raise with the intention of checking the river. This is a large pot. Your implied pot odds are 5 to 1 assuming at least the cutoff calls ($410/80). You only have to end up with the winning hand 1 in 6 times for raising to be correct. The cutoff could have many different hands since he posted preflop. He might have two pair or a set, but his call on the flop indicated weakness. He might just be betting out a pair in fear that you will take a free card with a flush or straight draw. The big blind probably has a draw and the early player two overcards. Raising forces them to pay two big bets to see the river. If you are reraised in this situation, you probably should fold.

Note how raising cost the same as simply calling the turn and river, but you improve your chances of winning the large pot if you can get the big blind or early player to fold. In the actual hand, the player raised, the big blind called, and the early player folded. Everyone checked the river card of J♥. The big blind showed J♣ 4♣ and the cutoff T♠ 8♦.

10/ $20-$40. You hold A♥ A♠ in the small blind. A strong middle player raises and a maniac calls from middle position. The maniac has been playing about 75% of his hands. You raise and three players see the flop of 8♣ 8♦ 2♦. You bet and both players call. The turn is the 2♠. You check, the middle player bets, and the maniac calls. There is $340 in the pot. What do you do?

Answer: Raise. It is unlikely the strong middle player was raising preflop with an 8 or 2 in his hand. You checked the turn because you did not want to give the maniac extra chips if he is holding an 8 or 2. When he only calls the turn, you most likely have the best hand.

11/ $20-$40. You raise first in from the small blind with Q♠ 9♠. The big blind reraises and you call. The flop is 7♠ 6♥ 4♠. The big blind bets and you call. The turn is the K♥. The big blind bets and you call. The river is the K♠. There is $240 in the pot. Should you bet or check-raise?

Answer: Bet. This is a scary board for your opponent as you could have a flush or trips. He might only have a hand like ace high or a weak pair and decide to check rather than risk a check-raise. Betting will ensure that you gain at least one big bet if the big blind has any kind of hand. Betting out also has the advantage that your opponent might raise if he has trip kings. In this case, you could reraise and gain three bets on the river. The one disadvantage to betting is that your opponent might fold if he has nothing.

Check-raising could induce a bluff in this case; however, your opponent three bet preflop and has acted strongly throughout the hand, so he probably has a hand at least worth a call. In the actual hand, the player bet, the big blind raised, and the player reraised with his opponent showing K♣ 3♣.

12/ $30-$60. You hold K♥ J♥ in the small blind. The cutoff raises, the button calls, and you call. The big blind calls and four players see the flop of J♣ 7♣ 6♥. You check, the big blind bets, and the button calls. You raise, the big blind reraises, and the button calls. You only call and the turn card is the 3♥. You bet, the big blind calls, and the button raises. You call and the big blind calls. The river is the 9♥. There is $870 in the pot. Should you bet or check-raise?

Answer: Check-raise. The button called a check-raise and reraise cold on the flop and then raised the turn. He most likely holds a set or possibly two pair. The river card is not too scary since he would not be expecting a backdoor flush. There is a very good chance he will bet and you will be able to raise gaining two big bets on the river.

Betting out is another option if you believe the big blind will call. You would still earn two big bets, and there is a small chance the button might even raise if he puts you on two pair. However, I believe you have a higher chance of earning two big bets by check-raising than by betting. It is difficult to know if the big blind will call since he may have been drawing to a flush or to two pair. In the actual hand, the player check-raised, the big blind folded, and the button showed 6♠ 6♣.

Deceptive Tactics

Deception is an important part of every successful player's strategy. If your bets and raises always mean your hand is strong and your checks always mean you have a weak hand, observant opponents will have a tremendous advantage since they will always know the strength of your hand. We have already discussed some ways to add deception to your game with bluffs, semi-bluffs, and check-raises. Other deceptive tactics include free cards, slowplaying, and inducing bluffs or calls.

Free Cards

A *free card* is when you receive a card without having to call a bet. In Hold'em, normally you try for a free card by either betting or raising on the flop, hoping that your opponents will check to you on the turn when the bets are more expensive. In reality, the card you receive is not free as you had to "pay" for it on the flop, but these flop bets are cheaper than calling a turn bet.

There are several advantages to try for a free card:
⇨ If your hand does not improve, you might be able to see an additional card for free that could help you win the hand. The main intention of trying for a free card is to allow you to see two cards for a cheap price. For example, you hold A5 on a KT5 flop. If an opponent bets, you might raise hoping that the bettor will check to you on the next round. If so, you are now able to see both the turn and river card without having to call a bet on the turn. In many situations, you are getting good pot odds when you are able to buy a free card successfully.
⇨ Your hand might improve on the next card and you can continue to bet having gained the additional small bet on the flop. In the example above, if an ace or 5 comes on the turn, you just continue to bet the hand.
⇨ Buying a free card is a cheap way of calling opponents to the river when you are not sure whether or not you have the best hand. Sometimes you are in situation where you are unsure whether or not to fold. For example, you hold A♣ 4♣ in late position and the flop comes A♦ 9♥ 2♠. A player bets into you who could have either a pair of aces or a hand like T9. You could raise hoping to take a free card on the turn with the intention of calling a river bet. You "save" yourself 1/2 of a big bet if your opponent has a better hand compared to simply calling your opponent on each street.

The problem with trying for free cards is that sometimes the strategy backfires if an opponent either reraises or comes out betting on the turn. Let's look at an example.

A middle position player calls and you call on the button with J♦ T♦. Three players scc thc flop of Q♦ 7♦ 5♣. The big blind bets and the middle position player folds. If you raise, four things could happen:

- Your opponent might fold if he only has a middle pair.
- Your opponent might call and check the turn. In this case, if no diamond comes you have the option of checking and seeing the river card for "free."
- Your opponent might call and bet out on the turn if a scare card does not come.
- Your opponent might reraise.

In the first two cases, your strategy is successful regardless of whether or not you hit the flush. In the last two cases, your strategy has backfired and will cost you more bets for your draw. Note that whenever there is even a small chance that your opponent might fold with a hand like middle pair you have even more reasons to try for a free card.

Let's reverse roles for a minute. When you expect that your opponent is trying for a free card, you should make them pay a higher price for playing by either reraising or betting out the turn.

Advanced Concept: Do not give free cards when you expect that your opponents are on a draw.

Internet Tip

On the flop, some players like to instantaneously raise on the flop by using the "raise in turn" button before you even bet. These players are sometimes trying to act strong so that they can get a free card on the turn. If your opponent is this type of player, reraise to charge him the maximum price for his draw.

Sometimes it is correct to just call a flop raise and then bet out the turn if no scare card comes. This becomes correct when there are many scare cards such as flushes and overcards that make your hand the dog on the flop but the favorite on the turn if it is favorable.

Slowplaying

Slowplaying is checking or just calling a very strong hand on one round of betting to win more bets on later rounds of betting. Generally, you slowplay a very strong hand when it is likely that your opponents will fold to a bet and a free card is not too dangerous. *Most players slowplay too often.*

You generally should not slowplay under the following conditions:
- A free card could beat you.
- The pot is large.
- A free card would not give your opponents a good second-best hand.
- There are many opponents in the hand.
- There are weak opponents in the hand.

Let's discuss each of these in more detail.

A free card could beat you

It usually is not wise to give a free card when that card could beat you. There are very few hands that are a lock on the flop. For example, if you flop a straight, you could lose to a higher straight or end up splitting the pot with one of your opponents. If you flop the nut flush, you could end up losing to a full house. If you flop a set, you could possibly lose to a straight or flush. If the pot is small and the flop is not too dangerous, you can sometimes risk giving a free card, but generally be hesitant in giving a free card that could beat you.

The pot is large

Slowplaying is not recommended when the pot is large. *Your main goal with a large pot is winning the pot rather than making it bigger.* In addition, when the pot is large, many opponents will give you action anyway even with their weak hands. One problem with slowplaying a large pot is the risk of backdoor flushes and straights. For example, you flop a set of queens on a Q♦ 7♣ 2♥ flop. Slowplaying is risky with a large pot since a free card like the J♦ could possibly give an opponent a good draw. With a small pot, you might be willing to take this risk to win extra bets, but not with a large pot.

There is one exception to this rule. Sometimes it is difficult to drive out opponents on the flop even by raising.

Advanced Concept: In a large pot, your opponents are often correct in calling a raise on the flop but are getting insufficient pot odds to call a raise on the turn; therefore, waiting to raise the turn is sometimes a better strategy to protect your hand and force your opponents to pay two big bets to see the river.

A free card would not give your opponents a good second-best hand.

Sometimes betting is the best play if giving a free card is unlikely to generate a lot of action anyway. This generally occurs when there is an ace or king on the flop since there are not many cards that can give an opponent a good second-best hand. For example, if you hold AA with a flop of A93, there are no overcards to give your opponents a decent hand. In these cases, it is usually best to go ahead and bet and hope that you get some kind of action from an opponent holding a weak pair or maybe even a set if you are lucky. Compare this to a flop of J73 when you hold JJ. A free card could give an opponent a good second-best hand allowing you to gain several more big bets.

There are many opponents in the hand.

This is really a combination of two of the other reasons given. With many opponents in the hand, the pot is usually large and the risk of giving a free card is greater since there are more opponents on a draw. With several opponents in the hand, you also will generally get good action on the flop in most types of games.

The exception to this rule is when you have a super strong hand like a full house and a raise would drive out several opponents. In this case, usually check if you are acting early since an opponent might raise directly behind you. If someone bets into you, tend to just call if your raise would drive out several opponents behind you.

There are weak opponents in the hand.

Go ahead and bet against weak opponents who call too many hands after the flop. These types of opponents tend to pay you off anyhow, so don't miss a good opportunity when you have a strong hand.

Let's look at some examples where you might slowplay. You hold TT with a flop of T52. You can slowplay this hand if the pot is not very large and you aren't against very many opponents. Any A, K, Q, or J on the turn could give you nice action.

You hold Q7 with a flop of Q77. You can slowplay this hand also with a small pot. You should still play this hand strongly with a large pot, especially if there is a decent chance your opponents hold a queen or 7. Although your hand is super strong, it is still vulnerable to an opponent hitting a higher full house. You could also end up splitting the pot against an opponent with a queen in his hand if the last queen hits the board.

One problem with slowplaying is that sometimes you lose bets you could have earned otherwise. As discussed before, weak opponents will often pay you off anyway. You also lose bets when an opponent has a strong hand also. For example, you might flop top set and they flop second set, or you flop the nut flush and an opponent has a flush also. You could lose a lot of bets if both of you are slowplaying!

Internet Tip

As discussed previously, players tend to bluff more online than in a live game; therefore, your opponents will not respect your raises on the flop as much since they may think you are bluffing. You should tend to slowplay less often online since there is an increased chance that you might get great action on both the flop and turn.

Sometimes a better strategy than slowplaying is to play your hand strongly hoping that an opponent has a strong hand also. Most opponents tend to back off when there is a raise on the turn, but they don't fear raises on the flop as much. For example, with a flop of T52 and you hold TT, you could either raise or slowplay until the turn. If you raise the flop, you might get a lot of action if an opponent has an overpair, hits an overpair on the turn, or already has a very strong hand like 55 or 22. Many opponents don't expect you to raise the flop with such a strong hand, so you might win a lot of bets on both the flop *and* turn.

Advanced Concept: Sometimes you win more bets by playing contrary to what your opponents expect. Playing strong hands strongly can sometimes confuse your opponents into thinking you have either a vulnerable hand or are bluffing. For this reason, usually only slowplay when the pot is small and your opponents are likely to fold if you bet.

To summarize, slowplaying is another deceptive tactic to confuse your opponents and gain additional bets when they would have otherwise folded. Slowplaying is risky however whenever free cards can hurt you and the pot is already large. Slowplaying also backfires sometimes when you would have gained bets anyway against weak opponents or an opponent who already has a strong hand.

Inducing Bluffs and Calls

Inducing a bluff or a call is the act of playing your hand weakly so that your opponents will either bet by trying a bluff or call with a weak hand (otherwise known as a crying call). For example, you hold K♥ Q♣ on a board of K♦ Q♦ 5♠ 2♣ 6♣. Your opponent called your flop and turn bets. You suspect that your opponent is on a draw. If your opponent is indeed on a draw and you bet, he will fold. If you check, your opponent might try a bluff if he suspects that you were on a draw also. You need to be fairly confident that your opponent was on a draw to try this move. If your opponent was planning on calling with a mediocre holding and then checks, you lose a bet.

Inducing bluffs or calls is also a good strategy when you have a good yet vulnerable hand. This strategy can either save bets against a monster hand or win an extra bet by inducing a bluff or a crying call. For example, you hold AA and raise on the button with one caller. The flop is Q82. You bet and your opponent calls. The turn is an 8 and your opponent checks. One option is to just check behind your opponent. If your opponent comes out betting on the river, then you call. You save two bets if he has an 8 and you gain a bet if he comes out betting the river with a hand he would have folded on the turn like 77. If he checks the river, then you can bet, and likewise your check on the turn may induce him to make a crying call on the river with a hand like 77. Note however that you probably lost a bet if your opponent holds a queen.

Do not try to induce bluffs against *rocks*. Since these players rarely bluff, you gain nothing. Also, do not give up bets against opponents who will call with many weak hands. For example, if you are playing with an opponent who will call with 77 down to the river, keep betting and gain those bets.

Let's look at another example. You raise on the button first in with A♦ 6♦ and are reraised by an aggressive player in the small blind. The most common raising hands by an aggressive player in this situation are either a pair or Ax. The flop comes A♣ Q♦ 5♥. Your opponent bets and you call. He now checks the turn of 7♣. If he is the type of opponent who will fold a weak pair if you come out betting and would check-raise strong hands, then a good strategy might be to check the turn. He might try a bluff on the river gaining you a bet. If he checks the river and you bet, he might call with a weak hand gaining you a bet. On the other hand, if he was planning a check-raise on the turn, you save two bets on the turn while gaining the possibility of improving to a better hand.

Chapter Review

❑ A *free card* is when you receive a card without having to call a bet. In Hold'em, normally you try for a free card by either betting or raising on the flop, hoping that your opponents check to you on the turn when the bets are more expensive.

- There are several advantages to try for a free card:
  - If your hand does not improve, you might be able to see an additional card for free that could help you win the hand.
  - Your hand might improve on the next card and you can continue to bet having gained the additional small bet on the flop.
  - Buying a free card is a cheap way of calling opponents to the river when you are not sure whether or not you have the best hand.
- The problem with trying for free cards is that sometimes the strategy backfires if an opponent either reraises or comes out betting on the turn. Conversely, do not give free cards when you expect that your opponents are on a draw.
- Beware of players who raise instantaneously on the flop. They may be trying for a free card.

❑ *Slowplaying* is checking or just calling a very strong hand on one round of betting to win more bets on later rounds of betting.

- Most players slowplay too often. You generally should not slowplay under the following conditions:
  - A free card could beat you.
  - The pot is very large.
  - A free card would not give your opponents a good second-best hand.
  - There are many opponents in the hand.
  - There are weak opponents in the hand.
- Sometimes it is difficult to drive out opponents on the flop even by raising when there is a large pot. In these cases, sometimes it is better to slowplay and wait to raise the turn so that the remaining opponents have to pay two big bets to see the river.
- One problem with slowplaying is that sometimes you lose bets you could have earned otherwise. This occurs against weak opponents who will pay you off anyway or an opponent with a strong hand also.

❑ *Inducing a bluff or a call* is the act of playing your hand weakly so that your opponents will either bet by trying a bluff or call with a weak hand. A good example is checking on the river to induce an opponent to bluff if you expect he was on a draw.

- Inducing bluffs or calls is also a good strategy when you have a good yet vulnerable hand. This strategy can either save bets against a monster hand or win an extra bet by inducing a bluff or a call.
- Do not try to induce bluffs against rocks since they rarely bluff and don't give up bets against opponents who will call with many weak hands.

Test Your Skills

1/ $15-$30. You hold A♥ 5♥ one seat before the cutoff. An early and middle player call. You limp in and the small blind calls. Five players see the flop of K♥ 8♣ 4♥. The middle player bets. There is $90 in the pot. What do you do?

Answer: Call. The pot is small, so I prefer to just call rather than driving out the remaining opponents. If the pot was large, I would raise to increase the chances that my outs to the ace would be good.

2/ $20-$40. You hold A♦ K♦ on the button. An early player raises, a middle player calls, and you reraise. The small blind calls and four players see the flop of J♠ 7♦ 4♦. The small blind bets and the middle player raises. There is $320 in the pot. What do you do?

Answer: Reraise. This is a large pot and you have a very strong draw. Since the pot is so large, you would like the small blind to fold increasing your chances of winning the pot against a lone opponent. If your opponents call, your reraise might buy you a free card on the turn. Even if your opponents cap the betting, you still have a strong draw. In the actual hand, the player reraised, the small blind called, and everyone checked the turn. The flush didn't come and his opponents showed Q♠ Q♥ and Q♣ J♦. The player had 14 outs on the flop, which is even money to improve.

3/ $1-$2. You hold T♥ 8♠ on the button. An early and middle player call. You decide to call with this weak hand and the small blind calls. Five players see the flop of J♦ 9♦ 4♥. It is checked to you. There is $5 in the pot. What do you do?

Answer: Bet. This is a decent flop now that you have played the hand. It is doubtful that you can win the pot outright against four opponents; however, betting may gain you a free card on the turn. In the actual hand, the player checked. The turn was the 9♣ and again it was checked to the player, who decided to bet this time. The middle player called all-in with KT and won the hand when a rag came.

4/ $20-$40. You hold K♦ T♦ on the button. An early player calls and you raise. The small blind and big blind call. Four players see the flop of A♦ 9♦ 2♥. It is checked to you and you bet. The small blind raises and your other opponents fold. There is $220 in the pot. What do you do?

Answer: Reraise. You raised preflop, so you can reraise to represent a pair of aces with a good kicker to try and buy a free card. In the actual hand, the player reraised and both players checked the turn. The river was a rag and the player folded when his opponent bet.

5/ $.50-$1. You are in the big blind with 7♠ 5♠ and get a free play with five other callers. The flop is 7♥ 7♦ 5♦. The small blind checks and there is $3.00 in the pot. What do you do?

Answer: Check. Since you are against many opponents, you do not want to bet and risk that a player raises behind you driving out the remaining opponents. Some of your opponents may be on flush and straight draws, so you should get lots of action at these low limits. In the actual hand, three bets went into the pot on the flop with this player only having to call and then the turn was capped! One of his opponents showed 8♦ 7♣.

6/ $5-$10. The cutoff posts $5. You call in early position with 4♣ 4♦ and the small blind calls. The big blind raises and everybody calls. Four players see the flop of K♠ 7♣ 4♥. The big blind bets. There is $45 in the pot. What do you do?

Answer: Raise. This is a decent size pot and you want to drive out the remaining opponents. Your opponents could get a good draw on the turn if you allow them to stay cheaply.

7/ $20-$40. You raise in middle position with A♣ A♦ and both the blinds call. The flop is A♠ K♥ 6♠. Both blinds check. There is $120 in the pot. What do you do?

Answer: Bet. This is a decent size pot. You want to charge your opponents for their flush or gut-shot straight draws. Sometimes it is difficult to gain a lot of additional bets by slowplaying when you were the preflop raiser, since your opponents tend to become suspicious if you check the flop and then show strength on the turn. In the actual hand, the big blind called to the river with K♣ T♣.

8/ $15-$30. You hold 3♣ 3♦ in the big blind. A middle player low on chips calls and the small blind calls. Three players see the flop of K♠ 3♥ 2♦. The small blind checks. There is $45 in the pot. What do you do?

Answer: Check. The pot is small and the flop is not too scary. Betting will scare away the middle player low on chips unless he has a pair. Even if he does have a pair, you can probably get the remaining chips from him on the turn and river.

In the actual hand, the player checked and called the middle player. He then check-raised the turn card of Q♥. His opponent called all-in on the river card of 4♦ showing 6♥ 5♥ for a straight. The turn card gave his opponent a flush and gut-shot straight draw. Given the small pot, slowplaying was correct to try and win some additional bets, but unfortunately the strategy backfired this time. This hand shows what can happen even with a strong hand on the flop and demonstrates why slowplaying would not be correct if the pot had been large.

9/ $20-$40. You hold 2♣ 2♥ in the small blind. A middle position player calls and the following middle player raises. You call and the big blind folds. Three players see the flop of K♣ K♦ 2♦. It is checked to the preflop raiser who bets. There is $160 in the pot. What do you do?

Answer: Raise. It is difficult to slowplay hands from early position. If you only call, your opponent will probably back off his hand on the turn unless he has a king. Raising in this situation can also be deceptive since many opponents expect you to slowplay trip kings. If you are lucky, your opponent will hold trip kings and you will gain a lot of bets on both the flop and turn before your opponent realizes you have a full house. In the actual hand, the player raised and his opponent folded on the turn.

10/ $15-$30. You raise in middle position with Q♥ Q♦. A strong middle player reraises, the small blind calls, and you cap the pot. Three players see the flop of Q♣ 7♥ 7♠. It is checked to you. There is $195 in the pot. What do you do?

Answer: Bet. You capped the betting, so continue betting as the aggressor. You could get great action if an opponent holds AA or KK. Checking after capping the pot preflop may look very suspicious and your opponents may not play as aggressively as otherwise.

In the actual hand, the player checked and both opponents took a free card. The turn was the J♣. The player bet and was called on both the turn and river. His opponent showed JJ. If this player had bet the flop, he would have won a lot of bets on the turn, as his opponent most likely would have capped the betting (assuming he called the flop). Slowplaying can sometimes be correct against weak opponents in this situation but can cost you bets against strong opponents who don't fall into traps.

11/ $15-$30. You raise first in from the cutoff with K♥ K♦ and both blinds call. Three players see the flop of T♦ 3♥ 3♣. You bet, the small blind folds, and the big blind check-raises. You reraise and the big blind calls. The turn is the A♥ and the big blind checks. There is $180 in the pot. What do you do?

Answer: Check to induce a bluff or call on the river. Checking is not too risky. The only danger is that your opponent hits another ten or hits a pocket pair, which will only happen once every 23 hands. You do not need to be worried about your opponent hitting two pair if he holds a ten since you already have him beat.

If you bet, your opponent will most likely fold a pair of tens unless he is a weak player; therefore, betting gains you nothing. However, if you check the turn, you might be able to get him to either bet out a bluff on the river or make a crying call. You also avoid a check-raise if your opponent has trips or AT. In the actual hand, the player checked and his opponent made a crying call on the river with T9.

12/ $15-$30. You call in early position with K♣ Q♦. A middle player and the button call. Four players see the flop of Q♥ 6♦ 4♦. The big blind bets, you raise, the button calls, and the big blind folds. The turn is the 5♥. You bet and the button calls. The river is the A♥. There is $205 in the pot. What do you do?

Answer: Check. The only hands that you can beat that your opponent might call with are QJ or QT, although a strong player would have folded these on the flop to a raise. The most probable holding of your opponent is a flush draw; therefore, betting will not gain anything since your opponent will almost never call with a hand that you can beat. However, checking gains you a bet if you can induce your opponent to try a bluff. Checking also saves you a bet if your opponent hit a hand like Axs and would raise if you bet, assuming you would call a raise. In the actual hand, the player checked and his opponent bet J♦ 7♦.

Starting Hands

Introduction

The first section of the book covered basic poker concepts that are useful in almost every type of poker game. In the next section of the book, we look at strategies specific to the four betting rounds of Hold'em: preflop starting hands, the flop, turn, and river.

One of the main differences between the players who win and the players who lose is the quality of starting hands played. In general, most players should only be playing about 15% to 25% of their hands. This varies depending if the game is loose or tight, but in either case, playing fewer hands than your opponents is a big advantage.

The main criteria in deciding your starting hand strategy include:
- Strength of Starting Cards
- Position
- Number of Callers
- Type of Game (Loose/Tight, Passive/Aggressive)
- Raised/Unraised Pot
- Type of Opponents
- Table Image
- Strength of Your Own Play

Let's look at each of these criteria in more detail.

Strength of Starting Cards

In the long run, everybody gets dealt the same starting hands on average. Winning players play mostly strong hands while losing players play both strong *and* weak hands. Playing the strong hands is easy. What is more difficult is folding those weak hands that have a negative expectation. We will discuss the quality hands played in each position. Be careful not to stray from these guidelines.

Position

In real estate, we all know the name of the game is location, location, location. In Hold'em, the name of the game is position, position, position. If you are not familiar with the various positions and their common names, please refer to the table in the chapter "About this Book."

Position is important because it determines how much information you have about how the hand is developing. In early position you have very little information about what your opponents will do, while in late position you already know what they have done. For example, in late position you know if the pot has been raised and how many opponents have entered the pot. This positional advantage also remains the same throughout the hand, whereas, in a game like 7-card stud it might change.

Additional information from late position allows you to make better and more profitable decisions. Sometimes you can use your position to win the entire pot. For example, if everybody checks, you may have an opportunity to steal the pot. Sometimes your position saves you bets that you would have otherwise invested.

For example, you hold JT with a flop of J74 against four opponents. If you are acting first, you might bet out. If an opponent then raises and another reraises, you will need to fold losing your bet. However, if you were in late position with the same hand, you could safely fold if the pot is raised before you have to act. Your position saves you a bet even though you have exactly the same hand.

Position is also helpful when you are on the river. Sometimes you are unsure whether you should bet with a mediocre hand into your opponents, especially when you are heads up. If you check the best hand, you lose an opportunity to gain a bet. If you are acting last and your opponent checks, you usually can safely bet since your opponent has indicated weakness.

There are many situations where your position will either save or gain you bets; therefore, you can play more hands in late position than early position since each particular starting hand has a higher expectation. Even pocket aces makes more money in late position than early position. You earn and save bets when acting last! Learn this concept well as it is critical in Hold'em.

Number of Callers

The number of callers in a hand can have a big impact on your decision to play certain hands. Small and medium pairs and suited connectors play best with many opponents, while high unsuited cards play best against only one or two opponents.

For example, hands like AK and KQ play well against one or two opponents and sometimes will even win with ace or king high. Against several opponents, you usually need at least a pair to win and your pair may be vulnerable to opponents hitting two pair or better. On the other hand, small pairs and suited connectors do not improve very often to big hands, but when they do, you can often win a big pot against several opponents. These hands need good implied odds to play, so they are not profitable against one or two opponents.

Let's look at a common example of playing small pairs to demonstrate how the number of players affects your pot odds and ability to play your hands. You generally will need to fold small pairs on the flop unless you are able to hit a set, which is 7.5 to 1 against improving; therefore, in a $10-$20 game you will play between seven and eight hands on average before you hit your set and in the process lose $10 each hand. Once you hit your set, you will need to win at least $75 on average to compensate for all those times you had to fold on the flop.

If you are only against one or two opponents, it is difficult to win $75 on average when there is only $20 or $30 in the pot. They might fold on the flop and you will only win a small pot. Your set will also lose sometimes to higher sets, straights, and flushes. Your wins need to be large enough to compensate for the occasional losses and for the times you have to fold when you don't hit your set. You need a lot of players in the hand to justify your odds. You can generally expect to make a profit with at least five players in the hand, including the blinds, and possibly four players if they don't play too well after the flop.

Type of Game (Loose/Tight, Passive/Aggressive)

The type of game criteria is related to the previous criteria of number of opponents. The type of game gives you an *indication* of how many players will see the flop and whether or not the pot might be raised.

I generally consider games where more than 30% of the players see the flop as a loose game and less than 30% a tight game.

Some games are aggressive where there is a lot of preflop raising while other games are passive where usually you can see the flop for only one bet.

Low-limit games tend to be loose and passive while high-limit games tend to be tight and aggressive. You will also find that some sites tend to be tighter than others so try to shop around for the best games.

The type of game criteria is used mainly by advanced players to play a few more hands from early or middle position if the conditions are right. For example, in a loose/passive game, you might be able to call with a few more hands such as suited connectors and small pairs. If the game is tight and aggressive, you might be able to raise with more hands such as 77 or even KQ. These borderline plays based on the type of game should usually only be tried by advanced players.

Raised/Unraised Pot

Many hands become unplayable when the pot is raised. This is a simple concept, but many players fail to understand this very important point. A raise indicates that your opponent has a strong hand *and also* lowers your pot odds. As a general rule, you should not call a raise with speculative hands such as medium pairs or suited connectors unless you expect to have at least five callers in the hand to justify your odds. Of course there are exceptions, but most players would not be giving up very much if they always folded these hands to a raise.

Under the number of players criteria, we showed how small pairs should only be played against many opponents; otherwise, you have poor pot odds compared to the chance of improving your hand. If an opponent raises, your pot odds are even worse! In a $10-$20 game, you will need to win at least $150 on average to compensate for all the times that you have to fold your small pocket pairs on the flop when you don't hit your set.

Hands like AT and KQ are also dangerous hands to play against a raise unless the situation is just right. Most players raise with premium pairs and hands like AK and AQ, so there is a good chance your hand is dominated. Be very selective in the hands you play once the pot has been raised.

Type of Opponents

Advanced players try to play more hands against weak opponents and less hands against strong opponents. Borderline hands are sometimes profitable against weak opponents, yet unprofitable against good opponents. Weak opponents make more mistakes after the flop, which means more profits for you.

For example, if there is a maniac who keeps raising every hand and you hold AT in late position, you might reraise with this hand to try and isolate yourself against this opponent. However, if the player who raised is a solid player, you would probably fold AT, as this hand does not play very well against a good player who is selective in the hands he raises.

Table Image

Your table image and that of your opponents can change how you play particular hands. For example, a tight table image may allow you to steal the blinds more often with some borderline hands. In addition, you might play a few more starting hands to take advantage of your tight image *after* the flop to steal a few pots with bluffs and semi-bluffs. On the other hand, players with a loose image will be less successful stealing the blinds so they should tend to raise less often preflop with borderline hands.

The table image of your opponents is also very important. You should play more hands against loose players and fewer hands against tight players. This is especially true when a tight player has raised. On the other hand, you might try to steal the blinds a little more often if there is a tight player in the blinds.

Table image is much more important in tight aggressive games that you see in the higher limits than in loose low-limit games. Generally there is a showdown in low-limit games so image is not very important.
Another important concept relates back to the advanced concept we discussed in the "Introduction to Internet Poker" chapter: table image is not as important online as in a live poker game. We'll discuss this more in the "Starting Hands – Advanced Concepts" chapter.

Strength of Your Own Play

The number of hands you play should also be dependent on how good a poker player you are. Advanced players are able to overcome the weakness of some starting hands by using their excellent post-flop skills to outplay their opponents. They make better decisions on the flop, turn, and river to minimize losses with weak hands and maximize their wins. This allows them to be able to play more hands profitably than the beginning player. Most beginning to intermediate players should play a very tight game until you gain more experience.

Now that we know the main criteria used in evaluating strategies for starting hand play, let's get more specific and look at what hands are playable in each position. The first chapter on starting hands is for beginning to intermediate players and shows a simple winning strategy based on tight play. The second chapter is for advanced players and discusses some other factors that may allow you to play more hands in certain situations.

Chapter Review

❑ Criteria for starting hand play include:
- **Strength of Starting Cards**
  - Winning players play mostly strong hands while losing players play both strong *and* weak hands.
  - It is important to play only the quality hands from each position.
- **Position**
  - Position is important because it determines how much information you have about how the hand is developing.
  - There are many situations where your position can help you save or gain bets or even win the whole pot.
  - You can play more hands in late position than early position since each particular starting hand has a higher expectation.
- **Number of Callers**
  - Small and medium pairs and suited connectors play best with many opponents, while high unsuited cards play best against only one or two opponents.
- **Type of Game (Loose/Tight, Passive/Aggressive)**
  - The type of game gives you an *indication* of how many players will see the flop and whether or not the pot might be raised.
  - Advanced players use this criteria to play a few more hands from early or middle position if the conditions are right.
- **Raised/Unraised Pot**
  - Many players fail to understand that many hands become unplayable when the pot has been raised.
  - A raise indicates that your opponent has a strong hand *and also* lowers your pot odds.
- **Type of Opponents**
  - Advanced players try to play more hands against weak opponents and less hands against strong opponents.

- **Table Image**
  - Your table image and that of your opponents can change how you play particular hands.
  - Table image is much more important in tight aggressive games that you see in the higher limits than in loose low-limit games.
  - Table image is not as important online as in a live game.
- **Strength of Your Own Play**
  - The number of hands you play should also be dependent on how good a poker player you are.

Starting Hands
Beginning/Intermediate Players

Early Position

Many players lose a lot of money playing too many hands in early position. There are three distinct disadvantages when playing from early position:
- You do not know how many players will be playing the hand.
- You are unsure of how much it will cost to play the hand since the pot could be raised or even reraised behind you.
- You will be acting before most of your opponents on every betting round.

For these reasons, *you should play very few hands from early position.* Compare this to when you are sitting in late position where you have much more information to make better decisions both preflop and after the flop. The same exact hand can be profitable in late position yet lose money in early position.

For example, let's say you play K♣ T♣ in early position with a flop of K♦ 9♥ 5♠. The big blind bets, so you raise with top pair. An opponent in middle position reraises and then the big blind caps! You should fold losing two bets since you are probably against either a set, two pair, or a pair of kings with a better kicker. If you were in late position, you could have safely folded to the raise by the middle position player without having committed money to the pot. You need strong hands from early position to compensate for acting first on every betting round.

Unraised Pots

You should usually raise with the following premium hands: AA, KK, QQ, AKs, AK, AQs, AQ, and AJs. Normally call with these hands: JJ, TT, 99, AJ, ATs, A9s, and KQs. You can raise with JJ if the game is rather tight; otherwise, it is better to just call in a loose game. If one player has already called, you can call also with 88, 77, A8s, A7s, KJs, and QJs.

By the way, in any position except for the blinds, once you have limped in, you should almost always call a raise. If your hand was good enough to call in the first place, it should be good enough to call one more bet with better pot odds. This leads me into a good general rule for playing starting hands. *Only call when a raise behind you wouldn't be so bad.*

For example, I would not be too happy having to call a raise with a small pair against a lone opponent; however, this is not such a bad situation if there are several callers. If you find yourself cringing a lot when an opponent raises, you are probably playing too many hands.

If the pot is reraised and you are faced with two more bets, you should usually fold unless you have a premium hand or your hand could play well in a multi-handed pot. For example, you should fold hands like 99, ATs, and QJs for two more bets, unless there are a lot of callers and you don't think the pot will be capped.

Raised Pots

If the pot has been raised, go ahead and reraise with AA, KK, QQ, AKs, and AK. Usually just call with JJ, AQs, AQ, and AJs. Against some opponents whose raising standards are not too strong, you might reraise with JJ or AQ. If you are against a very tight player, you might fold AJs and possibly even AQ.

Middle Position

You can begin to play a few more hands in middle position than you would from early position. On the other hand, some hands you might have played in early position may now be unplayable if the pot has been raised. In middle position, you have a little better idea of how many players will be in the pot, if the pot has been raised, and the caliber of players who have entered the pot. All of this additional information along with slightly better position allows you to play a few more hands.

Unraised Pots

Go ahead and raise with the same hands from early position. If you are the first one to enter the pot, you should also raise with JJ, TT, AJ, ATs, and AT. You can also add a few more hands to call with since there is now less of a chance that the pot will be raised: 99, A9s, A8s, A7s, KQs, KQ, and KJs.

If there are already callers, you can call with a few more hands since you are getting slightly better pot odds and your call may encourage others to call behind you. With one caller add 88, 77, Axs, KTs, QJs, and QTs. With two callers add 66, 55, and JTs. With three callers add 44, 33, 22, J9s, T9s, and 98s.

Note that *trap hands* should not be played from middle position: KJ, KT, and QT. These hands rarely win large pots, unless you hit a straight, and can lose a lot of money to hands with better kickers or players with good draws.

Raised Pots

If the pot has been raised, go ahead and reraise with AA, KK, QQ, AKs, and AK and call with JJ, AQs, AQ, and AJs. If the raise is a lone raiser from middle position and there are no other callers, you could reraise with all of those hands to try and drive out the remaining players and isolate yourself against the raiser.

Late Position

You will make most of your money from Hold'em in late position as you are able to act last on every betting round. You will know how many callers there are, who your competition is, and whether or not the pot has been raised. All of this solid information should allow you to make better and more profitable decisions.

Unraised Pots

One very important concept comes into play when you are in late position and nobody has called yet. If you are going to play your hand, you should almost always raise! Raising gives you a chance to steal the blinds or at least charge them a higher price for playing. If they do call, you will have good position on every betting round. In general, you can raise first in with all of the following hands: any pair 77 or higher, two cards jack or higher, two suited cards ten or higher, Axs, AT, and A9. There are situations when you can raise other hands, but for most beginners it is probably better to just play these hands.

With callers, raise with the same hands from early and middle position: AA, KK, QQ, AKs, AK, AQs, AQ, and AJs. If there is only one caller, you can also raise with JJ, TT, AJ, ATs, and KQs to try and isolate yourself against this lone opponent if possible. If there are already two or more opponents in the hand, you should normally just call with these hands.

You can play more hands with more callers:
One Caller: 99 88 77 AT Axs KQ KJs KJ KTs QJs QJ QTs JTs
Two Callers: 66 55 KT K9s QT Q9s J9s T9s
Three Callers: 44 33 22 K8s K7s JT T8s 98s
Four Callers: Kxs Q8s J8s 87s 76s

Raised Pots

When the pot has been raised and you are in late position, there are two important considerations in dictating your strategy: position of the raiser and the number of callers.

You should almost always reraise with AA, KK, QQ, AKs, and AK. If you are against a lone opponent, you can either reraise or call with JJ, TT, AQs, AQ, and AJs depending on their position and type of player. Either reraise or fold with 99. Generally you can call with KQs, although sometimes you can consider reraising a late position raiser. AJ is not nearly as strong a hand as most people think. Generally fold this to a raise unless you want to reraise a late position opponent.

If there is a raise and there are many callers, you can consider calling with other hands. Small pairs and suited connectors 98s and higher play well in a multi-handed pot. These hands generally need many opponents to give you good pot odds on your speculative hand, so you shouldn't be calling raises very often. With these hands you are hoping to hit a big hand on the flop; otherwise, you can safely fold losing just two small bets. You can consider calling a raise cold against three callers with 88 and 77. Against four callers add 66, 55, 44, 33, 22, QJs, and JTs. Against five callers add T9s and 98s.

The Blinds

You will lose money in the blinds no matter how good you are. You are forced to pay the blind money with many poor hands that you will be folding a lot. Your goal is to minimize your losses; however, many players lose more than they should by playing too many weak hands.

Play in the blinds is very subjective and dependent on many factors. It is here more than any other position that your post flop play is critical. Calling a raise with KJ might be OK for some players, but only if you know how to play the hand well after the flop. It takes a lot of experience to be able to play weak hands profitably out of position. It is recommended that beginning and intermediate players play conservatively from the blinds. In the following discussions, we will assume that there is at least one opponent in the hand other than the small blind and big blind. There is a separate section that discusses play when everyone has folded to the blinds.

Unraised Pots

You should almost always raise with AA, KK, QQ, AKs, and AK. If there are only one or two callers, you can also raise with AQs and AQ. Against one limper you can also raise JJ. When you are in the small blind, you can raise one limper with more hands such as TT, 99, AJs, AJ, ATs, and AT. You probably have the best hand and you would usually like the big blind to fold to isolate yourself against a lone opponent.

When calling a half bet from the small blind, you can play many hands since you are getting good pot odds on a half bet; however, you still need to be somewhat selective since you will be acting first on every round. As usual, the hands you should play depend a lot on the number of callers:

One caller: pairs, two cards T and above, two suited 8 and above, Ax Kxs
               T9 87s 76s
Two callers: 98 97s 65s 54s
Three callers: Qxs J7s T7s 87 86s 76 75s 65 64s
Four callers: 96s 85s 54 53s 43s 32s

One note about the limit you are playing. In most limits, the small blind is half the amount of the big blind; however, in some limits this amount could be more or less than half, so you need to adjust accordingly. For example, in a $15-$30 game, the small blind posts $10, which is 2/3 the amount of the big blind. You can play a few more hands since the cost of calling is only 1/3 of a bet. On the other hand, if you are playing $5-$10 and the small blind is only $2, you should be more conservative with the hands you play since the cost of playing is now 3/5 of a bet.

Raised Pots

When the pot has been raised, there are several considerations in determining your best strategy:

⇨ **What position did the raise come from?** An early position raiser usually has a premium hand, so you should be selective with the hands you decide to play. A late position raiser could be trying to steal the blinds, so you can play more hands.

⇨ **How many total players are in the pot?** The more players in the hand, the better your pot odds since you only owe one or one and a half small bets to play.

⇨ **Were there any cold callers?** There is a big difference in a player who limps and then calls a raise versus a player who cold calls a raise. If there is an early position raiser *and* a middle position caller, you should proceed very carefully, especially with the trap hands. Compare this to a middle position limper and late position raiser. In this scenario you could call a few more hands.

⇨ **Will your call close the betting?** Some players like to slowplay their premium hands from early position hoping to be able to reraise. If this type of player has called from early position and another player raises, you should fold more often than otherwise for the risk of a reraise and possibly even a capped pot.

⇨ **What type of player is the raiser?** Is he a rock who never raises without a premium hand? Is he a loose aggressive player who tends to overplay his hands post-flop once he has raised? Does the player try to steal the blinds a lot? With some players, you can narrow down their hands to the top premium hands, while other players might be raising with almost anything. Always consider the type of opponent you are against on borderline decisions.

When you are in the big blind and the pot has already been reraised, go ahead and cap with AA, KK, and sometimes QQ. Only call a reraise with the premium hands: JJ, AKs, AK, AQs, AQ, and AJs.

Against a raise, you should only reraise with the very best premium hands: AA, KK, QQ, and AKs. You can also reraise with AK, although sometimes you might just call against several opponents.

When you are in the small blind against a raiser, you should reraise with a few more hands to isolate yourself against one or two players. Generally reraise with AQs and AQ against one or two opponents, but call against three or more. Against a lone raiser, go ahead and reraise with JJ, TT, and 99. If you are against a lone late position raiser, you should almost always reraise if you play your hand. These hands include 88, 77, AJs, AJ, ATs, AT, and A9s. You can consider reraising with KQs or KJs depending on the type of opponent you are against, although you might just call if there is a weak opponent in the big blind.

Let's look now at calling raises from the big blind against a lone opponent. In these cases, the position and type of opponent is very important. Generally fold the small pairs against a lone opponent. Consider calling 88 and 77 against a lone middle or late position opponent and 66 or 55 against a late position opponent; otherwise, you probably should fold these hands. Other hands to consider calling against a lone early or middle position raiser include: TT, 99, any two suited T and above, AQ, AJ, AT, Axs, KQ, K9s, QJ, and QT. Against a lone late raiser, you can add A9, A8, KJ, KT, Q9s, and Q8s.

Against two or more opponents, you can usually call from the big blind with any pair, two cards ten and above, Q9s, Q8s, J9s, T9s, and 98s; however, be careful with the unsuited trap hands like KJ, KT, and QT. These hands are often counterfeited against several opponents in a raised pot, especially when there is an opponent who has cold-called a raise. You need to know when to fold these hands on the flop if you are going to play them profitably.

With more opponents you can play more hands from the big blind:
Three: Kxs Qxs J8s T9 T8s 98 97s 87s 76s 65s
Four: T7s 87 86s 76 75s 54s
Five: J7s 96s

When you are in the small blind, you still need a strong hand to call against several opponents since you must call 3/4 of a bet and you have to act first on every betting round. Against two opponents you can call with JJ, TT, 99, AJs, ATs, and KQs. Against three opponents you can play all pairs. Against four opponents you can add KJs, QJs, and JTs. Finally, consider calling T9s and 98s against five or more opponents. Note that even a hand like KQ should almost always be folded against a raise when you are in the small blind.

Small Blind vs. Big Blind

Players who play mostly in live games often do not have a lot of experience playing hands when everyone folds to the blinds. Many casinos allow the players to "chop," where each player simply takes back their blinds rather than playing out the hand.

Internet Tip

If you play mostly in live games and begin to play online, it is essential to learn to play well in small blind versus big blind situations, especially in the higher limits.

Small blind versus big blind situations still do not occur very often in full ring games at the lower limits since usually there are several callers in each hand. However, in the higher limits and in short-handed games, advanced players can earn a lot of money in these situations against the right opponents.

Everything changes when everyone folds around to the blinds. First of all, the big blind now has positional advantage over the small blind. On the other hand, the small blind only has to call a half a bet and beat only one opponent. In these heads-up situations, it is difficult to define starting hand guidelines since strategies are very dependent on the type of opponent you are against and your table image.

When you are in the small blind, you are getting 3 to 1 pot odds on a call, but at the same time will be acting first on every betting round. Your strategy to fold, call, or raise is dependent on several factors:

- **Does the big blind defend his blinds appropriately?** If he folds too much, you should raise with a lot of hands.
- **Does the big blind play his hands aggressively preflop?** What are the chances of being raised if you just call half a bet? If the big blind is aggressive, you will need to limit your calls since you may have to pay a high price for a mediocre hand out of position. By the way, if you call with a weak hand, feel free to fold if the big blind raises. This is one case where calling and then folding preflop can be correct since the pot is small, you are out of position, your opponent has indicated strength, and your hand is not very strong.
- **How does the big blind play post-flop?** Play more hands against opponents who make a lot of mistakes after the flop.

The following guidelines are for hands against typical players, but these can change dramatically depending on the type of opponent you are against and the conditions discussed above. In the small blind, you can safely raise with all pairs, any two cards jack and above, ATs, AT, KTs, KT, and QTs. Generally you can call with any two cards 8 and above, any two suited cards 7 and above, Ax, Kx, and Qxs; however, you should fold many of these hands if you are raised. Against weak opponents you could raise or call with even more hands.

When you are in the big blind against the small blind, you should generally play aggressively. If the small blind raises, generally reraise with all the hands you would raise with from the small blind: all pairs, any two cards jack and above, ATs, AT, KTs, KT, and QTs. You can call a raise with all of the hands you would normally call with from the small blind. If the small blind is a rock, you will need to be more conservative with the hands you reraise or call with.

If the small blind just calls, raise with many hands. The small blind has indicated weakness, and you have good position, so take advantage of it! Most players can safely raise with all the following hands: any pair, two cards ten and above, Ax, and K9(s). Again, you can raise with even more hands against weak opponents who play poorly after the flop.

Internet Tip

If you follow the starting hand guidelines in this chapter, you should be playing fewer hands than most of your opponents. Patience is a virtue in this game. Fortunately, it is much easier to be patient on the Internet than in a live game. In a live game, the action is much slower and your patience can sometimes run thin if you get a bad run of cards. On the Internet, you can play over 70 hands an hour even in a full ring game. Stay patient and you will get plenty of chances to play some strong hands.

Chapter Review

The tables on the following pages are a summary of starting hand play and are intended as a general guide for most situations. There are further explanations and considerations in the text for certain situations that may vary from these guidelines.

Most Hold'em books provide some type of tables for starting hands. Although many of these tables are very easy to understand, they sometimes put the user in unprofitable situations since they usually do not focus on the number of callers in the hand. In addition, many starting hand charts do not show strategies for raised pots.

The goal of these tables is to ensure that beginning players play hands in profitable situations. Before using the tables, be sure to carefully read the following instructions and reread them if necessary to ensure you have a clear understanding of how to use them.

To use the tables, the first step is to find the table for the related position. There are separate tables for early position, middle position, late position, and the blinds. The next step is to then find the row for the corresponding hand. Pairs are listed in the top column followed by hands starting with an ace, then king, queen, etcetera. Once you have found your hand, you then need to find the appropriate column depending on whether or not the pot has been raised.

The table then shows whether you should reraise, raise, call, or fold depending on how many callers there are in the pot. The following should help with the terminology in the tables:

Raise First In: You can raise when there are no limpers in the hand.

Raise: You can raise no matter how many players are in the pot.

Raise 1: You can only raise when there is one player in the pot or you are first in.

Call: You can call no matter how many players are in the pot.

Call 1: You can only call if there is *at least* one other caller in the hand; therefore, *you should fold if first in*.

Call 2: You can only call if there are *at least* two callers already in the hand.

Let's look at some examples.

Early Position	Unraised Pot	Raised Pot
88 77	Call 1	Fold
A8s A7s	Call 1	Fold

- In early position, only call with A8s or 77 if there is already at least one caller in the pot. Fold if you are first in or if the pot has been raised.

Middle Position	Unraised Pot	Raised Pot
98s	Call 3	Fold

- In middle position, only play 98s if there are already three or more callers. Do not call raises.

Late Position	Unraised Pot	Raised Pot
JJ TT	Raise 1, Call 2	RR 1 Option, Call All
99	Raise First In, Call 1	RR or Fold against 1 player, Call 3

- In late position, you should raise with JJ against one caller or first in, and call against two callers or more. You have the option of reraising a lone raiser; otherwise, always call a raise.
- Raise 99 when you are first in from late position; otherwise, call if the pot has not been raised. With a raised pot, either reraise or fold against a lone opponent and only call when there are at least three opponents in the hand.

Blinds	SB Unraised Pot	SB Raised Pot	BB Raised Pot
AQs AQ	Raise 1 or 2, Call 3	RR 1 or 2, Call 3	Call (raise 1 or 2 limpers)
A9s	Call	RR Lone Late, Fold	Call
KJ	Call	Fold	Call 2, or 1 Late

- In the small blind, you can raise or reraise one or two opponents with AQ, otherwise, call against three or more opponents.
- In the small blind, always call A9s against limpers. If the pot has been raised, you should reraise a late position player. You should fold if the raiser is in early or middle position or against two or more opponents.
- In the big blind, you can call with KJ against two opponents or a lone late player. Fold against a lone player from early or middle position.

With a little practice, you should be able to find the appropriate strategy very quickly. I recommend posting these charts next to your computer to provide you guidance as you play.

Early Position	Unraised Pot	Raised Pot
AA KK QQ	Raise	Reraise
JJ	Call	Call
TT 99	Call	Fold
88 77	Call 1	Fold
AKs AK	Raise	Reraise
AQs AQ AJs	Raise	Call
AJ ATs A9s	Call	Fold
A8s A7s	Call 1	Fold
KQs	Call	Fold
KJs	Call 1	Fold
QJs	Call 1	Fold

Middle Position	Unraised Pot	Raised Pot
AA KK QQ	Raise	Reraise
JJ	Raise First in, Call 1	Call
TT	Raise First in, Call 1	Fold
99	Call	Fold
88 77	Call 1	Fold
66 55	Call 2	Fold
44 33 22	Call 3	Fold
AKs AK	Raise	Reraise
AQs AQ AJs	Raise	Call
AJ ATs AT	Raise First in, Call 1	Fold
A9s A8s A7s	Call	Fold
Axs	Call 1	Fold
KQs KQ KJs	Call	Fold
KTs	Call 1	Fold
QJs QTs	Call 1	Fold
JTs	Call 2	Fold
J9s	Call 3	Fold
T9s	Call 3	Fold
98s	Call 3	Fold

Late Position	Unraised Pot	Raised Pot
AA KK QQ	Raise	Reraise (RR)
JJ TT	Raise 1, Call 2	RR 1 Option, Call All
99	Raise First In, Call 1	RR or Fold against 1 player, Call 3
88 77	Raise First In, Call 1	Call 3
66 55	Call 2	Call 4
44 33 22	Call 3	Call 4
AKs AK	Raise	Reraise
AQs AQ AJs	Raise	RR 1 option, Call All
AJ ATs	Raise 1, Call 2	Fold
AT Axs	Raise First In, Call 1	Fold
A9	Raise First In; otherwise Fold	Fold
KQs	Raise 1, Call 2	Call
KQ KJs KJ KTs	Raise First In, Call 1	Fold
KT K9s	Call 2	Fold
K8s K7s	Call 3	Fold
Kxs	Call 4	Fold
QJs	Raise First In, Call 1	Call 4
QJ QTs	Raise First In, Call 1	Fold
QT Q9s	Call 2	Fold
Q8s	Call 4	Fold
JTs	Raise First In, Call 1	Call 4
JT	Call 3	Fold
J9s	Call 2	Fold
J8s	Call 4	Fold
T9s	Call 2	Call 5
T8s	Call 3	Fold
98s	Call 3	Call 5
87s	Call 4	Fold
76s	Call 4	Fold

BLINDS	SB Unraised Pot	SB Raised Pot	BB Raised Pot*
AA KK QQ	Raise	Reraise (RR)	Reraise (raise limpers)
JJ	Raise 1, Call 2	RR 1, Call 2	Call (raise 1 limper)
TT 99	Raise 1, Call 2	RR 1, Call 2	Call
88 77	Call	RR Lone Late, Call 3	Call 2, or 1 Middle or Late
66 55	Call	Call 3	Call 2, or 1 Late
44 33 22	Call	Call 3	Call 2
AKs	Raise	Reraise (RR)	Reraise (raise limpers)
AK	Raise	Reraise or Call	Reraise or Call (raise limpers)
AQs AQ	Raise 1 or 2, Call 3	RR 1 or 2, Call 3	Call (raise 1 or 2 limpers)
AJs ATs	Raise 1, Call 2	RR Lone Late, Call 1	Call
AJ AT	Raise 1, Call 2	RR Lone Late, Fold	Call
A9s	Call	RR Lone Late, Fold	Call
A9 A8	Call	Fold	Call 1 Late, Fold
Axs Ax	Call	Fold	Axs Call, Ax Fold
KQs	Call	Call 2, or 1 Late	Call
KQ	Call	Fold	Call
KJs	Call	Call 4, or 1 Late	Call
KJ	Call	Fold	Call 2, or 1 Late
KTs	Call	Fold	Call
KT	Call	Fold	Call 2, or 1 Late
K9s	Call	Fold	Call
Kxs	Call	Fold	Call 3
QJs	Call	Call 4	Call
QJ QTs QT	Call	Fold	Call
Q9s Q8s	Call	Fold	Call 2, or 1 Late
Qxs	Call 3	Fold	Call 3
JTs	Call	Call 4	Call
JT J9s	Call	Fold	Call 2
J8s	Call	Fold	Call 3
J7s	Call 3	Fold	Call 5
T9s	Call	Call 5	Call 2
T9 T8s	Call	Fold	Call 3
T7s	Call 3	Fold	Call 4
98s	Call	Call 5	Call 2
98 97s	Call 2	Fold	Call 3
96s	Call 4	Fold	Call 5
87s	Call	Fold	Call 3
87 86s	Call 3	Fold	Call 4
85s	Call 4	Fold	Fold
76s	Call	Fold	Call 3
76 75s	Call 3	Fold	Call 4
65s	Call 2	Fold	Call 3
65 64s	Call 3	Fold	Fold
54s	Call 2	Fold	Call 4
54 53s 43s 32s	Call 4	Fold	Fold

* In the Big Blind, cap with AA, KK, and sometimes QQ. Only call reraises with JJ, AKs, AK, AQs, AQ, and AJs. Raise limpers where indicated.

Test Your Skills

1/ $15-$30. You hold KK in early position. An early player raises. What do you do?

Answer: Reraise. Always raise or reraise with AA and KK when one player has already committed chips to the pot.

2/ $1-$2. You hold 2♠ 2♦ in early position. What do you do?

Answer: Fold. To play small pairs, you generally want to be playing against many opponents and preferably in an unraised pot. In early position, you should fold since you are unsure if the pot will be raised and you do not know how many players will play the hand.

3/ $1-$2. You hold 5♠ 4♠ in the cutoff. A middle player calls. What do you do?

Answer: Fold. Small suited connectors are only profitable for their draw potential against many opponents.

4/ $1-$2. You hold K♠ J♣ in middle position. An early player calls and a middle player raises. What do you do?

Answer: Fold. Trap hands like KJ, KT, and QT are much weaker hands than most players realize. You should never call a raise that comes from early or middle position with these hands.

5/ $1-$2. You hold A♥ T♣ under the gun. What do you do?

Answer: Fold. AT unsuited is not profitable from early position.

6/ $15-$30. You are in early position with 9♥ 9♠. An early player raises in a tight aggressive game. What do you do?

Answer: Fold. This hand only plays well against one opponent or many opponents. In a tight aggressive game with a raise, there won't be many opponents. Even if you reraise to try and isolate, there are still many opponents behind you who could enter the pot. In addition, even if you do isolate, your opponent may have a higher pair or hit his overcards.

7/ $20-$40. You hold Q♣ J♣ in early position. An early player calls in a tight aggressive game. What do you do?

Answer: Call. This hand plays well in a multi-handed pot. The caller and your call should encourage others to enter the pot. Two callers also decreases the chance that the pot will be raised, except by opponents with the very best premium hands. Although you can play this hand, it is still a borderline decision and you will not be losing a lot by folding, especially if you are a beginning player.

8/ $5-$10. You hold Q♠ J♥ in middle position. What do you do?

Answer: Fold. Unsuited hands without an ace do not play well in early and middle position. KQ is a borderline call and QJ should be folded.

9/ $.50-$1. You are in early position with K♣ J♦. The first two players fold. What do you do?

Answer: Fold. KJ does not play well in early and middle position. Most beginners would do better if they never played this hand.

10/ $1-$2. You are on the button with Q♦ 9♦. An early player, a middle player, and the cutoff call. What do you do?

Answer: Call. This is not the best hand in the world since you can never have top pair with top kicker, the nut flush, and rarely the nut straight. However, since the hand is suited, it is playable on the button for one bet with several callers. If you always folded this hand, you would not be losing very much as it has only a very small positive expectation even with many callers.

11/ $.50-$1. You are on the button with 4♦ 4♥. An early player and a middle player call. What do you do?

Answer: Fold. Generally, you need three or more callers for small pairs to be profitable.

12/ $1-$2. You are in the cutoff with 5♣ 5♥. Two early players and a middle player call. What do you do?

Answer: Call. With three opponents you are getting good enough pot odds for small pairs to be profitable. The button and small blind could also enter the pot. Even if the button raises, there will be enough players to make your play reasonable even in a raised pot.

13/ $15-$30. You are on the button with A♣ A♥. A middle player raises. There is only $55 in the pot. Should you consider just calling?

Answer: No. With one opponent already committed to the pot, you should always raise or reraise with the premium pairs. The only exception to this is when you are in the blinds, when you *might* consider slowplaying against a lone aggressive opponent.

14/ $20-$40. You hold 5♠ 5♦ in the big blind. A player in early position raises and everyone folds. What do you do?

Answer: Fold. You will be forced to fold on the flop if any card jack or higher comes. Even if the flop is favorable, you still are not sure if your opponent holds a high pocket pair. The only way to win a large pot in this situation is to flop a set, and you are not getting sufficient pot odds to try for a set against only one opponent.

15/ $20-$40. You hold 5♠ 5♣ in the big blind. A player in early position raises and the small blind calls. What do you do?

Answer: Call. With the additional player you are getting sufficient implied odds to call. You currently are getting 5 to 1 pot odds and you will usually win additional bets when you hit your set.

16/ $20-$40. You hold A♦ 5♥ in the big blind. Two early players call, the cutoff raises, and the button calls. What do you do?

Answer: Fold. This will be a very large pot with four opponents paying two bets to see the flop. You only have to pay $20 for an expected pot of $210 should you call. The problem with calling here is that one of your opponents most likely has an ace with a better kicker; therefore, to win the hand you will need to flop a monster such as two pair, trip 5's, or the very unlikely straight. The odds against flopping one of these hands are too high to justify calling even with such a large pot. Many players call too often with Ax from the blinds.

Starting Hands
Advanced Concepts

This chapter discusses advanced concepts that may allow you to play a few more hands than recommended in the previous chapter. In addition, we discuss situations where you might add a little deception to your game. Most of these plays are borderline decisions that have an expected value of close to break even or are just slightly profitable for *advanced players*. Beginning players will probably lose money playing these additional hands; therefore, I recommend that beginning players skip this chapter until they have gained more experience and feel confident in all other aspects of the game.

A lot of the value in these plays is the advertising value of giving yourself a looser image to earn more profits later when you hold strong hands; however, I don't recommend plays just to boost your image unless you can at least break even on the play, especially on the Internet.

Internet Tip

As explained in the "Introduction to Internet Poker" chapter, table image is not as important online as it is in live games. Players do not stay in one game very long on the Internet and tend not to pay as much attention to the game; therefore, strategies that aim to create or take advantage of table image are generally not as profitable online as they would be in a live game. Of course, you can still use your table image online in the right circumstances, especially at some of the smaller sites where you play often against regular opponents. At larger sites, table image is less important since players are constantly moving in and out of games.

The plays discussed in this chapter are not necessarily for everybody. Some players are successful with a very tight strategy while others are successful with looser strategies playing every single borderline hand. Neither strategy is better than the other one is. Both players may win close to the same amount of money in the long run, although the player who plays more of the borderline hands will have larger fluctuations in his bankroll. This is just a matter of your own personal style.

Early Position

Premium hands such as AA, KK, and AKs do not come along very often. You would like to maximize your chances of winning a large pot with these hands if possible. If you are in a tight game where there is a decent chance that all of your opponents will fold if you raise, one strategy is to just call. If one of your opponents raises, you can then go ahead and reraise. Of course, the risk in just calling is that a player with a medium holding will play and hit something good on the flop.

I like to mix up my play by sometimes calling and sometimes raising, depending on how my opponents might perceive my play. If I have been playing a lot of hands, I would probably go ahead and raise since my opponents may not respect my raises as much. If I have been playing very few hands, I would probably just call since I do not want to raise and just win the blinds with these hands.

This strategy of only calling with premium hands should only be used in tight aggressive games. In loose games, you should usually go ahead and raise since you can expect to get some callers. Note that this strategy is most profitable from early position. When you raise from middle or late position, your opponents will call with more hands since they expect you to reduce your raising standards. Whenever there is one caller in the pot, you should also go ahead and raise since now you have at least one opponent to challenge you.

In tight games, you can consider raising first in with the medium pairs 77 and higher and AJ. Hopefully, you can win the pot outright or at least get the pot heads up to give you a good chance of winning the hand on the flop.

In the previous chapter, we discussed hands you could play once there was a caller. Advanced players can usually play these hands *first in* unless the game is very aggressive: A8s, A7s, KJs, and QJs. Axs is also a borderline hand playable from early position in both loose and tight games.

In almost all games, the following hands are unprofitable from early position: AT, KJ, KT, QJ, and QT.

Number of Callers

If you are playing in a loose passive game and there has already been one or two callers, you can play a few more hands such as 66, 55, KTs, QTs, and JTs. An additional caller benefits your hand in several ways:

- You are getting better pot odds.

- The remaining players are more likely to call, improving your pot odds further since they are getting better pot odds also. For example, most opponents will fold 67s in middle or late position with only one caller, but against two callers they might call.
- When two players have called the pot, opponents are less likely to raise behind you except with premium hands. For example, an opponent with AJ in late position would probably only call against two opponents while he might raise against one.

Even if the pot is raised behind you, at least there are several opponents playing to give you better pot odds for your hand.

Raised Pots

You can either call or reraise with JJ or AQs depending on the circumstances. With JJ, you should reraise against a weak player in a tight game if you think you can isolate him. Tend to only call if the game is loose.

When the pot has been raised, borderline hands include TT, AQ, AJs, ATs, and KQs. Strategies with these hands are dependent on the type of opponent who raised and the type of game. You could reraise with these hands against some opponents, just call in a loose game, or possibly fold against a strong opponent in a tight game.

Deceptive Plays

One play used by some advanced players is to raise occasionally with some of the middle connectors such as 98s. One reason for this play is to ensure that you get future action with your early position raises. If you only raise with AA, KK, QQ, and AK, your more observant opponents will not call too often.

Internet Tip

This is an excellent example of a deceptive play that does not work very well on the Internet. In a live game, this type of play might pay benefits for several weeks if you play against regular opponents. On the Internet, you normally are playing against a lot of new opponents for a short time period. In addition, if there isn't a showdown, most sites do not allow you to show your cards, so you might not even be able to show your opponents the "crazy" play you made. Even if you do get to show your hand, some opponents might not even notice if they are playing two tables or are otherwise distracted.

Middle Position

Advanced players should consider raising first in with any hand that you would call if you feel you have a reasonable chance of either stealing the blinds or controlling the flop with a good table image. Some hands to consider raising first in include: 99, 88, 77, A9s, A8s, A7s, KQs, KQ, KJs, KTs, QJs, QTs, and JTs. Important considerations in your decision include the type of game, what players are remaining, your table image, your exact position, and the type of opponent in the big blind.

Chances of success are better in seats seven or eight since you are closer to a steal position. Although it is only one seat, some of these hands like QTs and JTs should probably be folded from seat six, since there is a better chance that an opponent has a premium hand behind you. These raises work best in tight games, so it is probably best to just call if the game is loose or you have a loose player in the blind.

If one opponent has already called, there are circumstances when you can still raise the pot with borderline hands. The first thing you must determine is if you would like to play a multi-handed pot or try to isolate. If you are in a tight game and your raise could isolate yourself against the lone caller, raising might be correct if your opponent is weak, the big blind is very tight, your table image is very strong, etc. Some hands to consider raising against one caller include JJ, TT, 99, AJ, ATs, A9s, A8s, and A7s. Hands like QJs and JTs are best played in a multi-handed pot, so I would just call.

Note that small pairs should be folded from middle position unless there are at least a couple of callers. If there are no callers at this point, you are not getting sufficient pot odds to draw to a set.

Raised Pots

Your first consideration in a raised pot is the position of the raiser. A raise from a strong player in early position indicates a premium hand while a raise from seat seven could be quite different. For example, many opponents will raise with KQs or KQ from middle position but just call from early position; therefore, you can consider reraising some hands against a middle position player that you probably should fold against an early position player.

Hands to consider reraising against a lone middle position raiser include: JJ, TT, 99, AQs, AQ, AJs, and AJ. Against a strong opponent, consider folding TT, 99, and AJ. Reraising an early position opponent with these hands is mostly dependent on the type of opponent and those remaining behind you. AJ is a hand that you should probably almost always fold against an early position player. KQs is usually playable against a middle position raiser and is a borderline decision against an early position raiser. Throughout a hand, always be aware of the position of the raiser to help you determine his possible hands.

Late Position

You can raise first in with even more hands than discussed in the last chapter, especially if the blinds are tight or play poorly after the flop. Your positional advantage allows you to play even some weak hands profitably in certain situations. Hands to consider raising include all pairs, any two cards 9 and higher, any two suited 8 or higher, Ax, and Kxs. If the blinds fold more than 50% of the time and you have a strong table image, you could raise with even more hands.

Let's discuss how you can play QQ from late position. Of course, you should almost always raise with this premium hand; however, sometimes you might just call when there are three or four callers already in the pot. Calling can be a good play for two reasons. First, an ace or king will come on the flop 43% of the time, which is bad news against so many callers. The more important reason is that you have a better chance of driving out your opponents on a favorable flop by keeping the pot small. With a raised pot, your opponents will be correct to draw to many hands on the flop. If the pot is small, your bet or raise on the flop could drive out many of your opponents giving you a better chance of winning if an ace or king comes on the turn or river. You can still raise in this situation as either play is very close in regards to profit expectation, but just calling can add a little deception to your game to confuse your opponents.

Sometimes against one caller, raising is profitable even with average holdings such as 99, 88, 77, AT, KQ, KJs, KJ, and QJs. You need to decide whether you prefer to isolate yourself against the lone caller or play your hand against several players. These types of raises depend on several factors. If your opponent is a solid player from early position, you need to be selective in which hands you raise with. Opponents who only call first in from middle or late position are generally indicating weakness, as most opponents will raise with their strong hands; therefore, your hand might be the best hand justifying a raise. In loose games where the blinds call many raises, tend to call more since it is more difficult to isolate yourself against a lone opponent.

Advanced players can call with a few more hands in late position than indicated in the previous chapter. With one caller add K9s. With two callers you can usually play K8s, K7s, JT, and 98s. You can also consider calling with the small pairs against two opponents if they tend to play poorly after the flop.

With three callers you could add K6s, K5s, Q8s, J8s, T8s, 87s, and 76s. With four or more callers you might even add a few more suited hands.

Raised Pots

The skill level and position of your opponent is very important when determining strategy against raisers. A good guideline for advanced players is to either reraise a lone opponent or fold. For example, hands like TT, AQ, and AJs are borderline hands against raisers from early position. If you are going to play, you should generally reraise to use your positional advantage. Against a late raiser you can almost always reraise.

Against a lone raiser from seat eight or nine, advanced players can reraise with more hands if the conditions are right. Many players are trying to steal the blinds from this position, so you can reraise to try and use your positional advantage to take control of the hand. Against tight players, you still should only play the premium hands. Hands to consider reraising include all pairs, Axs, AJ, AT, A9, A8, KQ, KJs, KJ, and even QJ.

Note that QJ is not a real strong hand; however, if you can get this hand heads up, you have a couple of ways to win the pot. If a queen or jack flops, of course you are happy and can bet. If an ace or king flops, there is a decent chance your opponent will fold against this scare card; therefore, you can safely bet the flop with any A, K, Q, or J. If you are called with an ace or king on the flop, you should probably back off your hand on the turn since your opponent has probably hit a pair.

Deceptive Plays

If you are playing against strong players who play well after the flop, you might consider raising medium pairs when there are already at least three callers in the pot. This raise gains you two things. When you hit your set, your opponents are getting proper pot odds to draw to two pair, so you will get better action. If you don't hit your set, sometimes all the players will check to you and you can take a free card for that slim chance of hitting your set on the turn. These types of raises do not gain a lot against weak players since they will be chasing on the flop in any case without good pot odds. In this case, it is best to just call for a small price to see if you hit your set.

The Blinds

Advanced players can *sometimes* raise with a few more hands out of the blinds in an unraised pot. These hands might include TT, 99, 88, AJs, AJ, and

KQs, as well as other suited connectors and small pairs to vary your game. These raises are dependent on many factors: the number of callers, position of callers, skill level of your opponents, and your table image. For example, if there are many callers in the hand, then raising with a hand like 88 or KQs could be profitable since you are getting good implied odds should you hit a big flop. You might raise with AJ against a middle caller and the small blind simply because you feel you have the best hand. However, be careful not to try these kinds of plays too often.

Raising from the blinds decreases your pot odds. For example, there are three callers in a $10-$20 game. From the small blind, you would need to pay $5 to call, so you are getting 9 to 1 pot odds with $45 in the pot. You can play many hands with 9 to 1 pot odds. If you raise, you are paying $15 to win a pot of $75, assuming everyone calls except the big blind. In this case your pot odds have decreased to 5 to 1. You have decreased your pot odds, while at the same time you have decreased your chances of winning the pot since your opponents are less likely to fold on the flop or turn with a bigger pot. You also must overcome acting first on every betting round.

Note the difference: 9 to 1 pot odds with a better chance of winning the pot versus 5 to 1 pot odds and a decreased chance of winning. You should usually only raise with the premium hands that are strong enough to compensate for acting first on every betting round with decreased pot odds. When you raise in middle position or late position, it is true your pot odds decrease also, but your odds of winning the pot have increased as you are most likely minimizing the field as well as gaining position over your opponents.

Raised Pots

You can reraise with more hands from the blinds than indicated in the previous chapter when the raise comes from a lone player in a blind-stealing position. You sometimes need to "defend" your blinds against those aggressive opponents who try to steal your blinds too often with weak hands. Hands to consider a reraise include any pair 66 or higher, Ax, and any KT or higher. You don't always have to reraise with hands like A6 or KT, but it is important to sometimes be aggressive against your opponent. From the big blind you can also call against a late raiser with more hands than indicated in the previous chapter. Hands like small pairs and A7 through A2 are borderline decisions mainly dependent on the type of opponent you are against.

When you are in the small blind, you often should either reraise or fold against a lone raiser from any position. Reraising helps to drive out the big blind to isolate yourself against the lone raiser.

When heads up from the big blind, one strategy against an aggressive raiser is to just call with your premium hands such as AA, KK, QQ, AKs, and AK. This works best against an early or middle position raiser in order to disguise your hand when heads up. You are sacrificing the preflop reraise hoping to gain more bets later in the hand. Sometimes reraising from the blinds will cause your opponents to back off their hands, so just calling can sometimes be an effective strategy when heads up to add deception to your game and possibly win more bets.

Calling raises from the blinds is often a difficult decision. You are out of position playing against an opponent who has showed strength, yet you are receiving good pot odds on your bet. Often, your borderline decisions are dependent on the type of opponents you are against. If you are against opponents who tend to play poorly after the flop, you can call with a few more hands than indicated in the previous chapter. Calling is more profitable against opponents who will pay you off nicely if you hit your hand. Against opponents who play well after the flop, you should probably fold the borderline hands.

Small Blind vs. Big Blind

Small blind vs. big blind scenarios occur much more frequently in the high-limit games than the low-limit games since high-limit games tend to be tighter. They also occur a lot in short-handed games. As discussed in the previous chapter, many live players don't face these situations very often since they can "chop," but it is essential to learn good strategies for these situations on the Internet.

Let's look at some possible strategies. Let's assume you are in the small blind and you have the rare luxury of having a rock in the big blind. One option is to raise every hand! In a $20-$40 game, you are paying $30 to win the $30 already in the pot. If the big blind folds half the time, you will break even just on your raise and you will win money those times that you hit a big hand on the flop.

What if you are in the big blind and somebody in the small blind tries this strategy against you. An extreme counter strategy would be to reraise every time! Assuming the small blind raises every hand, you will have equal hands on average. By reraising every time, you now have three small bets in the pot while you have the best position and get to act last on every betting round. For this same reason, raising every time is also a possible strategy against a small blind who calls every time.

Of course, this is an extreme counter strategy. If a small blind attacked me every hand, I would probably reraise with about 60% to 70% of my hands. Although these two scenarios are very rare, the reason I show them here is to present the wide spectrum of strategies possible given the type of opponent you are against.

One other thing to consider is how your opponent plays after the flop. Some opponents make the mistake of folding too often on the flop. In this case, you want to play more hands in both the small blind and big blind and should consider raising more hands. For example, there is $40 in the pot in a $20-$40 game if you call from the small blind and the big blind doesn't raise. If you come out betting every flop, you are getting 2 to 1 odds on your bet. If your opponent folds more than 1 out of 3 times, you make an immediate profit on your bet!

Of course, you will also win some money for those times that he calls and you have the best hand. Note how these odds are even better if you raised preflop. Now you would be getting 4 to 1 pot odds on your flop bet and would make an immediate profit if your opponent folds more than 1 in 5 times!

For these reasons, starting hand guidelines for small blind versus big blind situations are very dependent on your opponent. If you can play many hands without a showdown, you can raise practically every hand and bet out every flop! Observe your opponents and adjust your strategies accordingly.

Chapter Review

❑ Advanced players can play a few more borderline hands and add some deceptive plays that have an expected value of close to break even or are just slightly profitable. Beginning players will probably lose money playing these additional hands.

❑ **Early Position**
- Consider slowplaying your premium hands AA, KK, and AKs in a tight aggressive game.
- Consider raising with medium pairs and a hand like AJ in a tight game.
- Consider calling first in with Axs, KJs, and QJs.
- Consider calling with a few more speculative hands like 66 and QTs when there has already been one or two callers.
- Rarely make a deceptive raise from early position on the Internet with a hand like 98s.

❑ **Middle Position**
- Consider raising first in with any hand that you would call if you feel you have a reasonable chance of either stealing the blinds or controlling the flop.
- Sometimes even consider raising some borderline hands against one limper if the conditions are right.

- Your first consideration in a raised pot is the position of the raiser.

❑ **Late Position**
- Consider raising with many hands when first in, especially if the blinds are tight or play poorly after the flop.
- Raise fairly often against a limper who calls from middle or late position.
- Against a lone raiser, you should generally either reraise or fold.
- Against several strong opponents, consider raising with your medium pairs. Generally just call against weak opponents.

❑ **The Blinds**
- Generally only raise with premium hands from the blinds since you are decreasing your pot odds while having to act first on every betting round. Consider an occasional raise with a borderline hand given the right conditions to add some deception to your game.
- Consider reraising against a lone late raiser to defend your blinds.
- The small blind should generally either reraise or fold against a lone raiser from any position.
- Consider slowplaying your premium hands from the big blind against an aggressive lone raiser.
- Starting hand guidelines for small blind versus big blind situations are very dependent on your opponent. Generally you should play aggressively, especially if your opponent plays too tight.

Test Your Skills

1/ $20-$40. You hold A♣ A♥ in early position in a tight aggressive game. What do you do?

Answer: Only call most of the time and raise some of the time. Since there usually are two or three players who see the flop in a tight game, I sometimes like calling in this situation and then reraising if given the chance. Even if nobody raises, you will have the element of surprise to possibly win a decent size pot after the flop.

2/ $15-$30. You hold A♣ A♦ in early position in a loose passive game with several weak players. What do you do?

Answer: Raise. Since there is a good chance that some of the weak players will not respect your raise, go ahead and raise with your premium hand. In general, I prefer raising more often playing $15-$30 than $20-$40 since the small blind is worth more than half a bet. The small blind will also tend to call more in a $15-$30 game since he has already paid 2/3 of a small bet.

3/ $20-$40. You are in early position with 6♣ 6♥ in a tight aggressive game. An early player calls. What do you do?

Answer: Fold. There are still many players behind you who might raise and generally only two to three players see each flop. Small pairs do not play very well in these types of games.

4/ $15-$30. You are in early position with 6♦ 6♥ in a loose passive game. An early player calls. What do you do?

Answer: Call. Calling in this situation does a couple of things. First, most players won't raise two opponents except with the very premium hands. Second, when two opponents have already entered the pot, more opponents tend to call giving you the pot odds you need to play this hand profitably.

5/ $20-$40. You hold Q♠ 9♠ one seat before the cutoff. An early player calls. What do you do?

Answer: Fold. This weak hand needs several players in the pot to be profitable. There is also the chance of a raise behind you.

6/ $20-$40. You hold K♠ J♠ on the button. A middle player calls. What do you do?

Answer: Raise. A middle player limping in usually does not have a very strong hand. Raise to force out the blinds and put the burden on your opponent to hit something on the flop. Even if the blinds call, you have built a better pot with a decent hand in good position.

7/ $20-$40. You hold 2♥ 2♣ on the button. A player in early position and the cutoff call. What do you do?

Answer: Fold. Generally you need three or more opponents in the pot to play the small pairs profitably. You can consider calling against two opponents if they both tend to play their hands too far after the flop.

8/ $20-$40. You hold A♥ 7♥ on the button. The cutoff raises first in. You want to play your hand against this opponent. What do you do?

Answer: Reraise. Even though you usually want to play suited cards against several opponents, this strategy changes somewhat against a lone opponent, especially if he is in late position. A player raising from the cutoff could have many hands. If you decide to play, you should reraise to drive out the blinds and put the burden on your opponent to hit something on the flop.

9/ $30-$60. You hold 9♥ 9♣ in the small blind. The cutoff raises first in. What do you do?

Answer: Reraise. You probably have the best hand and you want to force the big blind out of the hand. Raising allows you to bet out the flop and put the burden on your opponent to hit something.

10/ $15-$30. You hold K♥ J♥ in the small blind. A middle player raises and the button calls. What do you do?

Answer: Call, with folding a close second. Advanced players can consider a call in this situation. Note that you can call with more hands from the small blind in a $15-$30 game than a $20-$40 game since calling is only 1 1/3 bet compared to 1 1/2 bets in a $20-$40 game. A $20 call in this situation with two suited high cards is a decent play depending on the type of opponents you are against. Be careful however if you pair one of your cards and your opponents play back aggressively, since your kicker may not be any good.

11/ $20-$40. You hold K♠ Q♠ in the big blind. It is folded to the button who raises. What do you do?

Answer: Reraise. Opponents will raise with many hands on the button to try and steal the blinds, so you most likely have the best hand. You can safely bet out the flop with any A, K, or Q, since the ace will be a good scare card to your opponent if he doesn't have an ace.

The Flop

Introduction

The flop is a defining moment in Texas Hold'em. It is important to determine right away if your hand has value before you start committing chips to the pot. Many players consider the turn to be a more important round of betting since it is more expensive, but it is often the mistakes you make on the flop that create further mistakes on the turn and river. For example, if you make a weak draw on the flop and hit it on the turn only to lose to a better hand, it was probably a mistake on the flop that led you to lose several bets.

Let's look at the most important considerations you should evaluate on every flop.

⇨ **The strength of your hand** - How strong is your hand? Does it need to be protected? Can you slowplay? If you are drawing, how strong of a draw do you have? Each type of hand has its own chapter to discuss the considerations and strategies you might use.

⇨ **The type of flop** - How strong is your hand relative to each type of flop? In general, the following types of flops are dangerous unless they give you a very strong hand: all high cards, a high or low pair, three-suited, and three-connected. Two-suited flops or two related high cards also present dangers that require you to fold most of your weak draws. Later in this chapter we will discuss each type of flop in more detail.

⇨ **Number of opponents** - The more opponents you are against, the higher the chance an opponent has a strong hand. Against three or more opponents, you should normally assume that an opponent has a strong hand if they bet; therefore, against multiple opponents you need to limit your play to either strong hands or strong draws (unless the pot is very large, in which case you *might* be able to call with weak draws). You can consider bluffs and semi-bluffs against one or two opponents since there is a chance that no one has been helped on the flop. Bluffs against three opponents rarely work and are not recommended against four opponents.

⇨ **Possible hands of opponents** - You should try to determine the possible hands of your opponents based on their positions, the preflop betting, and the betting so far on the flop. Once you have an understanding of their possible holdings you can determine the relative strength of your own hand. Remember, the more players there are in the pot the more likely it is that someone has a strong hand such as a set or two pair. One important consideration when you are drawing is to evaluate the possibility that your draw is counterfeited. When you draw and hit your hand, you want to win!

⇨ **The pot size** - The size of the pot can have a big impact on the strategy you choose. When you have a very strong hand, you can sometimes slowplay when the pot is small, but should play it strongly when the pot is large. The pot size may dictate how you try to protect a vulnerable hand. Larger pots give you better pot odds to make more draws than small pots. Always be aware of the size of the pot when making decisions.

⇨ **Cost/Potential cost of bet** - Paying two bets can decrease your pot odds a lot. Always evaluate your position relative to the remaining players in the pot. Many times you need to fold hands that you would otherwise call when there is the possibility of a raise behind you. For example, when an early position player bets and you must act with a gut-shot draw, you should usually fold if there are many players behind you who could raise.

With every flop, you should go through some basic thought processes. First, evaluate the type of flop and then the strength of your hand *relative* to that flop. Next, compare your hand to the possible hands of your opponents. Finally, determine your best strategy based on the pot odds you are receiving. On the Internet you have about 20 seconds to evaluate all this information and make your decision!

Let's look at some examples to show how top pair can either be a strong hand or very weak depending on the type of flop. Notice how A♦ T♣ changes in value depending on the flop.

- T♦ 5♥ 2♣. This is a very good flop for A♦ T♣. You have top pair with the best kicker. There are no flush or straight draws available to your opponents.
- T♦ 5♥ 2♥. This is a good flop also, but now you could be against a flush draw.
- T♦ 5♥ 5♣. Whenever a pair comes on the flop and you don't have trips or a full house, you should proceed with caution. The risk is dependent on the number and position of the callers. If you are against a strong early position player, a T55 flop should not be too dangerous. If there are five callers in the pot including the two blinds, then a T55 flop would greatly diminish the value of your top pair.

- T♦ 9♥ 9♣. This flop also has a pair but now there are even more problems. The pair is relatively high, so it is more likely that a player would be holding a 9 than a 5. Many players will play J9, T9, Q9s, etc., whereas they generally fold hands with 5. The flop is also two-connected, so you could be against a straight draw.
- T♥ 9♥ 9♣. Add a flush draw to this very dangerous flop.
- T♦ 9♥ 8♣. Another very dangerous flop. You could already be against a straight or at least a good straight draw. Hands such as KJ, AJ, KQ, and QJ are all dangerous hands to your pair. You should probably fold if you are against several opponents and one or two of them are showing a lot of aggression.
- T♥ 9♥ 8♣. Add a flush draw to make this flop even more dangerous.
- T♥ 9♥ 8♥. Can it be any worse? You have top pair but must worry about flushes, straights, and overcards. If you are not already beat and drawing dead, any heart, K, Q, J, 9, 8, 7, or 6 could be bad news.

Let's look now at the main types of flops and the qualities and considerations of each. The purpose of this introduction to flop types is to help begin the thought processes that you should go through with each type of flop. The following chapters will look at each type of hand in more detail and the best strategies to use with the various flop types. Some of these flop types can be intertwined. For example, a flop with a high pair and a rag could also be two-suited, but these are discussed separately.

The main types of flops are as follows:
- Three of a Kind
- High Pair
- Low Pair
- Two-Suited
- Three-Suited
- Two-Connected
- Three-Connected
- All High Cards
- Rainbow with One High Card
- Rainbow of All Rags

Three of a Kind

Three of a kind flops like JJJ occur only once every 425 hands. If you are lucky enough to hold four of a kind, you should probably slowplay, although you could play aggressively if you believe an opponent will give you good action with a high pocket pair. Pocket pairs are very strong hands since four of a kind is an unlikely holding from one of your opponents. Obviously the higher your pair the better, and you must protect your medium and small pairs from overcards. In a heads-up situation, another playable hand would be ace high, unless there was a preflop raise by an opponent with a possible pocket pair.

High Pair

A flop with a high pair such as QQT or JJ6 is always dangerous since many players play high cards. You need a full house or trips to feel comfortable with your hand. In most cases, when the flop is bet and called by a second player, you are usually beat if you do not hold trips or better. High pocket pairs are decent holdings if you feel that the risk of an opponent holding trips is low. This is mainly dependent on the number of players in the hand. Against one opponent, a strong pocket pair usually is a good hand, but with four or five players seeing the flop you must play cautiously.

Flush and straight draws drop significantly in value with a pair on the flop. It's possible that you are drawing dead if an opponent already has a full house. For example, if you hold KJ with a QTT flop, you are drawing dead against TT and are in big trouble against QQ or QT. Also note that your straight draw only has four outs if an opponent holds AT or T9. Another problem with these flops is that even when you hit your draw on the turn, an opponent with trips has ten outs to beat you on the river. For these reasons, be careful playing flush and straight draws on the flop when there is a high pair. The exceptions are when you are relatively confident that an opponent doesn't hold trips or you are getting exceptionally good pot odds.

Low Pair

Compare QTT with a flop of Q55. Most good players will not play a hand with a 5 unless they were able to see the flop cheaply from late position or the blinds. If the pot was raised preflop and there are not many opponents, you usually can worry less about a low pair on the flop. Conversely, if the blinds are playing or there are many players in the pot, proceed with caution as indicated in the high pair section.

Two-Suited

One of the first things you should always look for on the flop is whether or not it is two-suited. You can always play flush draws when there is no pair and there are at least two callers. In heads-up situations, your draw is also almost always worth playing unless the pot is small and you are sure your opponent has a pair higher than the two cards in your hand.

If you don't have a flush draw, you must worry about other players having a draw. If there are several players who call a bet with a two-suited flop, it is almost guaranteed that at least one opponent has a flush draw. All hands go down in value against two-suited flops. This means that borderline hands with a rainbow flop should often be folded with a two-suited flop. Your stronger holdings such as top pair are usually still good hands, but you may need to fold if a third suited card comes on the turn or river. Overcards drop significantly in value with a two-suited flop.

If you hold an ace or king of the same suit as the two-suited flop, you have a backdoor flush draw, which adds a little extra to your hand. In big pots against several players, the addition of a backdoor flush draw to an otherwise mediocre hand may make your hand playable. For example, middle pair with an overcard might become playable if you have a backdoor flush draw also and the pot is very large.

Three-Suited

Three-suited flops occur about 5% of the time. If you flop the nut flush, you can consider slowplaying the hand. Generally you should play flushes that aren't the nuts strongly, since you need to protect your hand and can expect to get good action from players on draws.

If you have a flush draw with one of the top two available suited cards, you can always play the hand to the river. Usually fold draws to the third or fourth highest suited card unless your hand has other possibilities. If you have a set, you can play it strongly if you feel nobody has the flush; otherwise, you still can play to the river drawing to a full house. All other hands should be played with caution. Straights are still playable in most cases.

Straight draws are practically worthless unless your hand has other possibilities and you feel nobody has a flush. Middle or bottom pair should be thrown away in almost all circumstances. Top pair and overpairs should sometimes be played conservatively until the turn card, especially against several opponents. Overcards should almost never be played unless you have a good flush draw with your hand.

Two-Connected

An open-ended straight draw is a strong hand with rainbow flops. These draws become even stronger if you have overcards also. For example, Q♦ J♥ is a very strong hand with a flop of T♥ 9♠ 5♣. The only time you might consider folding an open-ended straight draw with a rainbow unpaired flop is when you are heads up, the pot is small, and you are sure your opponent has a pair higher than your two cards.

If you don't have a draw, you need to be worried that your opponents do, especially if the two connected cards are high cards. For example, if the flop has KQ, QJ, JT, T9, 98, or 87, there is a good chance your opponents have some type of draw or good hand. Since many players like to play connected cards, two pair is also a possibility. Two overcards increase in value when they give you a gut-shot straight opportunity.

Three-Connected

Three-connected flops are similar to three-suited flops and become very dangerous if they are two-suited also. Flopping the nut straight is not nearly as strong as flopping the nut flush. First of all, someone could draw to a flush and beat you. Secondly, your straight could lose to a higher straight or may have to split the pot. Straights should almost always be played strongly and never slowplayed.

If you are on a draw, be sure you are drawing to the high end. For example, holding A6 on a 987 flop is not a very strong hand, as a ten will give you a straight but could give someone else a higher straight. AT is a much better hand, as a jack or 6 gives you the straight and you could only lose to specifically QT.

Top pair and overpairs should be played with caution as you could already be against a straight or two pair. Any pair less than top pair should almost always be folded, unless your kicker gives you other possibilities. An overpair with a straight draw is a strong holding as it minimizes the probability that someone has a straight or can draw to a straight. These hands are strong because you have several outs if you are against two pair.

For example, JJ or TT would be a strong holding with a 987 flop. If an opponent has two pair such as 98, any jack, ten, 7, or 6 gives you the winner. When the flop is two-suited as well, top pair and overpairs are weak hands unless you also have a draw. AA might be thrown away in this case against a couple of callers on the flop.

Two overcards with a gut-shot draw can be played in some circumstances if they give you the nut straight. For example, QJ with a 987 flop is a decent drawing hand.

All High Cards

You need a strong hand to play a flop of all high cards such as AQ9, KQT, KJ9, or AT9. Drawing to weak hands is risky since an opponent could hold two pair or possibly even a straight with these types of flops. A two-suited flop complicates the hand even further. Generally you need at least top pair with a good kicker or some type of straight draw to play your hand. The same principle applies when there are two high cards, although obviously this is not quite as dangerous.

Rainbow with One High Card

These types of flops generally do not help very many players, so the field is usually limited very quickly. Examples include K76, A82, and J54. These are good types of flops to try bluffs, especially when the flop is a rainbow. Top pair with a good kicker is a strong hand, as you do not need to worry about straight or flush draws. When you have at least a pair of kings or better, you are not too worried about giving free cards, so a check-raise can be a good strategy. Pairs less than kings should usually be protected since they are more vulnerable to free cards.

Overcards can sometimes be played with these types of flops since there is less risk that you are drawing dead. When several players play this type of flop, be wary of an opponent holding a set. This is especially true if he starts raising on the turn.

Rainbow of All Rags

A rainbow flop of all rags, such as 8♠ 6♣ 4♦, 6♦ 5♠ 2♥, or 9♥ 6♣ 3♦, usually does not help anyone, unless they have hit a set or catch a decent hand playing out of the blinds. Sets or two pair are very strong hands with these types of flops. Limpers might flop a set, but this usually is not a concern against a preflop raiser. Overpairs should be played strongly to attempt to drive out your opponents. Overcards can sometimes be played depending on the situation and action.

A common situation is getting a free look out of the blinds and then flopping a small pair. For example, you hold 68 in the big blind and the flop comes 852. Unfortunately, you must act first on every betting round. Your options with these types of flops are to bet out, check and fold, or check and hope a late bettor will allow you to check-raise to try and minimize the field. Tend to bet out against one or two opponents and check against several opponents. If an opponent shows a lot of strength, then you should probably fold or possibly call a raise to see one more card.

Betting Strategies

After evaluating the relative strength of your hand given the type of flop and possible hands of your opponents, you then need to determine the best betting strategy on how to play your hand. These possibilities include all the basic poker concepts we discussed in the beginning of the book: bluffing, semi-bluffing, raising, check-raising, calling, slowplaying, buying a free card, betting, and finally folding. Let's review the various strategies you can employ:

⇨ **Betting out with the best hand.** Normally you should come out betting when you feel you have the best hand. One exception to this is when you want to check-raise the best hand or to also drive out opponents. Do not be afraid of betting into a preflop raiser.

⇨ **Betting out to protect your hand.** Sometimes you may not be sure your hand is best, but you have to bet out to protect your hand against a free card in case you have the best hand.

⇨ **Betting out to see where you are in the hand.** Sometimes a correct strategy is to bet out to see what happens behind you. If you are raised, you can then consider folding if you have a medium holding. If a couple of players just call, you might need to back off on the turn if your hand is not too strong. Betting to gain information can save you bets if it allows you to get out of the hand early, rather than checking and calling all the way down to the river.

⇨ **Betting a bluff or semi-bluff.** Against one or two opponents (and rarely with three), sometimes you can bet out as a bluff or semi-bluff.

⇨ **Calling / Checking and calling as a slowplay.** Simply calling to slowplay a really strong hand is a good strategy sometimes with a small pot. Checking and calling is also a good strategy against aggressive opponents to induce them to bluff on the flop and turn.

⇨ **Calling / Checking and calling mediocre hands.** When you have a medium holding, sometimes it is correct to just call to see how the hand develops. This is also correct when there are many dangerous cards that could hurt your hand. Rather than committing a lot of chips to the pot, you wait and see if the turn card is favorable.

When you are on a draw, checking and calling is the correct strategy when:
1/ You do not think you could win with a semi-bluff.
2/ You do not want to drive out other opponents either by betting or raising, or by betting and risking a raise directly behind you.
3/ There are not enough opponents to justify a check-raise (see below).

⇨ **Check-raising.** When you feel you have the best hand, you might check-raise to gain additional bets. You might also check-raise with the goal of driving out other players from the pot. You might check-raise your strong draws if there are a sufficient number of players in the pot to justify the pot odds. Finally, you can try a check-raise bluff or semi-bluff if you feel the bettor is bluffing and you want to try to win the pot immediately or set up a semi-bluff bet on the turn.

⇨ **Raising with the best hand.** When you feel you have the best hand and someone bets into you, you should almost always raise. The exception is when you want to slowplay your hand and wait to raise on the turn or river.

⇨ **Raising to protect your hand.** If your hand is vulnerable and you are not sure if you have the best hand, you still may need to raise to protect your hand against the remaining opponents acting behind you.

⇨ **Raising to try for a free card.** You can raise with your draw to try for a free card on the turn. When you have a hand that you are unsure is the best hand, you can also raise with the intention of checking the turn. In this case, you are minimizing your losses when an opponent has a better hand, while allowing you to play out the hand to the river.

⇨ **Raising as a bluff or semi-bluff.** You might raise with the hopes of winning the pot immediately.

⇨ **Checking.** Sometimes you find yourself in late or last position where checking would take the hand to the turn. In general you should almost always bet a strong hand, although there may be circumstances when you might check the flop and wait to see if the turn card is favorable. Checking your medium holdings is sometimes correct if betting is unlikely to drive out many opponents when the pot is large, or if you are at risk of being check-raised and you want to see the turn card cheaply.

⇨ **Folding.** Folding is correct under the following circumstances:
- You are not getting good implied pot odds that you have the best hand.
- You are not getting sufficient odds to draw.
- You are not getting sufficient odds to try a bluff or semi-bluff.

There is one exception. Sometimes you might fold even when you have the best hand on the flop. This occurs when the flop is so dangerous that it is doubtful that your hand could win on the river. For example, a medium pair against many callers on the flop is a dangerous situation. Even a relatively high pair is risky when there are many overcards, flushes, and straight draws that could beat you. For example, you might fold T♥ 5♦ against several opponents with a flop of T♣ 9♣ 8♠.

The flop is a defining moment in Texas Hold'em. Evaluate the relative strength of your hand given the type of flop and the possible hands of your opponents before deciding a betting strategy. The following chapters will look at the considerations and strategies for each type of hand in more detail.

Chapter Review

❑ The flop is a defining moment in Texas Hold'em. It is important to determine right away if your hand has value before you start committing chips to the pot.

❑ It is often the mistakes you make on the flop that create further mistakes on the turn and river.

❑ The most important considerations you should evaluate with each flop include:
  • The strength of your hand
  • The type of flop
  • Number of opponents
  • Possible hands of opponents
  • The pot size
  • Cost/Potential cost of bet

❑ The main types of flops are as follows:
  • Three of a Kind
  • High Pair
  • Low Pair
  • Two-Suited
  • Three-Suited
  • Two-Connected
  • Three-Connected
  • All High Cards
  • Rainbow with One High Card
  • Rainbow of All Rags

❑ Various strategies on the flop include the following:
  • Betting out with the best hand
  • Betting out to protect your hand
  • Betting out to see where you are in the hand
  • Betting a bluff or semi-bluff
  • Calling / Checking and calling as a slowplay
  • Calling / Checking and calling mediocre hands
  • Check-raising

- Raising with the best hand
- Raising to protect your hand
- Raising to try for a free card
- Raising as a bluff or semi-bluff
- Checking
- Folding

❑ Always evaluate the relative strength of your hand given the type of flop and the possible hands of your opponents before deciding a betting strategy.

Nut Hands

Nut hands on the flop include four of a kind, full houses, flushes, and straights. Nut hands are always strong hands, but some are still vulnerable to getting beat on the turn or river.

Four of a Kind/Full Houses

Four of a kind and full houses are very rare and practically guarantee that you will win the pot. Note that this chapter does not cover full houses where you hold a pocket pair and there is a flop of three-of-a-kind. That type of full house is played more like an overpair or middle pair depending on how high your pair is.

Let's look first at those fortunate cases when an opponent bets into you. If there are other opponents to act behind you, you should almost always just call to slowplay. Hopefully by just calling, you can get some more players in the hand to play pairs or maybe even a straight or flush draw.

If the pot is heads up and your opponent bets out, usually just call and wait to show your strength on the turn, or possibly on the river. If you suspect a player is on a bluff, let him continue to bluff as long as possible before showing your strength.

However, if there is a chance that an opponent might actually have a good hand, sometimes you can try to use reverse psychology. For example, an early position player raises and you call on the button with KQs. To your surprise the flop comes QQQ! The raiser bets out. One strategy is to raise!

The raiser probably would not expect you to raise with a queen in this situation since most players would slowplay such a strong hand. If you are lucky and your opponent has a high pocket pair, you could get some really good action before he realizes that you have four of a kind. Using reverse psychology by playing a strong hand strongly can sometimes gain you extra bets on both the flop *and* the turn; however, if you just call and wait to raise on the turn, your opponent might freeze up worried that you have the queen.

Now let's look at strategies when you act first. If there are several opponents, you should almost always just check and try to bring in as many opponents as possible. There is no use in betting and scaring away your opponents when a free card will not hurt you. Another risk by betting out is that the next opponent raises, forcing out all the other players.

One exception to betting out is when you were the preflop raiser. Your opponents might not expect such a monster hand since you generally bet out most of the time anyhow after raising preflop. Checking when you usually bet in this situation sometimes makes your opponents suspicious. For example, if you hold KK and the flop comes KQQ, usually go ahead and bet. You are hoping that an opponent holds a queen, and you could get good action if they put you on AA or AK. Checking may actually make them suspicious that you hold either KK or AQ since you almost always bet out in this situation. Of course, if you have checked the flop on several occasions after raising preflop, then slowplaying is a good consideration.

If you are heads up and acting first, there are several options to gain the most bets from your opponent depending on the situation. Again, if you raised preflop, you should usually still bet and hope that your opponent does not fold. However, if you did not raise preflop, you can check and call, check-raise, or simply bet out. If you suspect that your opponent does not have anything, you should always check to give your opponent a chance to bluff or possibly improve his hand on the turn.

If you suspect your opponent has something, consider checking and calling to slowplay your hand, especially against an aggressive opponent who will probably bet the turn. This can allow you to check-raise on the more expensive betting round; however, this type of play is risky since your opponent may decide to take a free card. For example, if the flop is K88 and you have 88, your opponent may not even bet a hand like AK on the turn. Generally only try this play against an aggressive opponent. Trying to check-raise the turn can sometimes result in losing a bet that you could have earned by betting.

One option is to check-raise the flop. This could gain you two bets on the flop and two bets on the turn and river, assuming your opponent calls you down. If you are worried that an opponent would fold to a check-raise, another option is to check and call. You can then decide whether to bet out the turn or try check-raising if there is a possibility your opponent will bet.

Another option is to bet out. Your opponent will not expect that you would bet out such a strong hand and could give you great action if he holds something or puts you on a bluff. However, this strategy is risky in that your opponent may simply fold.

Flushes

The odds of flopping a flush when starting with two suited cards are 118 to 1. If you are lucky enough to flop the *nut* flush, you can slowplay if the pot is not very large. Giving a free card is only risky in those cases where someone has a set and draws to a full house on the turn or river.

Against several opponents, I would usually just check allowing as many opponents as possible into the hand. I do not want someone to raise me early forcing out the other players. Raising is a good move once several opponents have already called. With flushes, you want to get in as many bets as possible while you still have several opponents. Waiting to raise the turn or river is risky since another suited card will dry up the action very quickly.

Advanced Concept: With very strong hands, generally try to gain extra bets on the current betting round rather than waiting until the next one if there are many potential scare cards that could dry up the action.

Generally play flushes strongly on the flop when you do not hold one of the top two available flush cards. Slowplaying is risky since an opponent who holds one of the top suited cards is going to draw to the flush. You need to charge your opponents as much as possible for their draws. Attempting a check-raise is risky since many players are reluctant to bet when the flop is three-suited; therefore, almost always bet out or raise unless you feel there is a good chance that a check-raise can be successful.

Straights

Flopping the nut straight is not nearly as strong as flopping the nut flush. First of all, someone could draw to a flush and beat you. Secondly, your straight could lose to a higher straight or may only win half the pot if one of your two cards comes on the turn or river. For example, JT with a flop of 987 is a great hand; however, if a ten comes on the turn, you could lose to QJ or split with anyone holding a jack. Finally, many players play connectors, so there is some chance that you are against two pair that could draw into a full house.

Generally you should play a flopped straight strongly and almost never slowplay. Check-raising is only a good option when you are confident that an opponent will bet. Remember, slowplaying is only a good play when the next card is not too risky and is likely to give someone a second-best hand. I cannot tell you how many pots I have lost after flopping the nut straight.

Advanced Concept: Flopped straights are vulnerable hands that should almost always be played strongly and almost never slowplayed.

Another reason not to slowplay straights is that you generally get good action anyway, especially when there are a couple of high cards on the board. Flops with several connected cards usually give your opponents additional outs for gut-shot or open-ended straight draws that allow them to play their hand further. For example, with a flop of 986, any player with QT, QJ, and any hand with a 7 will play, along with all those players who hold top pair or overpairs.

Not all straights are equal in value. With a flop of 987, JT is a strong hand while 65 is quite vulnerable. When you have the low end, you could already be beat and any jack, ten, or 6 on the turn or river is bad news. With JT, you are worried about a jack or ten coming also, but at least you would have a decent chance at splitting the pot. Straights are also much stronger with rainbow flops.

Chapter Review

❑ **Four of a Kind/Full Houses**
- When an opponent bets into you, you should almost always just call to slowplay if there are more players to act behind you.
- If the pot is heads up and your opponent bets out, usually just call and wait to show your strength on the turn, or possibly on the river.
- Using reverse psychology by playing a strong hand strongly can sometimes gain you extra bets on both the flop *and* the turn.
- When acting first into several opponents, you should almost always just check and try to bring in as many opponents as possible. One exception to this is when you were the preflop raiser.
- When heads up and acting first you should usually:
  - Bet when you were the preflop raiser.
  - Check when you suspect that your opponent does not have a hand.
  - Check and call to slowplay against an aggressive opponent who will probably bet the turn so that you can check-raise on the

more expensive betting round. However, this type of play is risky since your opponent may decide to take a free card.

- Check-raise when you suspect that your opponent has a good enough hand to call with, but a hand he might not bet on the turn if you check.
- Bet out occasionally as a deceptive strategy.

❑ **Flushes**
- You can slowplay the *nut* flush, unless the pot is very large.
- Raising is a good move once several opponents have already called.
- Generally play flushes strongly on the flop when you do not hold one of the top two available flush cards.
- Check-raises are risky since many players are reluctant to bet when the flop is three-suited.

❑ **Straights**
- Flopping the nut straight is not nearly as strong as flopping the nut flush.
  - Someone could draw to a flush and beat you.
  - Your straight could lose to a higher straight or may only win half the pot if one of your two cards comes on the turn or river.
  - Since many players play connectors, there is a chance that you are against two pair and your opponent could draw to a full house.
- Flopped straights are vulnerable hands that should almost always be played strongly and almost never slowplayed.

Test Your Skills

1/ $20-$40. You hold 4♣ 4♦ in middle position. Two early players call and you call. The small blind calls and five players see the flop of 5♣ 5♦ 4♥. The small blind bets and an early player calls. There is $140 in the pot. What do you do?

Answer: Raise. I like raising in this situation for two reasons. First, some opponents expect you to slowplay trips to the turn, so your raise may give you good action if they put you on a weak pair or a draw. Second, if one of your opponents actually holds trips, you should get great action on both the flop and turn. In the actual hand, the player raised and the small blind reraised. The early player folded and the player capped the betting. The small blind bet out the turn of T♦ and the player raised. The small blind showed J♦ J♠.

2/ $20-$40. You hold 5♥ 5♦ on the button. An early player and a middle player call. You call and the small blind calls. Five players see the flop of K♦ K♥ 5♠. The middle player bets. There is $120 in the pot. What do you do?

Answer: Call. Only one player has entered the pot and there still are three players left to act. One of them might be slowplaying trip kings, and you will be able to surprise them later if they raise or come out betting the turn. In the actual hand, the player only called and the small blind called. The turn was the 8♦. The middle player bet and the player only called, hoping that the small blind would continue to play or possibly even raise with trips. Both opponents called a bet on the river showing 99 and 66.

3/ $15-$30. You hold A♣ J♣ on the button. An early player raises, you call, and the small blind calls. Three players see the flop of 8♣ 7♣ 5♠. The small blind checks and the raiser bets. There is $120 in the pot. What do you do?

Answer: Call, with raising a close second. Calling gives you the chance to raise on the more expensive betting round of the turn. On the other hand, you also risk that another club comes on the turn, which would slow down the betting action. However, raising might drive out the small blind. One advantage to raising is the chance of getting some really good action if your opponents suspect that you are trying for a free card and one of them has an overpair. Both are decent options, but I prefer calling to try and keep the small blind in the hand and to give myself a chance of raising on the bigger betting round.

In the actual hand, the player called. The small blind called and bet out the turn card of the 8♥. The early player called and the player raised. The river was the 3♣ and the early player checked and called with K♣ K♥.

4/ $.50-$1. You are in the small blind with 8♣ 7♣. A middle player raises and the cutoff calls. You make a weak call from the small blind and the big blind calls. Four players see the flop of A♣ K♣ 6♣. There is $4 in the pot. What do you do?

Answer: Check-raise. There was a raise and a cold call preflop, so there is a good chance one of your opponents will bet this flop that has an ace or king. You also do not want to bet and then get raised directly behind you, causing the remaining opponents to fold. Your opponents will probably draw to the Q♣, J♣ or T♣, so you want to charge them as much as possible for their draw, which a check-raise accomplishes. Check-raising also ensures you will be betting out the turn rather than risk giving a free card.

In the actual hand, the player checked and called even though the preflop raiser bet and was called by the next player. The player then checked the turn and his opponents took a free card. If you have a strong hand and several opponents call the flop, it is rarely correct to slowplay.

5/ $15-$30. You hold Q♦ J♦ in the big blind. A middle player raises and the cutoff and small blind call. You call and four players see the flop of 8♦ 6♦ 4♦. The small blind checks. There is $120 in the pot. What do you do?

Answer: Bet. Slowplaying this hand is risky since your opponents may not bet this type of flop. You also must act first making a check-raise attempt on the turn risky also. Check-raising the flop also tends to give away your hand more than betting out with this type of flop. If you bet out, your opponents might suspect a pair or a flush draw and you could get some good action later on. Any player with an overpair or the A♦ or K♦ will most likely raise allowing you to reraise and charge them a lot to draw. In the actual hand, the player checked and called to the preflop raiser. The turn was the 7♦ and his opponent won with K♦ Q♥.

6/ $15-$30. You hold A♦ T♦ in middle position. A middle player raises and you call. The small blind calls and three players see the flop of Q♦ 9♦ 4♦. It is checked to you. There is $105 in the pot. What do you do?

Answer: Check. You have the nuts and are acting last. Both opponents have indicated weakness, so betting may drive them out. Checking could give your opponents a decent second-best hand with any A, K, J, T, or diamond. In the actual hand, the player bet and his opponents folded.

7/ $20-$40. You hold A♣ 6♣ on the button. An early and middle player call and you call. The small blind calls and five players see the flop of J♣ 9♣ 8♣. The early player bets and the middle player folds. There is $120 in the pot. What do you do?

Answer: Call. You still have both blinds waiting to act and you do not want to drive them out of the pot. With this type of flop, your opponents could have pairs and straight draws, so wait until the turn to show your strength. If you are lucky, one of the blinds will raise on the flop. In the actual hand, the player called and the small blind called also. Both opponents checked and called on the turn. The early player showed K9.

8/ $.50-$1. You are in the small blind with the Q♥ J♠. Six players see the flop of T♠ 9♣ 8♣. There is $3 in the pot. What do you do?

Answer: Bet. With so many opponents in the hand, there should be a lot of action with this flop. Players will have flush draws, straight draws, and possibly full house draws. There is no need to slowplay since you should get great action. Bet out and reraise if given the opportunity.

9/ $1-$2. You hold Q♥ J♥ in the big blind. An early player raises, a middle player calls, and the small blind calls. You call and four players see the flop of K♦ T♣ 9♠. You check. The early player bets and the middle player raises. There is $11 in the pot. What do you do?

Answer: Reraise. You should rarely slowplay a straight on the flop. Another queen or jack could be trouble for your hand. Even if it doesn't give an opponent a straight, the betting will usually dry up, so get in your raises on the flop. In the actual hand, the player reraised and ended up splitting the pot with the early player who held QQ. Although he still split the pot, his reraise on the flop made his opponent make a mistake by forcing him to call two more bets.

10/ $1-$2. You hold K♠ Q♦ in middle position. A middle player calls and you call. The button raises and the small blind calls. Four players see the flop of J♥ T♥ 9♦. The small blind bets and the middle player folds. There is $10 in the pot. What do you do?

Answer: Raise. Rarely slowplay a straight on the flop. If a K, Q, 8, or 7 comes on the turn, the betting action will usually dry up. In the actual hand, the player only called and the button called. The turn was the K♥ and he split the pot with the small blind who showed QQ.

11/ $15-$30. You hold Q♦ J♦ in the small blind. The button raises and you just call. Two players see the flop of A♦ K♠ T♥. There is $75 in the pot. What do you do?

Answer: Check-raise. Give your opponent a chance to bet a weak hand since he will almost always bet out in this situation. If you check-raise and your opponent has a strong hand like two pair, your opponent might reraise the flop or wait to raise the turn, allowing you to reraise and win a very large pot. In the actual hand, the player check-raised and his opponent called. The turn was the K♣ and his opponent called. The river was a rag and his opponent raised showing A♥ K♦. Although the player lost this hand, he probably would have won a large pot on the turn if an ace or king had not come.

12/ $20-$40. You hold K♠ Q♠ in the cutoff. A middle player calls and you raise. Two players see the flop of A♦ J♦ T♣. The middle player checks. There is $110 in the pot. What do you do?

Answer: Bet. You raised preflop, so go ahead and bet. If you are lucky, your opponent may have flopped two pair and will give you good action. Many players will draw to a gut-shot draw if they have a pair, so be sure not to give them any free cards for drawing. In the actual hand, the player bet and his opponent called to the river with A♣ 9♠.

13/ $20-$40. You post in the cutoff and are dealt 8♥ 7♦. A weak player one seat before you raises and you call. Two players see the flop of 6♦ 5♥ 4♦. The middle player bets, you raise, and the middle player reraises. There is $210 in the pot. What do you do?

Answer: Reraise. Capping in this situation does not give away your hand. Your opponent may not expect you to play such a strong hand so aggressively and might suspect that you are trying for a free card. If so, he still might bet out the turn giving you a chance to raise while also gaining the maximum bets on the flop. In the actual hand, the player capped the betting and his opponent bet out the turn of the 3♥. The player raised and his opponent showed K♥ 6♠ on the river.

Sets and Trips

A *set* is three of a kind when you hold a pocket pair that matches one of the board cards. The odds of flopping a set are 7.5 to 1. *Trips* is three of a kind when one of your pocket cards matches a pair on the board. You will only flop trips about 1.4% of the time. Sets generally win larger pots than trips. Any time there is a pair on the board, especially when it is a high pair, it is difficult to get a lot of action since your opponents generally will play cautiously.

Although sets are very strong hands, there still are dangers. Your first concern with a set is the possibility of flushes and straights; therefore, three-suited or three-connected flops are your biggest worry as it is possible that you are currently beat and must draw to a full house to win. If the flop is two-suited, two-connected, or contains two cards with one or two gaps, sets and trips are vulnerable to flush and straight draws.

Although flushes and straights are your main concern, sometimes you can lose to other hands. For example, you can lose to a higher set, or your trips can lose to an opponent who also has trips but with a better kicker. Another possibility is that an opponent holding two pair could hit a better full house if the board pairs on either the turn or the river. These secondary concerns usually will not dictate your strategy on the flop, although possibly on later rounds, since they are not very common; however, the possibilities of flushes, straights, or strong draws have a big impact on how you decide to play your hand.

Even with these potential dangers, you have at least a 33% chance of drawing out to beat any flush or straight; therefore, at the very least you have a good drawing hand. You are going to play your hand to the river, so you must determine the best strategy to maximize its value. Sometimes you should play your hand strongly on the flop, while other times you might slowplay until the more expensive betting round on the turn. Let's look first at dangerous and strong flops for sets and then we'll discuss strategies for trips.

Dangerous Flops

Three-suited and two-suited flops give your opponents flush opportunities. A three-connected flop or a flop with all high cards gives them straight opportunities. Even two-connected cards that are high can give opponents straight opportunities. You want to charge your opponents for drawing and try not to give a free card, especially when the pot is large. Even when your opponents have flopped a straight or flush, you still have a strong draw to a full house. With these types of flops, you should usually bet out or raise every opportunity from all positions. Only try check-raising when you are very confident that an opponent will bet.

There are a few exceptions when you might not play your hand strongly with these types of flops. For example, you can consider slowplaying in heads-up situations when the pot is small, especially with a two-suited flop. With small pots, you are not risking a large pot if you check and your opponent takes a free card.

There is also one scenario where you might slowplay with a very large pot. As discussed in the "Deceptive Tactics" chapter, sometimes it is difficult to drive out opponents on the flop even by raising. For example, some opponents with gut-shot draws might call a raise on the flop for two small bets. They could even be correct in calling if the pot is very large. In this case, you might wait to raise the turn to have a better chance of driving out your opponents.

Strong Flops

Rainbow flops of all rags or with just one high card are strong flops for a set. You do not have to worry about flush or straight draws, unless someone has some type of straight draw with all low cards. An ideal situation is when you flop a set, and one or two of your opponents hold either an overpair or top pair. For example, a great flop is J♣ 7♦ 5♥ when you hold 7♠ 7♥, especially if one of your opponents holds a jack and another opponent an overpair.

When the pot is large, you should almost always play your hand strongly by either betting out or raising. Your hand is very strong, but a free card could always give your opponents a backdoor flush or straight draw, so you want to drive them out of the pot. Check-raising is an option to drive out opponents of a large pot when you are sure an opponent will bet out; however, be careful in check-raising if you hold the highest set, since it is less likely that your opponents were helped by the flop and they may not bet.

For example, if you hold J♥ J♠ with a flop of J♦ 7♥ 5♠, it is unlikely that your opponents were helped with this flop. Note how slowplaying this seemingly very strong hand can be dangerous against several opponents when the pot is large. Any diamond, heart, spade, A, K, or Q could give your opponents a good drawing hand. A T, 9, 8, 6, 4, or 3 could also give your opponents a good drawing hand or possibly even a straight. Don't take the risk of giving your opponents a free card and a chance to win a large pot.

If the pot is small, you can consider slowplaying your hand. Ideally you want a couple players to play the flop to gain extra bets on the turn and river. Checking or just calling a bet can give your opponents a chance to bluff or possibly improve to a second-best hand on the turn. Slowplaying to the turn also allows you to raise on the bigger betting round. However, be careful in checking the turn if you must act first since your opponents may take a free card. Generally go ahead and raise once two players have entered the pot.

Even with a small pot, sometimes you might raise the flop or even bet out against a lone opponent as a deceptive strategy when you think he might also have a decent hand. You could gain a lot of extra bets if your opponent doesn't put you on such a strong hand.

Trips

Trips is a strong hand, but it is often difficult to conceal the strength of your hand making it difficult to win a large pot. For this reason, you should tend to play these hands stronger on the flop than you would sets since it is more difficult for your opponents to improve to a good second-best hand and your opponents will often back off on the turn.

You need to be worried about possible draws when the flop is two-suited or the third card is connected to the pair, especially if it is a high pair. Strategies in this case are similar to a two-suited or two-connected flop when you hold a set. You should almost always either bet out or raise, unless you decide to slowplay against a lone opponent when the pot is small.

Let's look at flops that are not too threatening. For example, you hold J♥ T♥ and the flop is T♣ T♦ 5♠. As usual, if the pot is large, you should play your hand strongly. Check-raising with these types of flops is risky since many opponents are reluctant to bet with a high pair on the board; therefore, almost always bet out or raise when the pot is large.

Slowplaying is an option when the pot is small. You can sometimes just call an opponent's bet to wait and raise the turn, especially if you feel your opponent doesn't have a very strong hand. However, it is more difficult to get a lot of action with trips than sets, so sometimes it is better to just go ahead and raise to gain that extra bet on the flop. The problem with just calling is that your opponent will be worried that you have trips and will often just check the turn once you have called the flop. This is an even bigger problem if your opponent acts behind you on the turn and takes a free card.

If an opponent bets and there are several players left to act behind you, tend to raise if they are strong opponents and just call if they are weak opponents. Strong opponents generally are reluctant to be a third caller on this type of flop, so generally it is better to go ahead and raise your lone opponent. However, if there are weak opponents left to act, consider slowplaying since they tend to call with many hands even with a scary board.

If you raised preflop and must act first, generally bet out your trips. Your trips are somewhat concealed since your opponents expect you to bet out most of the time anyway after raising preflop.

If you didn't raise preflop and must act first, checking is usually the best option when there is a good chance that your opponents will fold if you bet. If you do decide to check and an opponent bets, I would almost always check-raise since your opponents will usually back off on the turn as discussed above. Check-raising the flop can also add a deceptive quality to your play since some opponents expect you to slowplay such a strong hand to the turn.

One caution about playing trips when your kicker is not very good. If you start to receive a lot of action, you might need to back off. Since these types of flops are scary for your opponents, they will usually not play too aggressively unless they hold trips or maybe even a full house. You will still play to the river, but you may need to put on the brakes with your raises if the action is really strong.

Chapter Review

- ❑ Sets generally win larger pots than trips.
- ❑ Your main concern when holding sets or trips is your opponents holding a flush, straight, or a strong draw to one of these hands.
- ❑ Seldom slowplay dangerous flops where your opponents could have a good draw. Some exceptions include:
  - • When you are heads up with a small pot, especially with a two-suited flop.

- When there are many opponents with a large pot. In this case you might wait to raise the turn to have a better chance of driving out your opponents.

❏ Rainbow flops of all rags or with just one high card are strong flops for a set.

- When the pot is large, you should almost always play your hand strongly by either betting out or raising.
- Check-raising is an option to drive out opponents of a large pot when you are sure an opponent will bet out; however, be careful in check-raising if you hold the highest set, since it is less likely that your opponents were helped by the flop and they may not bet.
- If the pot is small, consider slowplaying your hand by either checking or just calling a bet.
- Generally raise once two opponents have entered the pot.
- Even with a small pot, sometimes you might raise the flop or even bet out against a lone opponent as a deceptive strategy when you think he might also have a decent hand.

❏ Trips should be played stronger on the flop than sets since it is more difficult for your opponents to improve to a good second-best hand and your opponents will often back off on the turn.

- You need to be worried about possible draws when the flop is two-suited or the third card is connected to the pair, especially if it is a high pair. You should almost always either bet out or raise, unless you decide to slowplay against a lone opponent when the pot is small.
- Slowplaying is an option when the pot is small; however, sometimes it is better to just go ahead and raise since many opponents will back off on the turn with these types of flops.
- If an opponent bets and there are several players left to act behind you, tend to raise if they are strong opponents and just call if they are weak opponents.
- If you raised preflop and must act first, generally bet out your trips.
- If you didn't raise preflop and must act first, checking is usually the best option when there is a good chance that your opponents will fold if you bet.

Test Your Skills

1/ $20-$40. You hold K♠ K♦ in middle position. An early player calls and you raise. A middle player, the cutoff, and button all call. Five players see the flop of K♣ 8♣ 6♥. The early player checks. There is $230 in the pot. What do you do?

Answer: Bet. You should not slowplay with a large pot. With a large pot and a two-suited flop, you will probably get some action anyway.

2/ $20-$40. You hold 3♦ 3♥ in the small blind. An early player and a middle player call. You call and four players see the flop of Q♠ 7♥ 3♣. There is $80 in the pot. What do you do?

Answer: Check. The pot is small. Your opponents may all fold if they didn't hit this flop. Giving a free card could give your opponents a good second-best hand. Betting can be deceptive if an opponent hits the queen, but you can still gain bets by check-raising and they still won't know how strong your hand is since you are in the small blind. In the actual hand, everyone checked the flop. The J♦ came on the turn. The player bet, the big blind called, and the middle player raised showing AJ on the river. Slowplaying gained a lot of additional bets for this player.

3/ $20-$40. You hold 9♣ 9♦ in middle position. An early player raises, you make a questionable call, and another middle player calls. Three players see the flop of 9♥ 6♥ 4♣. The preflop raiser bets. There is $170 in the pot. What do you do?

Answer: Raise. I would not slowplay with such a large pot. Allowing the remaining opponent to enter cheaply could be dangerous by giving him either a flush or straight draw. Raising the flop should also gain you a lot of bets on both the flop and turn if the preflop raiser has a high pocket pair.

4/ $20-$40. Continuing with problem #3. You raise the flop, the middle player calls, and the preflop raiser reraises. There is $270 in the pot. What do you do?

Answer: Call with capping a close second. Raising again is unlikely to drive out the middle player behind you who might be on a flush draw. It appears that the preflop raiser has an overpair and will be betting out the turn. Once the pot gets large, your main objective should be to choose the strategy that gives you the best chance of winning the pot rather than winning additional bets. Calling will allow you to raise the turn charging the remaining opponent two big bets to call to the river. As a secondary benefit, you will probably gain at least two big bets on the turn from the preflop raiser. Since the flop is two-suited, capping is also a good option since your opponent might still bct out the turn if he thinks you are on a flush draw. Cap against an aggressive player and tend to call against a conservative player. In the actual hand, the player only called and the preflop raiser showed AA.

5/ $5-$10. You hold 9♦ 9♠ on the button. An early player, two middle players, and the cutoff all call. You call and the small blind folds. Six players see the flop of Q♥ J♦ 9♥. The big blind and the early player check. The middle player bets, the next middle player calls, and the cutoff folds. There is $42 in the pot. What do you do?

Answer: Raise. This is a scary flop as there are straight possibilities and a flush draw; however, you most likely have the best hand. Even if an opponent has flopped a straight, you have a great draw to a full house. Go ahead and raise the flop and gain as many bets as you can while there still are a lot of opponents. In the actual hand, the player only called. The early player raised and was slowplaying a pocket pair of aces. The player did not raise the flop or turn. A middle player won with a straight when a ten fell on the river.

6/ $20-$40. You hold 7♣ 7♥ on the button. Two middle players call and you call. Four players see the flop of T♣ 7♠ 3♥. The first middle player bets and the next player folds. There is $110 in the pot. What do you do?

Answer: Call. You can slowplay in this situation. The pot is small and the flop is not very dangerous. The middle player's hand probably is not too strong since he limped in preflop. He probably is holding a hand like KT or JTs. You also wouldn't mind if the big blind stays in the hand with this small pot. In the actual hand, the player waited to raise the turn of the 3♦ and his opponent showed two pair with T♦ 9♦ when the 9♠ fell on the river.

7/ $15-$30. You hold 6♣ 6♦ in middle position. An early player calls and you call. The cutoff raises, the small blind reraises, and everyone calls. Four players see the flop of 9♣ 6♥ 3♦. The small blind bets, the early player calls, you raise, the small blind reraises, and the early player folds. There is $285 in the pot. What do you do?

Answer: Call. Your opponent will likely bet out the turn giving you the chance to raise when the bets are bigger. Capping the betting on a rainbow flop like this indicates a very strong hand, and your opponent might back off even with an overpair. If the flop wasn't a rainbow, you might cap the betting since your opponent still might bet out on the turn trying to protect against a free card. In the actual hand, the player waited to raise the turn and his opponent showed JJ.

8/ $.50-$1. You are in the big blind with T♠ 6♥ and there are five callers. The flop is T♦ T♥ 7♥. The small blind checks. There is $3 in the pot. What do you do?

Answer: Bet. You could slowplay since the pot is not very big, but you should get plenty of action with this type of flop since your opponents could have flush and straight draws. Checking is risky since your opponents may not bet with this scary flop. Giving a free card in this situation with so many draws is not wise. Betting out is also deceptive since many opponents will put you on a pair of 7's.

9/ $20-$40. You hold A♥ 4♥ in the small blind. Two middle players call and the cutoff raises. You call and four players see the flop of 4♦ 4♠ 3♣. There is $180 in the pot. What do you do?

Answer: Check-raise. The cutoff will almost always bet a flop of all rags allowing you to check-raise. The pot is quite large, so you don't want the other opponents to get a cheap play on the flop only to get some type of flush or straight draw on the turn. You also must act first on the turn, so check-raising the flop is a good lead into betting out the turn rather than risk trying a check-raise on the turn.

10/ $20-$40. You hold K♦ 4♦ in the cutoff. An early player calls. You make a poor call in this situation. The small blind calls and four players see the flop of K♣ K♥ 3♦. The early player bets. There is $100 in the pot. What do you do?

Answer: Raise. Slowplaying will not give any opponent a good second hand. Calling in this situation would look suspicious, as many opponents will worry that you are slowplaying trips. Raising can be deceptive as many opponents will not expect you to raise such a strong hand on the flop. In the actual hand, the player raised and was called by the early player who bet out the turn of T♠. The player only called the turn as he was either beaten badly or a huge favorite. Only calling also lets the bettor continue to bluff or will keep him in the hand with a weak pair. The early player bet out the river showing 55.

11/ $15-$30. You raise with A♥ Q♠ in early position. A middle player reraises and the cutoff calls. Three players see the flop of Q♦ Q♥ 7♠. There is $160 in the pot. What do you do?

Answer: Check-raise. The middle player will almost always bet since he showed so much strength preflop. Even if both opponents check, your hand is very strong with this flop and they may not put you on queens when you bet out the turn. Betting out could be deceptive, but it is difficult to be very deceptive when there was so much preflop action. In the actual hand, the player check-raised both opponents. The next player reraised and the cutoff folded. The player capped the betting and his opponent folded on the turn.

12/ $20-$40. You hold K♣ J♦ in middle position. An early player calls, you make a weak call, and the cutoff raises. The small blind calls and four players see the flop of J♣ J♠ T♥. The early player bets. There is $200 in the pot. What do you do?

Answer: Raise. The pot is large and there are a lot of straight draws that your opponents could hold. You want to raise to force any opponents with gut-shot draws to fold or pay two bets to draw. Raising may also be deceptive as your opponents might expect you to slowplay trips. In the actual hand, the player raised and only the bettor called. The early player check-raised the turn of 8♥ and showed Q♥ 9♥ on the river for a straight.

Two Pair

The strategies presented in this chapter are for two pair when you match both your hole cards with two of the flop cards. If there is a pair on the flop, then strategy is more like playing either an overpair/top pair, or middle/bottom pair. For example, if the flop is T55 and you have JT, I treat this like top pair for strategy purposes. You will flop two pair matching both hole cards approximately once every 50 hands.

Similar to sets, your main concerns with two pair are flushes, straights, and strong draws to these hands. One good thing about two pair is that you can be less worried about your opponents holding a set since you have two of the flop cards in your hand.

Two pair can also lose to a higher two pair, so your hand is more vulnerable when you have bottom two pair. For example, if you hold 97 with a J97 flop and your opponent holds a jack, your hand is vulnerable to another jack landing, a running pair on the next two cards, or your opponent hitting his kicker card. Another situation that can occur is when you are against an overpair and flop two pair. If the board pairs and it is not one of your two pair, you will lose to a higher two pair.

Strategies for two pair are similar to the strategies when you hold a set; however, if you hold top two pair, it is less likely that an opponent will bet since you hold two of the top flop cards in your hand. Therefore, you need to be even more careful not to give free cards. Let's look at the different flop types and discuss potential strategies.

Three-suited or Three-connected

These types of flops are very dangerous for two pair. You could already be beaten or there is a good chance that an opponent has a good draw. Almost always bet out into one or two opponents since you do not want to give a free card. If an opponent bets, you can either raise the flop, or just call and wait to see if the turn card is favorable.

Your betting strategies may change somewhat when there are several opponents in the hand. There is a higher chance that you are already beat, and if not, it is likely that you are against a good draw. In situations like these, it may be best to just check and call and wait to see if the turn card is favorable. If the turn card is favorable and you feel you have the best hand, you can either bet or raise to drive out players. If you suspect that you might be against a made hand, you need to decide whether you should fold or continue playing to the river with a draw.

Note that two pair cannot be played as strongly as a set. A set can almost always be played to the river since you have so many outs; therefore, you can usually stay the aggressor by raising or reraising even though there is the possibility that you are beaten. Compare this to two pair, which only has four outs if an opponent has you beaten. Your draw is not nearly as strong; therefore, sometimes you will need to fold when it becomes obvious that an opponent holds a better hand.

Two-suited or Two-connected

You should almost always play two pair strongly with these types of flops since you do not want to give a free card and you want to collect bets from your opponents making draws. This is especially true when the pot is large or you are against several opponents.

When the pot is large, almost always bet out or raise at every opportunity. Only consider check-raising if you are confident an opponent will bet and your check-raise will force your opponents with gut-shot or backdoor flush draws to call two small bets. Check-raising with top two pair is risky since it is less likely that your opponents were helped by the flop. You should usually only try a check-raise against an aggressive preflop raiser in late position who will almost always bet.

Similar to sets, if the pot is very large and it would be difficult to drive out opponents on the flop, you might wait to raise the turn if this will give you a better chance of driving out opponents.

If the pot is small and you are acting first, check-raising is a good option against one or two opponents. Betting out will likely cause your opponents to fold since it is unlikely they were helped by the flop when you hold two of the flop cards in your hand. If they have a draw, they will likely bet out and you can check-raise charging them a higher price for their draws. If they take a free card, it is not too dangerous since the pot is small and you have a strong hand.

Internet Tip

As discussed previously, players tend to check-raise more on the Internet than in a live game. Since players check-raise on the Internet so often, your opponents won't respect your check-raises quite as much as they would in a live game and will call more often. Many players on the Internet feel committed to the pot once they bet and it is very easy to just click the call button to see one more card; therefore, *check-raising on the Internet can be especially effective in earning additional bets.* If they call, you win at least two more small bets on the flop, and the turn card might improve them to a second-best hand.

When the pot is small and an opponent bets, you can either raise the flop or consider slowplaying to the turn. You do not want your opponent to fold, so tend to just call against strong opponents and raise against weak opponents who will call many hands.

Consider slowplaying when one or two opponents check into you and the pot is small. Many opponents bet out their flush draws, so you are less worried about giving a free card. There is a decent chance they might fold the flop, so slowplaying could improve their hand to earn you some additional bets. For example, an early player calls and you call with A♦ 9♦ in late position. The big blind checks. Three players see the flop of A♣ 9♥ 4♥. Consider checking with this small pot.

All High Cards

You should get a lot of action with two pair and a high card flop. Many opponents will hold pairs and/or straight draws. Your opponents could flop a straight or a set, but you should generally play aggressively until your opponents let you know that you might be beat. Against several opponents, almost always bet out or raise. You do not want to give a free card and you want to charge your opponents for drawing. One exception to betting out is trying a check-raise when the pot is large to drive out players on weak draws such as gut shots.

If you are against a lone opponent, tend to bet out more as opposed to the two-suited or two-connected flops. Check-raises are risky since many opponents may not bet in fear of a check-raise and may take a free card with a weak draw. You can consider waiting to raise the turn if a lone opponent bets into you.

One note about holding the two smallest pair with a high card flop. You should still play aggressively, but if your opponents start raising and reraising, you may be in trouble. For example, if you hold KT with a flop of AKT and two opponents are raising and reraising, you should probably fold. AA, KK, TT, AK, AT, and QJ are all possible hands that would have you beat.

Rainbow with One High Card

This is a very favorable flop for two pair, although sometimes it is difficult to get a lot of action. With a large pot, you should bet out, raise, or reraise as usual if given the opportunity. If an opponent raises with a suspected overpair, you can reraise and bet out the turn. Check-raising is risky with these types of flops since you hold two of the board cards in your hand. One exception to raising the flop is when the pot is very large and you think you have a better chance of driving out opponents on the turn.

With a small pot, you have a few more options since giving a free card is not as risky. You have a strong hand and would like to gain more bets. When acting first against one or two opponents, usually check unless you were the preflop raiser. Against a preflop raiser, sometimes check-raise and sometimes just check and call to wait and show your strength on the turn. With more than two opponents, you should usually go ahead and bet out or raise if given the opportunity.

Rainbow of All Rags

Strategy for a rainbow flop of all rags is very similar to strategy for a flop with only one high card. The difference is that betting out is not as likely to scare off opponents since they will often play two overcards. A common situation for flopping two pair with an all rag flop is when you get a free play out of the blinds. Since it is difficult for opponents to put you on any kind of hand, you should usually bet out if your opponents are the type who will call with overcards. If someone raises, you can decide whether to reraise the flop or wait until the turn to show your true strength. Be careful however in giving a free card if the pot is large.

If a player bets into you on the flop, then again your options are open. If the pot is large, usually raise to try to drive out opponents with weak draws. If the pot is small, raising or slowplaying are both good options depending on how your feel you can extract the most bets from your opponents.

Chapter Review

❑ Your main concerns with two pair are flushes, straights, and strong draws to these hands. Sets are less of a concern since you hold two of the flop cards in your hand. Two pair can also lose to a higher two pair.

❑ Three-suited and three-connected flops are very dangerous for two pair. You could already be beaten or there is a good chance that an opponent has a good draw:

- Against one or two opponents, almost always bet out. If an opponent bets, you can either raise the flop, or just call and wait to see if the turn card is favorable.

- Against several opponents, it may be best to just check and call and wait to see if the turn card is favorable.

❑ Generally play two pair strongly with a two-suited or two-connected flop:

- When the pot is large, almost always bet out or raise at every opportunity. Usually only try a check-raise against an aggressive preflop raiser in late position.

- If the pot is small and you are acting first, check-raising is a good option against one or two opponents.

- When the pot is small and an opponent bets, you can either raise the flop or consider slowplaying to the turn.

- Consider slowplaying when one or two opponents check into you and the pot is small.

❑ All high card flops will usually generate a lot of action as many opponents will hold pairs and/or straight draws:

- Against several opponents, almost always bet out or raise. One exception to betting out is trying a check-raise when the pot is large to drive out players on weak draws such as gut shots.

- Against a lone opponent, tend to bet out more as opposed to the two-suited or two-connected flops. Check-raises are risky since many opponents may not bet in fear of a check-raise and may take a free card with a weak draw.

- You can consider waiting to raise the turn if a lone opponent bets into you.

❑ A rainbow flop with one high card is a very favorable flop for two pair, although sometimes it is difficult to get a lot of action:

- With a large pot, you should bet out, raise, or reraise as usual if given the opportunity.

- With a small pot, you have more options since giving a free card is not as risky. Consider check-raising or slowplaying to try and gain more bets.

❑ Strategy for a rainbow flop of all rags is very similar to strategy for a flop with only one high card. The difference is that betting out is not as likely to scare off opponents since they will often play two overcards.

  • Generally bet out when you get a free play out of the blinds and flop two pair. If someone raises, you can decide whether to reraise the flop or wait until the turn to show your true strength.

  • When a player bets into you, usually raise if the pot is large. With a small pot, raising or slowplaying are both good options.

Test Your Skills

1/ $15-$30. You hold J♥ 4♣ in the big blind. An early player and the small blind call. Three players see the flop of J♠ 7♠ 4♦. The small blind checks. There is $45 in the pot. What do you do?

Answer: Check with the intention of raising. The pot is small, so you are willing to risk giving a free card. Even if your opponents get a flush or open-ended draw on the turn, they will not have correct odds on the draw. Rather than winning a small pot, giving a free card could allow you to win a couple more big bets. If the early player bets, go ahead and raise in case he is on a flush draw. In the actual hand, everyone checked the flop and the J♣ came on the turn. He decided to check to try and induce a bet from the early player who bet with 6♦ 6♠.

2/ $15-$30. You hold K♠ J♣ in the big blind. The button raises and you call. The flop is K♦ J♠ 5♣. There is $70 in the pot. What do you do?

Answer: Check-raise. You have several options with this hand. Betting out is risky since you have two of the top cards on the flop. Your opponent could fold and you would only win a small pot. Trying to slowplay to the turn and then check-raising is risky since your opponent might take a free card. Checking and calling the flop and then betting out the turn is a decent option. Your opponent may think you are betting out a weak hand and raise, allowing you to make it three big bets.

I prefer check-raising the flop. This option will gain you at least another small bet on the flop, as your opponent will almost always bet out. Your opponent will not know how strong your hand is since you could be raising in a heads-up situation with any pair or a draw. You could gain a couple of bets on the flop and your opponent still might raise the turn with a decent holding. In the actual hand, the player planned on check-raising the turn only to see his opponent take a free card. He showed J♥ T♥ when the 5♠ fell on the turn.

3/ $20-$40. You hold K♥ Q♠ in the cutoff. Two middle players call and you call. Four players see the flop of K♠ Q♦ 6♠. The first middle player bets and the next middle player folds. There is $110 in the pot. What do you do?

Answer: Raise. This type of flop is dangerous with many gut-shot possibilities and the flush draw. Raise and make your opponents pay two bets for their draws. In the actual hand, the player raised and only the bettor called. The bettor bet out the turn of A♥ and called the player's raise. He also bet out the river of the 8♠ and showed the nut flush with A♠ 7♠. The player lost the hand, but his raises maximized the cost of the draw for his opponent.

4/ $20-$40. You hold K♦ Q♦ on the button. The seat before the cutoff posts $20. A middle player raises, the player who posted calls, the cutoff calls, and you call. The small blind calls and five players see the flop of K♥ Q♣ 2♣. The preflop raiser bets and the cutoff calls. You raise, the preflop raiser reraises, and the cutoff folds. There is $340 in the pot. What do you do?

Answer: Reraise. It is doubtful that your opponent holds KK or QQ since you hold one card of each. Your opponent probably holds AA or maybe AK. If you only call the reraise, your opponent will almost always bet out the turn allowing you to raise when the bets are bigger. However, many opponents will put you on a draw with this type of flop. You could have either a flush or a straight draw, so even if you cap the flop, your opponent will still probably bet out the turn to protect from giving you a free card.

Capping the flop allows you to gain more bets on the flop without jeopardizing your chance of being able to raise the turn. If the flop was a rainbow, I might lean towards calling the reraise to wait and raise the turn. In the actual hand, the player capped the flop and his opponent bet out AQ on the turn. The player raised and his opponent called to the river.

5/ $.50-$1. You are in the big blind with the K♦ T♦. An early and middle player call. Three players see the flop of K♣ T♥ 2♠. There is $1.75 in the pot. What do you do?

Answer: Check-raise. The pot is small, so giving a free card is not too risky. Betting out may only win you a small pot since you hold two of the flop cards. An opponent on a gut-shot draw or one pair may bet out allowing you to check-raise. In the actual hand, the player bet out and the flop was capped! The middle player showed T♣ 2♣ on the river.

6/ $20-$40. You call in middle position with A♠ 6♠. The small blind calls and the big blind raises. You call and the small blind folds. The flop is A♦ 9♣ 6♣. The big blind bets. There is $120 in the pot. What do you do?

Answer: Raise. This is a situation where reverse psychology comes into play. If you just call in this situation, your opponent might become suspicious and back off if he holds a hand like KK or QQ. On the other hand, if he holds AK or AQ, you might get great action on both the flop and turn before he realizes you have two pair. The two-suited flop also disguises your hand somewhat since your opponent may put you on a flush draw. In the actual hand, the player raised and was called. His opponent check-raised the river with TT when a ten fell. This is exactly the kind of play we want our opponents to make, even though once in a while it will cost us a pot.

7/ $15-$30. You call in early position with A♦ 4♦. Only the small blind and big blind call. Three players see the flop of A♥ 6♦ 4♥. Both blinds check. There is $45 in the pot. What do you do?

Answer: Check, although betting is a close second. Both players have checked, which probably indicates that they do not have a flush draw. The pot is small, so you are not risking too much by giving a free card. Even if your opponents get a good draw on the turn, they would not be getting good pot odds on their draw, especially if they bet the turn and you raise. Betting out is a close second given that a free card would not give your opponents a very good second-best hand with an ace on the board. In the actual hand, the player checked and the 8♠ fell on the turn. The big blind bet out with 8♣ 5♥.

8/ $20-$40. You raise with Q♥ J♥ from middle position and both blinds call. Three players see the flop of Q♦ J♦ 4♦. A weak player from the big blind bets. There is $140 in the pot. What do you do?

Answer: Call, with raising a close second. Your opponent would most likely slowplay a flush. He is most likely on a flush draw since you hold two of the flop cards. This weak opponent is acting before you and will probably bet out the turn continuing his bluff. I prefer waiting to the turn to raise. This does two things. You can see if another diamond comes on the turn before investing more money in the pot. If the diamond doesn't come, you can raise on the larger betting round allowing you to charge your opponent a higher price for his draw. In the actual hand, the player waited to raise the turn and his opponent folded on the river.

9/ $15-$30. You hold A♥ 6♥ on the button. An early player and the cut-off call. You call and the small blind folds. Four players see the flop of A♠ T♦ 6♠. The big blind bets and the early player raises. There is $115 in the pot. What do you do?

Answer: Reraise, with calling a very close second. You most likely have the best hand, so go ahead and reraise. Reraising may get the big blind to fold a hand like A8. You also might be able to buy a free card if a spade falls on the turn. Calling is also a valid option. Waiting to raise the turn has two potential benefits over raising the flop. You can simply call if another spade comes on the turn, hoping that your hand is best or that you hit a full house on the river. If a spade doesn't come, you can raise the turn charging your opponents two big bets to draw to the river. In the actual hand, the player waited to raise the turn. Both opponents folded on the river.

10/ $1-$2. You hold 9♦ 3♣ in the big blind. The cutoff posts $1. An early player, a middle player, and the small blind call. Five players see the flop of 9♥ 6♦ 3♠. The small blind checks. There is $5 in the pot. What do you do?

Answer: Bet, with check-raising a close second. With several opponents, you should still get calls with opponents playing overcards and gut-shot draws. It is difficult for your opponents to put you on a hand with this type of flop, so you could get good action if an overcard comes on the turn. Check-raising is valid also since one of your opponents might bet this flop. Even if your opponents don't bet the flop, a free card is not too dangerous with a small pot and this type of flop. In the actual hand, the player bet out and was called by three opponents. The player in the cutoff hit a gut-shot straight on the river holding 42.

Top Pair/Overpair

Unfortunately, we are not so lucky to flop two pair or better very often. A much more common situation is flopping top pair or an overpair. Sometimes top pair/overpair can be a strong hand, and at other times it could be a hand we are folding on the flop.

The relative strength of your hand depends on the following factors:

⇨ **How high your pair is**

When the flop is favorable but your pair is vulnerable to overcards, you generally should choose the best strategy that will drive out your opponents by betting, raising, or check-raising. The higher the pair the more risks you can take since a free card is less likely to hurt you.

⇨ **How high your kicker is when holding top pair**

A high kicker adds a lot of value to top pair. This is why AK is such a strong hand. If an ace or king falls on the flop, you are at least guaranteed top pair with top kicker. Whenever an opponent holds an overpair, a kicker higher than their overpair adds value to your draw.

⇨ **The number of players playing the hand**

The more players in the hand, the higher the probability someone holds two pair or better, or a good drawing hand. In a heads-up situation, top pair is always worth playing with a favorable flop. On the other hand, if your pair is not very high or you have a weak kicker, your hand may need to be folded against many opponents.

⇨ **The possible strength of your opponents' hands, especially in a raised pot**

In pots where an opponent raised or reraised preflop, there is a higher probability of someone holding an overpair to your pair or a better kicker. It is less likely that an opponent holds a premium hand in an unraised pot.

⇨ **The flop type. Flops that are more dangerous than others include:**
- A high or low pair
- Two- or three-suited
- Two- or three-connected
- Two or more cards 9 or above

Let's look at an example of a dangerous flop for your top pair. For example, you get a free play in the big blind with T♣ 4♦ and four opponents see a flop of T♦ 9♥ 8♥. Your hand is vulnerable to any card above a 5 falling on the turn or river, except a ten, and your hand could already be beat. You should fold this hand against several opponents.

Note that the relative strength between top pair and an overpair can sometimes be very different. An overpair is a much stronger hand since you can beat any opponent with top pair and your hand is less vulnerable to overcards; however, strategies are generally very similar so they are discussed together in one chapter. When reading through the chapter, take note when I mention just top pair versus top pair and/or an overpair.

Strategies with top pair or an overpair can vary a lot depending on the particular circumstances. Since you will be playing top pair quite often, we will look at many different considerations for each flop type.

Rainbow with One High Card

A rainbow flop with one high card is a good flop for top pair or an overpair, as your opponents cannot have too many draws to hurt your hand. Examples include KK, AQ, or QJ with a flop of Q53.

Although top pair is usually a good hand with a flop with only one high card, some common situations where you should consider folding include:

♣ The pot is raised before you act and you have a weak kicker.
♣ Several players pay a bet on the flop and you have a weak kicker.
♣ Several players pay a bet on the flop and your top pair is not very high; for example, you hold T8 with a flop of T42.
♣ The bettor is a tight player who never bluffs and you hold a weak kicker.

There are other situations where you may need to fold top pair, but these listed above are some of the more common. Sometimes you might even fold an *overpair* when the action is very aggressive both preflop and on the flop. The general rule is to consider folding against several opponents on the flop when you can't justify a draw and your pair is not very high or your kicker is weak.

Let's look first at those strong hands that are not very vulnerable to overcards. Examples include a pair of aces or kings, or a pair of queens with an ace or king kicker. Whenever the pot is small, you can either play these hands aggressively on the flop, or wait until the turn to raise. Check-raising the flop is an excellent play to try and get an opponent to commit some chips to the pot. If he decides to take a free card, you still might get action if he improves to a second-best hand.

If the pot is large and you hold a premium pair, almost always play your hand strongly. Choose the best strategy to drive out your opponents to give you the best chance at winning the pot rather than try winning additional bets.

Let's look now at hands that are not so strong and more vulnerable to overcards. You should usually bet out or raise to drive out your opponents. One exception when you might consider check-raising is when you are acting first and betting out is unlikely to drive out many players and you think a player in late position will bet. For example, you hold A♣ T♦ with a flop of T♥ 8♠ 5♦ or 9♠ 9♦ with an 8♠ 5♥ 3♣ flop. If an opponent raised before the flop, it usually is difficult to drive out your opponents with a bet since they are getting decent pot odds on a draw to overcards. However, if the pre-flop raiser is acting last and bets, check-raising could force the remaining opponents to pay two bets to continue playing.

With pots that are very large, it is sometimes very difficult to drive out many opponents even by raising. As discussed in other chapters, your main concern in large pots is selecting the best strategy to help you win the pot. This might mean waiting until the turn to try and drive out your opponents. With a favorable turn card, a raise or check-raise to two big bets can be more successful in driving out your opponents than a raise on the flop.

Sometimes it is difficult to know whether or not you have the best hand on the flop. If an opponent has an overpair to your top pair, you only have five outs. Even worse is when he holds the same top pair but with a better kicker, since now you only have three outs. In these cases, you want to find out as early as possible where your opponents stand. One option is to bet out with your medium holdings. If you are raised or several players call, you can usually safely fold your hand or back off on the turn. However, if you are against many opponents, you might just check to see what happens behind you. If an opponent then bets and another raises, you can safely fold saving yourself a bet.

Advanced Concept: Try to avoid just checking and calling your borderline hands to the river since this can be much more expensive than gaining information early in the hand that might allow you to safely fold.

For example, you hold A♣ 4♣ with a flop of A♦ T♥ 2♠. If you bet out and an opponent raises, you can safely fold against most opponents. This is less expensive than simply checking and calling all the way to the river. If you are against many opponents, you might just check to see what your opponents do behind you before committing chips.

Related to the above concept, when you are acting last, sometimes the correct strategy is to raise with a borderline hand. If you are reraised, you can safely fold. If your opponent just calls, you might have the option of taking a free card on the turn. Successfully buying a free card saves you a bet on the turn while still allowing you to showdown your hand for a possible win.

One other common situation is when you are in late position and all of your opponents have checked. In general, you would almost always bet top pair; however, there are some special situations when you might check the flop and wait to see if the turn card is favorable. For example, if the pot is large and you are worried about a check-raise from a better hand, you might check to see if you can improve your hand on the turn. Another example is when the pot is so large it is doubtful that a bet would drive out very many players. In this case, you might just check your top pair to give yourself a better chance of driving out your opponents on the bigger betting round.

Rainbow of All Rags

Strategies for a rainbow flop of all rags are similar to those when the flop includes a high card, but low to medium pairs are always more vulnerable to overcards. Straight draws are also more common, especially against opponents from the blinds. Since there is not a high card on the flop to scare your opponents, many will play overcard draws. In addition, your hand could already be losing against an opponent holding a medium high overpair such as 99 or 88.

When you hold a small top pair, important considerations in determining strategy include:
- **The number of opponents:** You should almost always play your hand strongly against one or two opponents by either betting out or raising. When there are several opponents in the hand and you feel you have the best hand, choose the strategy that has the best chance of driving out your opponents such as a check-raise.
- **The size of the pot:** Against several opponents in a raised pot, top pairs are rather weak with an all rag flop since you could already be beat by an overpair and it is nearly impossible to get many opponents to fold their overcard draws. When the pot is large, you actually might play top pair as a draw to five outs.
- **Your kicker card:** A high kicker card can add some value to your hand by giving you a stronger draw or by counterfeiting your opponent's overcard.

Let's look at a couple of examples where you flop a low top pair. One common situation is when you get a free play out of the blinds. For example, you hold 9♣ 7♥ with a 7♦ 4♥ 3♣ flop. Against one or two opponents, you should almost always bet out. Checking is risky since you do not want to give free cards. Against three opponents, you are usually in a borderline situation where you might bet out or check with the option of folding, calling, or raising should someone bet. Tend to bet out in a tight game and check in a loose game. Also tend to bet out more if your kicker is high. Sometimes checking and calling is correct when you don't feel your hand is currently best but you are getting sufficient pot odds to draw.

Against four or more opponents, you might check and then determine your best strategy based on the action behind you. If a late opponent bets, you could check-raise to try and drive out the other players. If several opponents play the flop or there is a raise, consider folding or possibly calling if you are getting decent pot odds on a draw.

Another common situation is when you are in late position and play a hand such as A7s or 98s against several players. In these situations, you at least get to see what your opponents do before you have to act. If it is checked to you, almost always bet out. All of your opponents have indicated weakness, so you probably have the best hand unless an opponent is going to check-raise out of the blinds.

Two-Suited

Your strategies will change somewhat when the flop is two-suited. Let's first look at strategies when you flop top pair and a flush draw. In those situations where you may have folded a vulnerable pair against several opponents, you would now play since you have a flush draw. You are also less worried about driving out your opponents with these types of hands if the pot is small. For example, if you hold A♦ J♦ in early position with a flop of J♣ 7♦ 4♥, you would be concerned with driving out opponents to protect your top pair; however, if the flop is J♣ 7♦ 4♦, your main strategy may not *always* be to drive out players on the flop. For example, you might not raise with a small pot so that other players will play behind you; however, you should usually raise when there is a large pot. Flush draws are discussed in more detail in a later chapter.

When you hold top pair or an overpair but don't have a flush draw, you now must worry that your opponents have a draw. This has two significant meanings for you. First, you should be more inclined to check and fold your borderline hands than otherwise, especially when there are several players in the hand. Second, with your stronger hands, be careful not to give free cards since you have a better chance of being paid off with players on flush draws.

Depending on how many players are in the pot, you need to choose the best strategy that will charge the highest price for your opponents to draw. On the flop, you can either bet out, check-raise, raise, or just call and wait until the turn to raise. Waiting until the turn to show your power can sometimes be the best play by making your opponents pay two big bets to see the river card. This also allows you to back off or possibly fold if a scare card comes on the turn.

If you bet out, beware of players who raise from late position. In many cases, they are trying to buy a free card on the turn. If you suspect that you indeed have the best hand, you should reraise, or at the very least, call and bet out the turn if a scare card does not come. If raised again on the turn, you will need to decide whether or not you have the best hand based on the likelihood that your opponent would raise the turn as a semi-bluff or with a hand weaker than yours.

Three-Suited

A three-suited flop is always dangerous, unless you happen to have a flush draw with one of the top two remaining suited cards. For example, top pair with an ace or king of the same suit as the flop is a very strong holding. However, if you do not have a flush draw, you must be very careful in how you play your hand. The danger is that an opponent already has a flush or at least a strong draw.

Let's look first at when you have top pair and a good flush draw. There are two scenarios. You could hold a pair not vulnerable to overcards, such as A♦ K♣, and you are fortunate enough to flop K♦ T♦ 5♦. There is a small chance that you could be beat by a flush or a set, but even then you still have a strong draw to win the hand. In these situations, you can either play your hand aggressively or wait until the turn to raise on the more expensive betting round. Usually it is better to just go ahead and bet or raise the flop since the betting action could dry up if another suited card comes.

The second scenario is when you hold a medium pair with a high kicker, such as A♦ J♣ with a flop of J♦ 7♦ 4♦. Similar to the two-suited flop, your main strategy may not *always* be to drive out players on the flop if the pot is small.

When you don't have a flush draw, you should proceed cautiously, especially when your pair is not very high or your kicker is weak. If someone comes out betting, you first must determine the probability that you are already beat. Against many opponents, it may be best to go ahead and fold. Even when you are ahead, there is still a good chance that an opponent will outdraw you, especially if your pair is vulnerable to overcards also.

For example, if you hold Q♦ J♦ with a flop of J♥ 7♥ 3♥ and someone bets into you with many opponents left in the hand, you should probably fold. First, your kicker is not very strong. Even if you do have the best hand, you must worry about any ace, king, or another suited card coming, which is basically even money with two cards to come.

If your hand is A♦ J♦, now you have a somewhat better hand since you have top kicker, but your hand is still very vulnerable. Your betting strategies in this type of situation are usually dependent on how many opponents you are against. If you are against one, you might play aggressively; two or three you might play conservatively to see the turn card; and you might fold a weak kicker against a lot of action from several players.

Two-Connected

Two-connected flops present some of the same problems as two-suited flops, especially when the two connected cards are medium to high. Your opponents could have open-ended or gut-shot straight draws along with overcards, so you want to be sure that they pay for their draws. Two pair is also a concern.

Your opponents are often getting decent pot odds to try for gut-shot draws for only one small bet; therefore, raise your strong hands if given the opportunity so that any remaining opponents acting behind you will have to call a raise cold on their weak draw.

If your pair is vulnerable to overcards, you should protect your pair as discussed in the previous sections. When your top pair is not very high and your kicker is weak, you may need to fold your hand if several players are playing the hand and there is a lot of action. For example, if you hold T♣ 9♠ and the flop is 9♦ 6♥ 5♣, you should usually fold if there are several callers on the flop or the flop is raised. The two connected cards give your opponents more outs to draw and beat you *if* you are ahead. In fact, with the above flop, the only cards that can come that are not dangerous to your hand are another ten or 9!

Three-Connected

Like the three-suited flop, a three-connected flop can be dangerous, especially with medium to high cards. An opponent could already have a straight, set, two pair, or a strong draw. However, these flops add a lot of value to top pair or an overpair when you also have a strong straight draw. Examples include either Q♣ J♦ or Q♣ Q♥ with a flop of J♥ T♠ 9♣. You should almost always bet out in this type of situation and generally raise if an opponent bets. If the pot is large, it may be difficult to drive out opponents with these types of flops, so sometimes it is better to wait and raise the turn to charge them a higher price for their draws.

Sometimes you might just call when the pot is small to keep the remaining opponents in the hand with your draw. Remember however that these types of draws are relatively weak, as there is a good chance of splitting the pot and your straight could possibly lose to a higher straight.

When you don't have a straight draw, you should proceed with caution just like you would with a three-suited flop. This is especially true when the flop has high cards. Flops such as JT9 or T98 are very dangerous. There are too many hands that your opponents would play that present problems for you. For example, if you hold AJ with a JT9 flop, any K, Q, T, 9, 8, or 7 could present big problems. Even if you have the best hand on the flop, there are many ways for you to be beaten on the turn or river. In fact, with several players playing the hand, you probably are not the favorite to win the hand even though you might currently have the best hand.

Against a lone opponent you should usually come out betting or raising. You do not want your lone opponent to get a free card with these types of flops. With several players in the hand, consider checking to see what develops behind you, especially if your pair is vulnerable to overcards or your kicker is weak. You should usually fold if you have to call a raise cold on the flop. If several players are paying a bet on the flop and it is your turn to act, you might also go ahead and fold. If you call and the turn card is favorable, you can then decide whether to raise or just continue to call.

All High Cards

An all high card flop is another dangerous flop for top pair or an overpair. Your hand is vulnerable to straights, sets, two pair, and straight draws. For example, flops of AJT, KT9, and QT9 could all hit big hands for your opponents.

Top pair is especially vulnerable against several opponents playing the flop. You may need to fold against a lot of action, unless you have some type of draw to a straight also. If you hold a weak kicker, generally check if you are acting early to see what happens behind you. If several players enter the pot or you must call a raise cold, you should usually fold. If one player bets into you and there are still several opponents to act behind you, you might also consider folding.

Whenever there are only one or two opponents playing the flop, your hand has a better chance of holding up, especially if one of the players played from the blinds. In these situations, you should probably go ahead and bet. If you are raised, then make an evaluation of the player's hand and decide whether or not to proceed. If nobody shows any strength and a rag comes on the turn, go ahead and bet again. Generally fold if raised on the turn with these kinds of flops.

If you are acting last against one or two opponents, almost always bet out if it is checked to you. If you are check-raised, consider folding against most typical opponents. If you are heads up and an opponent bets into you, you have several options depending on the type of opponent you are playing and their likely hand. One option is to simply call to the river. Another option is to raise and then determine your best move on the turn. You might even consider folding top pair weak kicker against tight opponents with these types of flops.

High Pair

For purposes of this chapter, when there is a pair on the flop and you have two pair, strategy is similar to having top pair or an overpair since everyone has at least one pair. For example, you have AQ with a QTT flop, or KJ with a QQJ flop. You always need to worry about trips with a pair on the flop, especially when the pair is high. Of course, this risk is dependent on how many players are in the hand and their position.

Strategy often depends on whether or not you need to protect your pair. For example, if the flop is T99 and you are holding T8, your hand is vulnerable to any jack or higher falling. If you decide to play the hand, you usually should bet out since you cannot afford to give a free card and you need to drive out your opponents. On the other hand, if you hold AK with a flop of A99, your only major worry is that an opponent holds a 9. The AK hand can be played more conservatively since a free card is unlikely to hurt your hand.

Let's look at some of the betting strategies that can be employed with top pair or an overpair when a high pair is flopped:

⇨ **Checking and folding.** Consider checking against several opponents when you hold a weak kicker or a pair vulnerable to overcards to see what develops behind you. You should generally fold when two or more players call the flop or you call and a third opponent raises.

⇨ **Calling or checking and calling.** You can generally call with a strong kicker or strong pair against a lone opponent when you are unsure whether or not your opponent has trips.

⇨ **Check-raising.** Check-raising against several opponents is risky. Many players slowplay trips, so any other opponents who check behind you could be holding a strong hand. You also risk giving a free card since many opponents will not bet into a flop with a high pair. In general, avoid check-raising if you do not want to risk giving a free card. If you are against a lone opponent, check-raising can be effective to try and get your opponent to bluff.

⇨ **Betting out.** Generally bet out pairs that are vulnerable to overcards against one or two opponents to avoid giving a free card. If you are raised or two players enter the pot, you can then decide whether or not folding is correct. One exception to betting out is when your hand is relatively weak against several opponents (see Checking and folding).

⇨ **Raising the best hand.** Consider raising with your strong pairs since most players slowplay trips and their bet probably indicates a weak hand or a bluff. This is especially true if the bettor is betting into only one or two opponents.

Internet Tip

Most weak opponents on the Internet tend to always slowplay trips, whereas in a live game players tend to bet out more. This is in line with the general rule that Internet players play more deceptively than live players do. Of course, this is a generalization and there are exceptions, but you can generally assume that an unknown player will not bet out trips, especially if he is a weak player. In these cases, you can safely raise if you have either an overpair or a good kicker card.

If you believe your opponent is bluffing and your pair is not vulnerable to overcards, you might just call his bets down to the river rather than drive him out of the hand. Against strong opponents, it is sometimes difficult to know their holding. Some strong opponents will always bet out their trips while others always slowplay. With your regular opponents, keep notes on their play and see if you can pick up some of their tendencies on how they play certain types of flops.

⇨ **Raising to try for a free card.** When you are unsure if you have the best hand and your pair is relatively strong, you could try a raise and then check the turn. In this case you are minimizing your losses when your opponent has trips, while allowing you to play out the hand and win the pot when you have the best hand.

Let's look at an advanced concept that many players do not consider. Sometimes you might check and call even though you feel your opponent *probably* has trips. Let's assume you think there is a 70% chance that your opponent holds trips. You might play your hand if there is a large pot and your hand would win the 30% of the time your opponent doesn't have trips.

Advanced Concept: Sometimes it is correct to check and call to the river even though you feel your opponent probably has flopped trips. This becomes correct in a large pot when the pot odds are enough to call in the small probability that your opponent doesn't hold trips combined with the probability that you could improve to the best hand.

Low Pair

Top pair or an overpair with a low pair on the flop is played practically the same as a high pair on the flop, except that you can sometimes decrease the risk that someone is holding trips. For example, a strong player in early position is not likely to be holding a low card and you can probably assume he does not have trips. On the other hand, if both of the blinds are playing the hand or several players from late position are in the hand, trips is a possibility and strategies should be employed as discussed above in the high pair section.

In those cases where you are not too concerned about trips, you can play your hand similarly to how you play a rainbow flop of all rags or with one high card. This generally means betting and raising your strong hands for value. If your pair is vulnerable to overcards, you should try to minimize the field either by betting, raising, or check raising, although check-raising is risky with these types of flops since your opponents may not bet.

One common situation is flopping top pair in the blinds with a flop of a small pair and another rag. For example, you hold 85 in the big blind and the flop is 522. Many players like to play overcards for only one bet. If you bet out trips sometimes in these situations, your more observant opponents will not know what hand to put you on and might fold their overcards.

Internet Tip

As discussed before, opponents on the Internet are not as observant as in live games. They will generally expect you to slowplay trips unless they are a regular opponent of yours and have seen you bet out trips often; therefore, expect most opponents to call with overcards since they will assume you are betting a pair.

Some players are going to fold their overcards and some will call. Generally bet out against one or two opponents and check against four or more. Against three opponents, tend to bet out in a tight game and check in a loose game. Against four or more opponents, there is a decent chance now that an opponent has a medium pair or trips. If an opponent then bets, you can decide whether to check-raise if you think you have the best hand, fold if you don't have the best hand, or possibly call if you are getting good pot odds to draw with a high kicker.

Chapter Review

❑ One of the more common situations on the flop is playing top pair or an overpair. The relative strength of your hand depends on the following factors:
  • How high your pair is
  • How high your kicker is when holding top pair
  • The number of players playing the hand
  • The possible strength of your opponents' hands, especially in a raised pot
  • The flop type. Flops that are more dangerous than others include:
    ▪ A high or low pair
    ▪ Two- or three-suited
    ▪ Two- or three-connected
    ▪ Two or more cards 9 or above
❑ A rainbow flop with one high card is a good flop for top pair or an overpair.
  • Although top pair is usually a good hand with this type of flop, some common situations where you should consider folding include:

♠⃰ The pot is raised before you act and you have a weak kicker.

♠⃰ Several players pay a bet on the flop and you have a weak kicker.

♠⃰ Several players pay a bet on the flop and your top pair is not very high.

♠⃰ The bettor is a tight player who never bluffs and you hold a weak kicker.

- Whenever the pot is small and you hold a strong hand that is not very vulnerable to overcards, you can either play your hand aggressively on the flop, or wait until the turn to raise. If the pot is large, choose the best strategy to drive out your opponents.

- With pairs more vulnerable to overcards, choose the best strategy to drive out your opponents. This might include betting out, check-raising, raising, or just calling and waiting to the turn to try and drive out your opponents.

- Try to avoid just checking and calling your borderline hands to the river since this can be much more expensive than gaining information early in the hand that might allow you to safely fold.

❑ Strategies for a rainbow flop of all rags are similar to those when the flop includes a high card, but low to medium pairs are always more vulnerable to overcards.

- When you hold a small top pair, important considerations include:
  - The number of opponents
  - The size of the pot
  - Your kicker card

- Against several opponents in a raised pot, top pairs are rather weak since you could already be beat by an overpair and it is nearly impossible to get many opponents to fold their overcard draws.

❑ Two-suited flops either increase the value of your pair when you have a flush draw, or give your opponents a better chance to draw out on you.

- When you hold a flush draw, your borderline hands are now playable and you are less worried about driving out opponents.

- When you don't have a flush draw, you should be more inclined to check and fold your borderline hands than otherwise.

- With your stronger hands, be careful not to give a free card.

❑ A three-suited flop is always dangerous, unless you happen to have a flush draw with one of the top two remaining suited cards.

- With a high flush draw, slowplaying is an *option* if your pair is not vulnerable to overcards. With pairs vulnerable to overcards, generally bet or raise to try and drive out your opponents unless you want to keep players in the hand when the pot is small.

- You should proceed cautiously when you don't have a flush draw, especially when your pair is not very high or your kicker is weak. Strategy is usually dependent on how many opponents you are against.

❑ Two-connected flops can give your opponents two pair or open-ended or gut-shot straight draws along with overcards.
- Almost always raise your strong hands to make it two small bets for the remaining opponents who may be on gut-shot or other weak draws.
- Always try to protect a vulnerable pair if possible. You may need to fold your weaker holdings if there is a lot of action on the flop.

❑ A three-connected flop can be dangerous, especially with medium to high cards. An opponent could already have a straight, set, two pair, or a strong draw.
- With a straight draw, generally bet out or raise. You can consider slowplaying if the pot is small and your hand is not too vulnerable to overcards.
- When you don't have a straight draw, usually bet out or raise against a lone opponent. With several players in the hand, consider checking to see what develops behind you, especially if your pair is vulnerable to overcards or your kicker is weak.

❑ Flops of all high cards make top pairs and overpairs vulnerable to straights, sets, two pair, and straight draws.
- Consider folding against several opponents unless you have some type of straight draw also, especially if you have a weak kicker.
- Usually bet out against one or two opponents.

❑ You always need to worry about trips with a pair on the flop, especially when the pair is high. Strategy often depends on whether or not you need to protect your pair.
- Consider checking against several opponents when you hold a weak kicker or a pair vulnerable to overcards to see what develops behind you.
- You should generally fold when two or more players call the flop or you call and a third opponent raises.
- You can generally call with a strong kicker or strong pair against a lone opponent when you are unsure whether or not your opponent has trips.
- Check-raising against several opponents is risky.
- Generally bet out pairs that are vulnerable to overcards against one or two opponents to avoid giving a free card.
- Consider raising with your strong pairs since most players slowplay

trips and their bet probably indicates a weak hand or a bluff.
- When you are unsure if your hand is the best and your pair is relatively strong, consider raising to try for a free card.

❑ A low pair on the flop is played practically the same as a high pair on the flop, except that you can sometimes decrease the risk that someone is holding trips.
- In those cases where you are not too concerned about trips, you can play your hand similarly to how you play a rainbow flop of all rags or with one high card.
- When flopping a small top pair from the blinds, generally bet out against one or two opponents and check against four or more. Against three opponents, tend to bet out in a tight game and check in a loose game.

Test Your Skills

1/ $20-$40. You limp in with K♥ Q♥ under the gun. The cutoff raises, the button and the big blind call. Four players see the flop of Q♦ T♠ 3♣. The big blind checks. There is $170 in the pot. What do you do?

Answer: Bet. Do not be afraid to bet into the preflop raiser. This kind of flop is also one where the preflop raiser might take a free card with hands like AK, AJ, or a medium pair. In the actual hand, the player bet and was raised by the preflop raiser who showed AK.

2/ $15-$30. You hold T♠ 8♦ in the small blind. Five players call and you call for $5 more. Seven players see the flop of T♣ 9♥ 2♠. You check, the next player bets, two players call, and the button raises. There is $180 in the pot. What do you do?

Answer: Fold. This is one of those hands where top pair is no good. With the two-connected flop of T9, any A, K, Q, J, 7, or 6 could be bad news, assuming you even have the best hand. Even an 8 could be bad news if it gives someone a straight. Your kicker is too weak to be able to call a raise cold against so many opponents.

3/ $20-$40. You hold K♠ Q♦ on the button. An early and middle player call and you call. Four players see the flop of Q♣ 7♠ 6♣. The big blind bets and the early player raises. There is $150 in the pot. What do you do?

Answer: Reraise. Reraise to force the big blind to either fold or pay two bets to play a draw. In the actual hand, the player reraised and the big blind folded. His opponent folded to a turn bet.

4/ $15-$30. You hold K♥ 3♠ in the big blind. An early player and two middle players call. The small blind calls and five players see the flop of K♠ T♠ T♦. The small blind bets. There is $90 in the pot. What do you do?

Answer: Fold. The only hand you can beat is a draw and there still are three players to act behind you. There could be a lot of raising with this type of flop with players on straight and flush draws or trip tens. In the actual hand, the small blind showed QJ and a middle player KT.

5/ $20-$40. You hold Q♠ J♠ on the button. A middle players raises and another middle player calls. You call and the big blind calls. Four players see the flop of Q♣ 8♣ 2♦. It is checked to you and you bet. The preflop raiser raises and the next middle player reraises. There is $290 in the pot. What do you do?

Answer: Fold. You are lucky if you have three outs. Your opponents could have an overpair, a set, AQ, KQ, or a flush draw. One of them has you beat. In the actual hand, the preflop raiser capped and won on the turn when his opponent folded.

6/ $20-$40. You raise in early position with A♠ Q♥. Only the cutoff and small blind call. Three players see the flop of A♦ J♥ T♣. The small blind bets, you call, the cutoff raises, and the small blind reraises. There is $260 in the pot. What do you do?

Answer: Fold. Here is a hand where you flop a pair of aces with a queen kicker and have to fold. There is not one hand that your opponents could have that you could beat based on the flop and the betting. You are losing to AK, AJ, AT, KQ, JT, JJ, and TT. If you draw to the king, you may have to split the pot. If you hit the ace or queen, you still may not win as an opponent could be improving to a full house or a straight. In addition, you face the possibility that the cutoff will cap the betting. In the actual hand, the player folded. The cutoff showed KQ and the small blind AJ. Don't get married to top pair!

7/ $20-$40. You hold Q♦ J♦ in middle position. Two early players call and you limp in. The button raises and the big blind calls. Five players see the flop of Q♥ 6♠ 4♦. It is checked to you. There is $210 in the pot. What do you do?

Answer: Bet. Check-raising is risky as the preflop raiser might take a free card against so many opponents. In the actual hand, the button raised with KK and the big blind called with Q4. Although you were beaten, you can't be afraid to bet into the preflop raiser on the flop with top pair; however, you should probably fold on the turn if an opponent bets. With this type of flop, an opponent raising and another opponent calling a raise cold indicates that at least one of them has a premium hand.

8/ $15-$30. You hold J♣ 9♣ in the small blind. An early player calls, a middle player raises, a middle player calls, and you make a weak call. The big blind reraises and everyone calls. Five players see the flop of J♦ 6♣ 6♥. You check, the big blind bets and only the preflop raiser calls. There is $255 in the pot. What do you do?

Answer: Fold. Whenever the big blind reraises a pot, he usually has a premium pair unless he is a maniac simply trying to build a large pot. You also have an additional caller in the hand that you have to beat. Therefore, you are most likely beat on this flop, and even if you aren't, your opponents have a lot of outs. This hand should be treated as a drawing hand. One problem with this flop is the pair of 6's. Even if you hit your 9, you would lose to an overpair, which is a likely hand in this situation; therefore, you should fold with only two outs. In the actual hand, the player folded. The big blind showed JJ and the preflop raiser TT.

9/ $15-$30. You hold Q♦ J♥ in middle position. An early player calls and you make a weak call. The small blind calls and the big blind raises. Everybody calls except the small blind. Three players see the flop of J♠ 5♦ 4♠. The big blind bets and the early player folds. You raise and the big blind reraises. There is $180 in the pot. What do you do?

Answer: Call. Note how this hand is different than the hand before. In the hand before, there was a small pair on the flop, so the player probably only had two outs. In this hand, you again are most likely beat; however, you have five outs to improve your hand compared to the previous example of only two outs. You should probably fold the turn if you don't improve, unless your opponent is an aggressive player who raises often from the big blind. Your opponent might have AK, but he is indicating a premium pair by reraising the flop and it will cost you two big bets to find out.

10/ $5-$10. You hold 9♦ 6♦ in the big blind. The cutoff raises and you call. The flop is 9♠ 5♦ 2♠. You check and the cutoff bets. There is $27 in the pot. What do you do?

Answer: Raise. The problem with calling here is deciding what you are going to do on the turn. If you check the turn, your opponent might take a free card. The best strategy is to go ahead and raise and then bet out the turn. In these types of situations you should either bet out the flop or check-raise.

11/ $30-$60. You hold Q♣ Q♠ on the button. A wild early player raises and a middle player raises all-in to $90. You cap the betting and the small blind and early player both call. Three players and an all-in player see the flop of 8♣ 7♦ 2♦. The early player bets. There is $510 in the pot. What do you do?

Answer: Call. The wild early player could have anything. Your main concern with such a large pot is maximizing your chance to win it. The small blind called a capped pot, so it will be difficult to drive him out of the pot on the *flop*; however, if you wait to raise the turn, you have a better chance of driving out this player by forcing him to call two big bets. This will give you a better chance of winning the pot if an ace or king falls on the river.

In the actual hand, the player called and the early player checked the turn card of 7♠ ruining the player's strategy to make it two big bets on the turn. The player bet, the small blind called, and the early player folded. The river card was the 3♠ and the small blind called with 4♣ 4♠. Even at $30-$60 you find players who love small pairs!

12/ $20-$40. You hold A♥ Q♠ in the big blind. An early and middle player call and you just check. Three players see the flop of Q♥ 8♥ 4♠. There is $60 in the pot. What do you do?

Answer: Bet or check-raise. This is one of those hands where I believe either strategy is very close in regards to profit expectation. If you bet, they will most likely think that you hold a small pair allowing you to surprise your opponents if they hold some kind of hand, while if you check-raise, they will assume you have a queen. On the other hand, they may fold if you bet and you will only win a small pot. Check-raising is not too risky since the pot is small and the only dangerous free card would be a king. Check-raising will allow you to gain at least another small bet if one of your opponents either bets a weak hand or a bluff. Strategy is mostly dependent on the type of opponents you are against. You should lean towards checking against aggressive opponents and betting against tight opponents.

Middle/Bottom Pair

Middle or bottom pair is when you hold a pair but there is another card on the board higher than your pair. For example, you hold JJ, QT, or A8, with a flop of KT8. One of the more common mistakes made by weak players is drawing too often with poor pot odds to middle or bottom pair.

You need very good pot odds to play middle or bottom pair when you suspect an opponent has at least top pair. Your hand is 8 to 1 to improve on the next card, and only 23 to 1 if you have a pocket pair. With five outs, you are getting slightly better odds than a gut-shot straight draw, but you are drawing to a hand that is not nearly as strong:

♠ You could be drawing practically dead to an opponent's set or two pair.
♠ An opponent's hand could counterfeit your kicker card, giving him two pair, a straight, or a flush.
♠ You could hit your card on the turn, only to lose on the river by an opponent hitting one of his outs to a flush, straight, three of a kind, or two higher pair.

Drawing to a middle or bottom pair is risky when you only have a 1 in 9 chance of improving, and you aren't even sure if that will be good enough to win. You usually need pot odds much better than 8 to 1 to justify all these risks. In addition, only consider drawing when your call will close the betting, as a raise behind you will generally ruin your pot odds.

When you do draw, you want to give yourself the best chance of winning when you improve to two pair. Holding a kicker card above the highest card on the flop improves your chances of winning the hand. When you hit an overcard kicker higher than your opponent's two cards and he only has a pair, he only has two outs to beat you on the river. When you have a low kicker, your opponent has eight outs. We will discuss this concept in more detail later in the chapter.

You should be folding middle or bottom pair often, but not always. There are four scenarios when you can play your hand:
- You feel there is a good chance that you hold a better hand than your opponents.
- You have a kicker higher than the highest card on the table and are getting sufficient pot odds to draw to a hand that you feel could finish as the best hand.
- Your kicker is weak, but the pot is giving excellent pot odds to draw.

- Your hand is probably not the best, but you are able to justify a semi-bluff bet or raise by the combination of the probability that you could get your opponent to fold the best hand, with the probability that you could improve to the best hand.

Note that middle or bottom pair is sometimes the best hand. In these cases you can sometimes be the aggressor. Let's look now at strategies to consider for each type of flop.

High or Low Pair

With a pair on the flop, you really are holding top pair. There is not much difference in strategy between holding AT with a QQT flop or AQ with a QTT flop, except that the AT hand has more exposure to overcards. Please refer to the chapter "Top Pair/Overpair" for strategies on how to play a pair when there is a pair on the flop.

Three-Suited

With a three-suited flop, your middle or bottom pair is almost worthless. Your opponents could have a flush, set, two pair, a higher pair, or a strong flush draw with overcards to your pair. You can only play your hand if you have a high flush draw in addition to your pair (see "Flush Draws" chapter for strategies) or sometimes as a semi-bluff against one or two opponents.

A bluff attempt with this kind of flop against three opponents is very risky, even when they have all checked. If you are against two opponents and they both check, a bet might win the pot. If you get check-raised, you should probably fold. If you must act first against two opponents, usually just check and fold.

Even when you are heads up you should be inclined to fold to a bet unless you have a flush draw also. In those cases where you might have the best hand, your opponent still has a lot of outs that could beat you. On the other hand, if your opponent checks, you should bet and probably fold to a check-raise. If you must act first, you can bet out sometimes to see how your opponent reacts. Again, if he raises, you probably ought to fold.

Three-Connected

Strategy with three-connected flops is very similar to three-suited flops, especially when the three connected cards are medium or higher. You should almost always check and fold against three or more opponents and follow the same strategies for the three-suited flop against one or two opponents.

All High Cards

Generally you should not play middle or bottom pair when the flop has all high cards. One exception is when you have a straight or flush draw. Even top pair is not always a great hand with these types of flops, so middle or bottom pair is very weak. Your opponents are just too likely to hold a better pair, two pair, or a straight. There is also a good chance that your draws are counterfeited.

For example, when you hold AT and the flop is KJT, your hand is especially vulnerable. An ace could give someone two better pair or a straight, so your only outs may be the ten for trips or the queen for a straight, although you might have to split the pot with the queen. A hand such as J9 is very weak, as a queen would give an opponent a higher straight if they hold an ace, and a 9 would give an opponent a straight if they hold a queen. You could be drawing to only two outs and possibly are drawing dead. You need an exceptionally large pot to even consider playing these hands. One exception is when you have an open-ended straight draw, such as QJ, but you still might have to split the pot.

Against several opponents your best option is to check and fold middle or bottom pair. The only time to consider betting is if you are against one or two opponents and you think you might be able to win the pot by betting. If you are against two opponents and they both check, you should probably go ahead and bet. If heads up, usually bet if your opponent checks or bet out if acting first. When you are playing heads up, aggression is usually best since your opponent could have a variety of hands. For example, if the flop is KT9, your lone opponent could be holding a middle pair such as 88 or a hand such as A7s. In these cases, you want to go ahead and bet rather than give your opponent a chance to steal the pot or hit a miracle card on the turn.

If you bet and an opponent raises, you should usually assume that your opponent has a better hand as it takes a very aggressive player to bluff into these types of flops. You should usually fold to a raise unless you have some type of straight draw that might justify calling or the pot is large enough to justify calling with a weak draw.

Two-Suited

When the flop is two-suited against several opponents, you should usually fold if you suspect that the bettor has at least top pair. Your outs are reduced;

and even when you do hit your hand, there is a decent probability you could lose on the river.

Advanced concept: Almost always fold middle or bottom pair when the flop is two-suited and you are against three or more opponents, unless the pot is very large.

To demonstrate this concept, let's look at your possible outs assuming at least one of your opponents has a better hand and one opponent has a flush draw. You could have either 5, 4, 3, 2, 1, or 0 outs depending on the circumstances. For example, with a flop of J♦ 7♣ 5♦:

- 5 outs: You hold A♦ 5♣
- 4 outs: You hold A♣ 5♣ (the A♦ is counterfeited)
- 3 outs: You hold A♣ 7♠ (A♦ and 7♦ is counterfeited)
- 2 outs: You hold A♣ 7♦ and an opponent has A♦ J♠
- 1 out: You hold A♣ 7♠ and an opponent has A♦ J♠
- 0 outs: You could be drawing practically dead depending on your opponents' holdings.

The *best case* scenario in this example is that you have five outs, which has the added benefit of a backdoor flush draw. However, calling against several opponents is usually not justified since there is a higher probability that your outs are counterfeited.

Strategy against one or two opponents is more complicated. You could have the best hand. A bettor may be semi-bluffing with a flush draw. When they do hold a hand, you may have all five outs since there are not so many opponents to counterfeit your hand.

Generally bet out against one or two opponents to see how they react, especially when they have already checked and you are acting last. If raised, you have a difficult decision to make that is often based on the type of opponent you are against. Most opponents who check-raise probably have a strong hand, while a raise in late position may just be an attempt to buy a free card. A good understanding of your opponent's playing style should help you with these difficult decisions.

The same thinking applies when you are against one or two opponents and an opponent bets into you. Are they the type of opponent who would bet out a flush draw? You might have the best hand depending on the type of opponent you are against. It is difficult to give concrete rules when playing against one or two opponents, as there is a greater chance that your opponents could be semi-bluffing. Study your opponents and evaluate their tendencies to help you make better decisions in these situations.

Two-Connected

When there are two connected high cards, you should usually fold against several opponents. You have to worry about straight draws and the possibility that you are already against two pair since many opponents play connected cards. An opponent's hand might counterfeit your kicker card. For example, with a QJ7 flop and you hold A7 or AJ, be inclined to fold against several opponents. If you hit your ace, an opponent could either be hitting a straight or two better pair.

Against one or two opponents, strategy is usually dependent on the pot odds and the bettor's tendency to semi-bluff. If the two connected cards are low, you do not need to worry so much about straight draws, unless an opponent played out of the blinds or from late position.

Rainbow with One High Card

So far we have shown that you generally should not draw with dangerous types of flops that are two- or three-suited, two- or three-connected, or have a lot of high cards. You can sometimes play a rainbow flop with only one high card since your draw is less likely to be counterfeited.

Advanced Concept: Holding a kicker higher than the highest card on the flop significantly improves your odds that your hand can win; otherwise, an opponent with top pair will have a decent draw to two higher pair or better.

When your kicker is lower than the highest card on the flop, you need even better pot odds to justify a draw. Let's look at an example of this concept.

You hold A♠ 7♠ with a J♦ 7♣ 5♥ flop and an early position player bets. If you are acting last, a call could be correct with decent pot odds; however, you would need even better pot odds to call with a hand like 8♠ 7♠. The problem with drawing and improving to two small pair is that your opponent has a better chance of drawing to beat you on the river when he holds the highest pair.

If your opponent has Q♠ J♣, any queen, jack, or 5 on the river would beat 8♠ 7♠ (if an 8 comes on the turn). However, if the turn card is an A♦ and you have A♠ 7♠, your opponent can only beat you with a jack on the river. Your opponent has six additional outs on the river to beat two small pair compared to two high pair. This sometimes can be the difference between calling and folding on the flop, especially against several opponents.

Remember however, you still need excellent pot odds to justify drawing to a hand that is 8 to 1 against improving and could possibly be drawing dead. For example, you hold 98 with a A86 flop. You feel that an opponent has at least a pair of aces, so you will need to improve by hitting one of your five outs. If your opponent holds A8 you are drawing dead to the turn card. If he holds A9 or A6, you only have two outs to the 8. Even if you improve to two pair on the turn, your opponent will have at least eight outs to improve to an even better hand on the river. *Drawing to bottom or middle pair requires excellent pot odds.*

Whenever you are against one or two opponents, there is a decent chance that you might be holding the best hand. If you are acting first, you should usually bet and see how your opponents react. You might have the best hand, and even if you don't, you still have outs. Whenever an opponent bets into you, you need to determine the chances that you are holding the best hand. Against rocks you should almost always fold since it is unlikely you are getting good odds to draw. Tricky players could be betting a good hand, bottom pair, or even as a bluff. Sometimes you will need to call or raise against these types of players if you feel there is a decent chance that your hand could win.

Rainbow of All Rags

This is the best type of flop as you may have the best hand. Strategy is very similar to holding top pair with an all rag flop since these types of flops usually do not help your opponents. Please refer to the previous chapter for strategies. However, if you are playing against a player in the blinds, you need to be concerned that he has hit top pair.

Chapter Review

❑ One of the more common mistakes made by weak players is drawing too often with poor pot odds to middle or bottom pair.

❑ The best you can hope for when drawing is five outs, which is 8 to 1 against improving; however, these odds are often worse:

♠ You could be drawing practically dead to an opponent's set or two pair.

♠ An opponent's hand could counterfeit your kicker card, giving him two pair, a straight, or a flush.

♠ You could hit your card on the turn, only to lose on the river by an opponent hitting one of his outs to a flush, straight, three of a kind, or two higher pair.

❑ There are four scenarios when you can play middle or bottom pair:

• You feel there is a good chance that you hold a better hand than your opponents.

• You have a kicker higher than the highest card on the table and are getting sufficient pot odds to draw to a hand that you feel could finish as the best hand.

• Your kicker is weak, but the pot is giving excellent pot odds to draw.

• Your hand is probably not the best, but you are able to justify a semi-bluff bet or raise by the combination of the probability that you could get your opponent to fold the best hand, with the probability that you could improve to the best hand.

❑ When you are getting decent pot odds to consider drawing, you generally need a favorable flop so that the risk that your outs are counterfeited is minimized:

• Favorable flops include rainbow flops of all rags or with just one high card.

• Generally you should fold with these dangerous flop types unless you have some type of flush or straight draw to add value to your hand: three-suited, two-suited, three-connected (especially medium to high), two connected high cards, and all high cards.

❑ Whenever you are against one or two opponents, there is a decent chance that you might have the best hand. You can sometimes bet out hoping to win the pot immediately, especially if you are acting last. Whenever a lone opponent bets or raises, strategy is often dependent on the type of player you are against, but folding is usually the best play.

Test Your Skills

1/ $30-$60. You hold 8♣ 8♦ in the cutoff position. A middle player raises and you reraise. The flop is A♥ Q♣ 3♣. The middle player checks. There is $225 in the pot. What do you do?

Answer: Bet. You should almost always bet the flop when you reraise preflop and are against a lone opponent. Betting may get your opponent to fold pocket pairs JJ and lower. You should fold if he check-raises and should usually back off on the turn if he only calls.

2/ $20-$40. You call in early position with A♥ 7♥. Only the blinds call. Three players see the flop of T♠ 7♠ 5♥. Both blinds check. There is $60 in the pot. What do you do?

Answer: Bet. Your opponents have indicated weakness and you have middle pair with a good kicker.

3/ $20-$40. You hold T♥ T♠ on the button. A middle player raises and the cutoff calls. You call and three players see the flop of A♦ 7♥ 2♦. The preflop raiser bets and the cutoff folds. There is $170 in the pot. What do you do?

Answer: Fold. A preflop raiser is betting into two opponents with an ace on the flop. There is a high probability he has you beat. Even if he doesn't have the ace, he could hold KK, QQ, or JJ. Calling to the river is your worst option since it will cost you $100 to see if you have your opponent beat, and you still might lose if a K, Q, or J comes on the turn or river. Drawing to the ten is a bad play since you are 23 to 1 against improving on the next card. If you want to play your hand, the only option is raising the flop as a bluff hoping that your opponent will fold a hand like a medium pair or KQ. However, you need to know your opponent well to make this type of raise.

4/ $20-$40. You hold Q♠ J♠ in middle position. A middle player calls and you raise. The button and big blind call. Four players see the flop of K♦ Q♥ 2♣. It is checked to you. There is $170 in the pot. What do you do?

Answer: Bet. Two players have indicated weakness by checking, so you may have the best hand. If you bet and are raised, you can probably take one more card on your draw. Checking in this situation puts you in a vulnerable position since you won't be sure that an opponent's bet indicates a strong hand or a semi-bluff. Stay aggressive until your opponents tell you otherwise. In the actual hand, the player bet and was called by the big blind and the middle player. The big blind folded on the turn and the middle player showed Q♦ 8♦.

5/ $15-$30. You hold A♦ 5♦ in middle position. A middle player calls and you call. The button raises and the big blind calls. Four players see the flop of 7♣ 5♥ 4♦. It is checked to you. There is $130 in the pot. What do you do?

Answer: Bet. Your hand is good enough to call, so go ahead and bet. The button might raise driving out the other opponents, which is good if he only has overcards. In the actual hand, the player bet, the button raised, and the big blind called. The turn was the 6♦. The player bet and only the big blind called. The river was the 8♦ giving the player a flush and his opponent showed 65.

6/ $20-$40. You hold Q♦ Q♣ in the cutoff. An early player calls and you raise. The button and the big blind call. The early player reraises and everyone calls. Four players see the flop of K♥ J♣ 4♠. The early player bets. There is $270 in the pot. What do you do?

Answer: Fold. The most common hands for someone to only call and then reraise preflop from early position are AA or KK followed by AKs. In all three cases you are beaten. You could draw for another queen, but you are not getting good enough pot odds and you still might lose to KK. To make it worse, you still have opponents behind you who might raise. Don't get married to pocket pairs. In the actual hand, the early player showed KK and the button KJ.

7/ $15-$30. You hold 9♥ 9♠ on the button. A middle player raises and you reraise. The small blind calls and three players see the flop of A♠ K♠ J♥. It is checked to you. There is $150 in the pot. What do you do?

Answer: Check. You are against a preflop raiser and a player who called two and a half bets cold before the flop. With two or three high cards and one of them an ace, you are most likely in big trouble. Take the free card and hope for a 9 on the turn.

8/ $15-$30. You hold A♦ 7♦ in the big blind. The button raises first in. The small blind calls and you call. Three players see the flop of K♠ 9♦ 7♣. The small blind checks. There is $90 in the pot. What do you do?

Answer: Bet. You would probably call in this situation against most opponents with five outs and a backdoor flush, so go ahead and bet to try and win the pot outright. You could very well have the best hand against only two opponents. In the actual hand, the player bet and his opponent on the button called. The turn was an ace and the player successfully check-raised with his opponent showing KJ.

9/ $15-$30. You hold J♣ J♦ on the button. A middle player raises and you reraise. The big blind calls and three players see the flop of A♠ 6♣ 3♥. The middle player bets. There is $160 in the pot. What do you do?

Answer: Fold. When a player raises preflop and then bets a flop with an ace on the flop, you must proceed carefully. It can be very expensive calling to the river with a pocket pair and only two outs if your opponent has an ace in his hand. The other problem in this hand is that you still have the big blind to act behind you. Even if you have the middle player beat, the big blind could have the ace also. In the actual hand, the player folded and the middle player showed AK, only to be beat by a backdoor flush from the big blind.

10/ $20-$40. You call in early position with A♣ 6♣. The cutoff calls, the button raises, and the big blind calls. Four players see the flop of 8♦ 6♦ 3♣. The big blind checks. There is $170 in the pot. What do you do?

Answer: Bet. This flop probably has not helped anyone. Betting into the cutoff should force him to fold two overcards since he must worry about a raise from the button. If the preflop raiser has two overcards, you are in good shape, especially if one of them is an ace. In the actual hand, the player bet and was called by the button and big blind. The button then raised the turn when the Q♣ fell. The player caught a backdoor flush on the river and his opponent showed KQ.

11/ $20-$40. You raise in the cutoff with A♥ 5♥ and only the big blind calls. The flop is J♠ 5♣ 4♥. The big blind bets. There is $110 in the pot. What do you do?

Answer: Raise. Your opponent could have many hands unless he is a rock. Many opponents would check-raise a pair of jacks. Raise and keep the pressure on your opponent. In the actual hand, his opponent reraised with T4.

12/ $5-$10. You hold 9♣ 9♥ in middle position. Two early players call, you call, the cutoff calls, and the button calls. The small blind raises, the big blind calls, and everybody else calls to the cutoff who reraises. Everyone calls. Seven players see the flop of T♠ 5♦ 4♥. It is checked to you. There is $105 in the pot. What do you do?

Answer: Bet. This is a large pot and you have the reraiser acting right behind you. You are not too concerned that the raiser or reraiser has a high pocket pair, because the small blind did not cap preflop or bet out the flop, and the cutoff didn't raise preflop until there was a lot of money in the pot. It appears he was probably just trying to build a big pot. There is a decent chance that you hold the best hand. Bet and hope that the cutoff will raise to help you drive out the other opponents.

In the actual hand, the player bet and the cutoff only called. The big blind and two early players called to see the turn card of 7♠ and the river was the K♠. An early player showed 6♠ 4♠, the other early player A♥ 2♥, and the cutoff 6♥ 5♥.

Flush Draws

Strategies for flush draws with a three-suited flop are very different than with a two-suited flop. Strategies for two-suited flops can vary depending on other qualities of the flop. For example, the flop could also have a pair or connected cards. Flush draws increase in value when you add other elements to your hand such as straight draws, pairs, or overcards.

Let's look quickly at odds. Flush draws are approximately 2 to 1 against improving by the river, but this could improve depending on the pair and straight possibilities of your hand. Add a gut-shot straight draw or an over-card and you are about 1.2 to 1 against improving. An open-ended straight and flush draw is .9 to 1. Add overcards to any of these and you have even better odds. As you can see, at worst you are 2 to 1 against improving, and this is even better when you have other elements to your hand.

Two-Suited

Let's look first at flush draws when the flop is two-suited. When the flop is two-suited, you are almost always getting sufficient odds to draw to the flush with these few exceptions:

- You are heads up in a small pot and don't have a pair, and you are confident that your opponent has a pair higher than your two cards.
- There is a pair on the flop and a decent chance an opponent holds trips. With a pair on the flop, it is much easier for someone to hit a full house to beat your flush; however, you can still draw sometimes depending on the action and size of the pot.
- The action is so strong on the flop that your small flush draw could be drawing dead to a higher flush draw. Be careful in getting into a betting war with a drawing hand that could be second-best. The worst case scenario is when someone has a set and the other player has a nut flush draw with a top pair. These two players could be raising a lot and you would be stuck in the middle drawing dead. Play your draws, but be prepared to back off when the action gets too heavy on the flop.

Flush draws are very strong. Even with the exceptions listed above, there may be times when drawing to the flush is still OK. For example, if the pot is large with several opponents, sometimes you can draw to the nut flush when there is a pair on the flop.

Let's look first at draws when there are three or more players in the hand. In these cases, you usually prefer to keep as many players in the hand as possible to help improve your odds; therefore, you should normally check when acting first, especially when there is a preflop raiser. You do not want to bet and then get raised immediately behind you, causing the other players to fold. If you were the preflop raiser, go ahead and bet out as usual. If someone bets into you and there are still opponents to act behind you, normally just call to allow the other players to come in cheaply.

There is one exception in trying to keep as many opponents in the hand as possible with your flush draws. This occurs when there is a large pot and you have other elements to your hand that could help you win the pot. For example, if you have an ace overcard with a weak kicker and you believe a raise could get an opponent to fold a hand like Ax, you might raise to give yourself a better chance at winning a large pot. Generally, deciding whether to drive out players or keep them in the hand is a function of the size of the pot and how strong your secondary draws are.

If there are already several callers, raising is an option. Raising increases the size of the pot when you are getting good pot odds on the bet. If you are in late position, you also might be able to get a free card on the turn. Check-raising is an option when there are several callers in the hand, but you must act first on the turn thereby eliminating your chance at a free card. Check-raising in these situations is much better when you have other strong elements to your hand, such as a pair, two overcards, or a straight draw.

Against one or two opponents (and sometimes even three), it is possible to win the pot on a semi-bluff. Whenever you feel there is a chance to win the pot outright by betting or raising, you should usually do so.

Advanced Concept: Whenever you have a strong drawing hand, you should bet or raise if you feel you have a decent chance to win the pot outright, especially against one or two opponents.

Semi-bluffs with flush draws are very strong plays. You could win the pot immediately, and if you don't, you still have a good chance at winning the pot on your draw; therefore, if you act first against one or two opponents, usually bet out if you feel you have some chance that your opponents will fold. Otherwise, usually it is better to just check and call.

If someone bets and you feel there is some chance he is bluffing, semi-bluff raising can be correct. If you act last and no one has bet, you should almost always bet out. If both players have already bet, you must decide whether to raise or just call. Raising is an option if you could receive a free card. Otherwise, only raise when you have other elements to your hand.

There are times when reraising with flush draws is correct. For example, a hand like Q♦ J♦ with a flop of T♣ 9♦ 5♦ gives you a super strong hand. You have a good flush draw for nine outs, an open-ended straight draw for an additional six outs, and finally a queen or jack may also give you the winner for an additional six outs. You will hit a straight or flush 54% of the time and an overcard an additional 24% of the time! Heads up you should almost always reraise with hands such as these. Against several opponents, always reraise unless you prefer to just call rather than drive out opponents who might have to pay two bets. With small pots, you prefer there to be several opponents in the hand; however, if the pot is large, you might try to drive out opponents if one of your overcards could potentially win the pot.

Three-Suited

With a three-suited flop, you should generally only draw to the flush if you have one of the top two remaining flush cards in your hand. For example, with a flop of A♥ Q♥ 8♥, you would need either the K♥ or J♥ to draw. If the flop is 8♥ 5♥ 3♥, you would need either the A♥ or K♥. Remember, you will only hit your hand about 36% of the time, so when you do, you want to be confident that you have a winning hand. Drawing to the J♥ or T♥ is a losing play most of the time.

Normally it is difficult to get multi-way action with these types of flops. Against several opponents, you could already be against a flush, so you should normally just check and call. Raising in late position to try for a free card is risky, as many opponents with a good hand will protect their hand. They will either reraise the flop or call and bet out on the turn if another suited card does not come. With at least three callers on the flop, you could raise since you are getting good odds on the play.

When there are only one or two opponents and you have the nut flush draw, you can often play the hand aggressively as a semi-bluff by either betting out or raising. You are hoping that your opponents will fold, but if they call, you still have a strong draw with many outs.

When you have additional possibilities that add value to your draw, you might play a little more aggressively. For example, if you raise preflop with AA or KK and flop a flush draw and overpair with a three-suited flop, you should usually bet out. If someone bets into you, you can either raise or call. Calling can be a good play here since you have a high pair and are not worried about overcards or opponents on flush draws. You are either losing on the flop or have the best hand with little worry about being beat by the turn or river card.

The following is a hand that shows the potential benefit of just calling against weak opponents. A middle player called preflop and I raised on the button with A♥ A♣. Both blinds called. Four players saw the flop of J♥ 7♥ 4♥. An aggressive weak player in the small blind bet out and the middle player called. I debated between raising and calling but decided to call as I felt that the small blind might already have a flush.

The turn was the 6♥. The small blind bet and the middle player raised! I decided to just call and the small blind reraised (remember this is an aggressive weak player)! The middle player and I called. The small blind bet out the river and the middle player called. I raised and got called by both! The small blind had the Q♥ 5♥ and the middle player had the K♥. If I had raised the flop, I would have greatly reduced the action I received on later streets.

I show this example for two reasons. First, although I had a strong hand, I was still beaten on the flop. You always need to be concerned about flopped flushes when someone leads into a large field. Second, notice how playing contrary to what is "normal" can lead you to win a large pot.

Advanced Concept: Deception is a key part of strategy for advanced players. You create deception by playing contrary to what your opponents expect. When used in the right situations, deception can sometimes result in gaining several additional bets that you would not have won otherwise.

Chapter Review

❑ Flush draws are strong hands, as they are only 2 to 1 against improving by the river. These odds are improved further when you add other elements to your hand such as straight draws, overcards, or a pair.

❑ You can usually draw to flushes with a two-suited flop with these few exceptions:

- You are heads up in a small pot and don't have a pair, and you are confident that your opponent has a pair higher than your two cards.
- There is a pair on the flop and a decent chance an opponent holds trips; however, you can still draw sometimes depending on the action and size of the pot.
- The action is so strong on the flop that your small flush draw could be drawing dead to a higher flush draw.

❑ With a three-suited flop, you should generally only draw to the flush if you have one of the top two remaining flush cards in your hand.

❑ When playing flush draws against three or more opponents, usually choose a strategy that will keep as many players in the hand as possible. If several players have already called, consider raising, especially when you are in late position.

❑ Against one or two opponents, you can bet out or raise as a semi-bluff if you feel there is a decent chance you can win the pot outright.

❑ Whenever you have other elements to your hand such as straight draws, overcards, or a pair, you can play your hand more aggressively than otherwise.

Test Your Skills

1/ **$20-$40.** You hold Q♥ J♣ on the button. Two early players and the cutoff call. You call and five players see the flop of 7♥ 6♥ 4♥. The early player bets and the cutoff calls. There is $150 in the pot. What do you do?

Answer: Fold. When drawing with a three-suited flop, you should usually be drawing to either the nut flush or second highest flush. In this case, either the A♥ or K♥ will beat you. You also have two overcards, but these outs are reduced to five with a three-suited flop and there is no guarantee that you would even win with a pair.

2/ $20-$40. You hold A♥ 9♣ in the cutoff. A wild middle player calls and another weak middle player raises. You make a bad call and the small blind calls. Four players see the flop of 9♥ 7♥ 3♥. The preflop raiser bets. There is $200 in the pot. What do you do?

Answer: Raise. There still are two opponents yet to act behind you. Normally you do not want to drive out your opponents when you have the nut flush draw; however, you have top pair and top kicker with a large pot. Raise to protect your pair and try to force the other opponents out of the pot. Even if they have a better hand, you still have a great draw. In the actual hand, the player raised and only the small blind folded. The 5♠ came on the turn, giving the first middle player a straight when he showed 8♠ 6♠. The flush did not come on the river.

3/ $20-$40. You raise in early position with K♥ K♣. A middle player and the big blind call. Three players see the flop of Q♣ 5♣ 3♣. The big blind bets. There is $150 in the pot. What do you do?

Answer: Call with raising a close second. There are only three aces that could hurt your hand, so I prefer just calling rather than driving out the middle player. You can then decide whether or not to raise the turn. Raising is also a good play, especially since the pot was raised preflop. In the actual hand, the player only called and the middle player called. The big blind checked the turn card of the 2♦ and the player bet. Only the middle player called and he showed 6♠ 5♦ on the river card of the J♥.

4/ $20-$40. You hold A♥ 9♥ in middle position. An early player calls, you call, and the button and small blind call. Five players see the flop of K♥ 3♥ 2♣. It is checked to you. There is $100 in the pot. What do you do?

Answer: Bet. Three players have already checked, so there is a small chance you could win the pot outright with this flop. Even if you get callers, you might be able to take a free card on the turn. Worst case in betting is that the button raises driving out some of the other players. In the actual hand, the player bet, the button and small blind called, and the early player raised with KT. His raise actually gave you good pot odds against three opponents with the nut flush draw and an overcard. The flush did not come.

5/ $20-$40. You hold A♥ 5♥ in middle position. A middle player calls and you call. The button and small blind call. Five players see the flop of Q♥ T♥ 3♣. The middle player bets. There is $120 in the pot. What do you do?

Answer: Call. There still are three opponents to act behind you. You do not want to raise and drive out the other opponents with this small pot. If the pot had been raised preflop, then raising would be OK to give your ace a chance at winning.

6/ $20-$40. You hold A♠ 9♠ in the small blind. A middle player calls and the cutoff raises. You call and three players see the flop of T♠ 9♣ 5♠. You check and the cutoff bets. There is $160 in the pot. What do you do?

Answer: Raise. You should drive out the remaining opponent from the pot. Generally you like to play flush draws against several opponents, but with a pair, your hand currently may be the best. In the actual hand, the player raised, the middle player called, and the cutoff reraised. A spade came on the river.

7/ $15-$30. You raise in middle position with A♥ 6♥ and only a middle player calls. The flop is 5♥ 3♥ 2♣. You bet and the middle player raises. There is $130 in the pot. What do you do?

Answer: Reraise. You are slightly better than even money with 15 outs against a pocket pair (nine outs to a flush, three outs to a straight, and three to the ace). Stay the aggressor representing a high pocket pair and you might be able to get your opponent to fold his hand on the later streets if a scare card comes. In the actual hand, the player reraised and hit a flush on the turn with his opponent showing Q♠ Q♦.

8/ $15-$30. You hold A♣ 6♣ in the cutoff. Two early players and a middle player call. You call, the button calls, and the small blind raises. The big blind folds and everyone else calls. Six players see the flop of Q♣ 9♣ 5♥. The small blind bets and the two early players call. There is $240 in the pot. What do you do?

Answer: Raise. With three players already in the pot, you are getting good pot odds for each bet that goes into the pot on the flop. Raise and reraise if given the opportunity. In the actual hand, the player raised, the small blind reraised, and the player capped. The flush came on the turn and two players called to the river. One advantage with capping the flop is that the pot becomes so big your opponents will make crying calls to the river with weak hands.

9/ $15-$30. You hold Q♣ 6♣ in the small blind. Two early players call, an early player raises, a middle player calls, and the button calls. You call and the big blind calls. Seven players see the flop of 9♦ 9♣ 2♣. The pre-flop raiser bets. The middle player folds and the button calls. There is $240 in the pot. What do you do?

Answer: Call. With such a large pot, you can draw to your flush; however, raising in this situation is not very wise. The pair on the flop effectively reduces your outs and you are not drawing to the nut flush. There still are three players to act behind you, and you prefer that they stay in the hand increasing your pot odds. You also must act first on the next round, which is not ideal. In the actual hand, the player called and two more players entered the pot. The K♣ came on the turn and only one opponent called when the player bet out.

10/ $20-$40. You hold Q♠ 2♠ in the big blind. An early player, a late player, and the small blind call. You get a free play and four players see the flop of K♠ 6♠ 5♣. The small blind checks. There is $80 in the pot. What do you do?

Answer: Bet. There is only one high card on the flop and one opponent has already checked. You will play this to the river, so go ahead and bet hoping to win the pot on the flop. In the actual hand, the player bet and was raised by the late player. His flush did not come and he folded on the river.

11/ $5-$10. You hold Q♥ J♥ in middle position. A middle player calls, you call, and the cutoff calls. Four players see the flop of A♠ 9♥ 6♥. The big blind checks and the middle player bets. There is $27 in the pot. What do you do?

Answer: Call. It is difficult to steal a pot with an ace on the flop against three opponents, especially since one has already bet. You also prefer that the remaining opponents stay in the hand. In the actual hand, the player called and both of the remaining opponents called. The turn was the 8♠ and three players saw the river of the 5♥. The player bet and was raised by the cutoff who showed 7♦ 6♦. The cutoff probably would have folded (or should have) on the flop if you had raised.

12/ $20-$40. You hold A♥ 5♥ in the small blind. A middle player raises and the cutoff calls. You call and the big blind reraises. Everyone calls and four players see the flop of 8♥ 6♥ 3♦. There is $240 in the pot. What do you do?

Answer: Check, with betting out a close second. The problem with betting out is that the big blind will most likely raise, driving out the remaining opponents when you have a very strong flush draw. On the other hand, this pot is quite large. Driving out your opponents may be beneficial so that your ace could possibly win if it pairs. However, it is doubtful that an opponent will fold a big ace even to a raise on the flop with such a large pot, so checking is probably your best option. If all three opponents call a flop bet, you can raise with the good pot odds you are getting on your draw.

Straight Draws

There are three main types of straight draws: open-ended using two cards in your hand, open-ended using one card in your hand, and gut-shot draws. Let's quickly summarize the odds for straight draws. An open-ended straight draw is approximately 2.2 to 1 against improving by the river. A gut-shot draw is approximately 5 to 1, but is 11 to 1 when you plan on just taking one more card. An open-ended straight with a pair has 10 good outs (eight for the straight and two for trips), which is 1.6 to 1. An open-ended with two overcards should hit a little over 50% of the time, so you are even money. Be careful however with an overcard out since it could be counterfeited by giving an opponent a straight.

Since we are discussing straight draws, this is a good time to discuss why connected cards are higher valued starting hands than one-gapped or two-gapped hands. Two connected cards can have up to four different straight draws, while a three-gapped hand only has one possibility. For example, if you start with 98, there are four combinations that could give you a straight: QJT, JT7, T76, and 765. Compare this to when you hold 97: JT8, T86, and 865. Now look at two-gapped hands such as 96: T87 and 875. Connected cards give you much better odds of hitting the straight; therefore, they are more profitable than gapped hands.

Straight draws also increase in value like flush draws, depending on other qualities of your hand. For example, you could have a pair or overcards, which might add value to your draw. On the other hand, straight draws decrease in value whenever the flop is two- or three-suited or paired.

An open-ended straight draw has eight outs, but this might only be six outs if an opponent is on a flush draw. There is also the risk that you hit your draw on the turn only to lose to a flush on the river, so your straight will only hold up 4 out of 5 times; therefore, you need to discount your pot odds accordingly. Playing straight draws with a paired flop or two-suited flop depends on the size of the pot and the overall likelihood of your opponents being on a draw. In a heads-up situation, the chances are less likely that your opponent has a strong draw. If there are multiple players in the hand and a few have already called the flop, you can probably assume to be against a flush draw or a set and play accordingly.

It is difficult to discuss strategy for every type of straight draw with every type of flop; therefore, we will first look at open-ended straight draws when using both cards in your hand, and then look at those open-ended draws when you are using only one of your pocket cards. The final section of the chapter will discuss gut-shot draws. All of the discussion assumes a rainbow flop unless otherwise noted.

Open-ended Draws Using Two Cards in Your Hand

Open-ended straight draws are played similarly to flush draws as long as the flop is a rainbow. In fact, you should use the same strategies presented under the flush draw section. There are several main differences between open-ended straight draws compared to flush draws:

⇨ Straights have eight outs while flushes have nine outs.

⇨ Straights can be beaten by flushes or higher straights, so they win less often than flushes. Even with a rainbow flop, an opponent could still win with a backdoor flush. You must discount your odds, especially when the flop is two-suited.

⇨ Straights can be counterfeited so that you have to split the pot. For example, you hold J♣ T♦ with a flop of 9♥ 8♠ 5♣. The Q♠ falls on the turn giving you the nut straight. However, if a jack or ten comes on the river, you may have to split the pot with one of your opponents, or possibly lose the entire pot if they hit a higher straight.

⇨ Straights are more concealed than flushes, so it is easier to gain additional bets. Many players start backing off their hands when the board is three-suited, but if you hit a straight you could get great action from someone with a set or even two pair.

Overall, straight draws are not as valuable as flush draws, but strategies are similar, especially with a rainbow flop. With rainbow flops, you can almost always play your open-ended straight draws with a couple of the same exceptions given for flush draws:

⇨ You are heads up in a small pot and don't have a pair, and you are confident that your opponent has a pair higher than your two cards.

⇨ There is a pair on the flop and a decent chance an opponent holds trips. With a pair on the flop, it is much easier for someone to hit a full house to beat your straight, although you can sometimes still draw depending on the action and size of the pot.

Overall betting strategy for straight draws is very similar to the strategies presented in the flush draw sections. Just remember that when the flop is two-suited, you must now adjust your strategies accordingly. This will often dictate a fold, unless the pot odds are very good or you are against a lone opponent so that the chance of a flush draw is low.

Open-ended Draws Using One Card in Your Hand

Sometimes you hold an open-ended draw using only one card in your hand. For example, you hold A♣ T♠ with a 9♦ 8♥ 7♠ flop or a J♦ 9♥ 8♠ flop. The first thing you must realize is that these types of draws are not nearly as strong as straight draws using both cards in your hand:

- You could already be beat by a flopped straight.
- If you hit your straight, you will have to split the pot with an opponent holding the same card as you.
- When you hit your straight, you will not get a lot of action since the board will be too scary for your opponents. For example, if you hold AT with a flop of 987 and a jack or 6 comes, the betting action will quickly dry up. When you are using two cards, your hand is more concealed, so you can sometimes raise or even reraise and get a lot of action.

Let's look first at three-connected flops and the various possible hands. We will use the 987 flop as an example. Obviously, JT would be the best hand, which gives us the nut straight followed by T6 and 65. Straights would be followed by sets like 99, 88 or 77. Two pair would also be good hands, yet very vulnerable.

All of these hands would then be followed in strength by TT, which is a good open-ended straight draw with an overpair. The fact that you hold two of the four tens also reduces the possibility of a flopped straight by your opponents and reduces the chances of having to split the pot. Another strong hand would be JJ as you now have an overpair with a gut-shot draw. These overpairs also have some additional outs if you happen to be against two pair. Finally, another strong hand would be top pair with the open-ended straight draw, such as T9 in this example. In general, all of these hands are strong and can usually be played aggressively until your opponents indicate otherwise.

Whenever you draw using only one card and you don't have other possibilities, your hand is much weaker. You *might* play a hand such as T4 in the right circumstances, but remember to include the possibility that your outs could be counterfeited by another player or that you might have to split the pot. However, if the flop is two-suited, you should usually fold.

When you decide to draw using only one card with a three-connected flop, you almost always want to be drawing to the high end. For example, holding A6 with a 987 flop is not a very strong hand. A ten would give you a straight, but an opponent with a jack would have a higher straight. The only time you might play this hand is when you are heads up under the proper conditions, or when the pot is large and you play the hand like a gut-shot draw to the 5.

Three connected cards with a gap could also give you a straight draw. For example, you hold A8 or 85 with a flop of T97. In general, strategies are practically the same as discussed above when the flop is three-connected. The main difference is that now at least one of your cards is not an overcard. With a 987 flop, there are times when you might hold AT and a ten comes giving you a pair, which holds up and wins the pot. You would not have this possibility with a hand like 85 and a T97 flop; therefore, these types of draws are slightly less valuable. Having said this, strategies are still very similar as we discussed with a three-connected flop. Decent hands like K8 or T8 play well with these types of flops.

Straight draws are always more risky with suited flops. When the flop is three-suited, you should almost always fold your draw, unless you have a semi-bluffing opportunity against a lone opponent or have added value to the hand such as top pair. Two-suited flops also create a lot of problems for these types of straight draws. Against several opponents, you should usually fold. You probably only have six outs and there is a decent chance you could be beat on the river. Against one or two opponents, you might play the hand, depending on your assessment of what your opponents might be holding, the pot odds, and if your draw has any other added value such as pairs or overcards.

Gut-shot Straight Draws

Gut-shot straight draws only have one card that can improve your hand; therefore, you only have four outs rather than the eight outs of an open-ended draw. For example, you hold T♣ 8♦ with a flop of A♥ J♦ 7♣ and need specifically a 9. With only four outs, you are approximately 11 to 1 against improving your hand with one card to come, so you need good pot odds to be able to draw. In addition, when you are drawing on the flop you still need to discount your outs for the risk of losing on the river to a full house, back-door flush, or a higher straight.

Generally you are not getting sufficient pot odds to draw to gut-shot straights unless the pot has been raised before the flop. The only exception is when there are a lot of callers on the flop. For example, let's say there are five players who call preflop in a $10-$20 game for a total pot of $50. If one player bets out and two players call, you could probably call. Your pot odds are 8 to 1 and you can expect to earn additional bets should you improve with so many players in the hand. However, most games on the Internet require a raise preflop to justify calling since games are usually not this loose.

Whenever you decide to draw to a gut-shot straight, you need to be sure that the pot will not be raised behind you. Paying $10 to win a $110 pot is fine, but if the pot is raised and you have to pay $20 to win $140, your pot odds are now only 7 to 1. The best time to play gut-shot draws is when your call will close the betting.

Advanced Concept: When drawing to long-shot hands such as gut-shot draws, you should almost always fold if there is a risk of someone raising behind you.

When the flop is two-suited, you should almost always fold, unless the pot is exceptionally large. You may only have three outs rather than four, decreasing your odds to 15 to 1. Even when you do improve on the turn, you still have the worry that an opponent could hit a flush or better on the river.

Gut-shot draws using only one card in your hand are very weak draws. Sometimes you will lose to higher straights, and there is also a decent chance you will have to split the pot. In addition, it is very difficult to win more bets if you improve since your opponents will not give you a lot of action with such a scary board. For example, 62 with a board of T87 is a very weak hand. A 9 would give you a straight, but you would lose to an opponent holding a jack and would split with anyone holding a 6. If you held J6, at least you would be drawing to a high straight (although you could still lose to QJ), but it still is difficult to win many more bets with this type of board.

A lot of the value in playing gut-shot draws is the additional bets you hope to gain on the turn and river. Since it is difficult to gain these bets when using only one card in your hand, you should generally fold unless you have other outs to your hand such as an overcard or a pair.

One exception to these guidelines about gut-shot draws is when the pot is extremely large. If the pot is very large, you can sometimes justify calling two bets on the flop, playing against a two-suited flop, or calling using only one card in your hand. For example, with a pot of $200 in a $10-$20 game, you could call a raise for $20 on the flop or play a gut-shot draw with three outs for $10.

Betting strategies for gut-shot draws are generally straightforward. You should usually never bet out first or raise, unless you have a semi-bluffing opportunity or other value to your hand. However, to try a semi-bluff, the probability that your opponents will fold should be pretty high since you do not have very good odds to improve your hand.

Like other draws, gut-shot draws increase in value when you have a pair or overcards. For example, with a T86 flop, all of the following hands would have additional outs: T9, A9, K9, T7, or QJ. You would have nine outs holding T9 if you were confident that you were against an overpair. You now are only 4 to 1 against improving instead of 11 to 1. An overcard can add three outs. For example, if you are against KK and hold A9, you would have seven outs. As always, remember to discount your outs for the possibility that they are counterfeited.

Two overcards and a gut-shot draw can also be a good drawing hand, especially if you are drawing to the nut straight. For example, you hold QJ with a 987 flop. However, a hand like KJ is much weaker since you may have to split the pot or possibly even lose to QJ.

You have additional betting strategies when you add other outs to your gut-shot draws. Top pair with a gut-shot draw is a strong hand, so you can usually bet out or raise. When holding middle or bottom pair or an overcard with the gut-shot draw, these are usually just calling situations unless you have a semi-bluffing opportunity.

Chapter Review

❏ Open-ended straight draws are played similarly to flush draws as long as the flop is a rainbow; however, there are a few differences between flush and straight draws:
  • Straights have eight outs while flushes have nine outs.
  • Straights can be beaten by flushes or higher straights.
  • Straights can be counterfeited so that you have to split the pot.
  • Straights are more concealed than flushes, so it is easier to gain additional bets.
❏ Straight draws decrease in value when the flop is two-suited. You may only have six outs rather than eight, and there is a decent chance you could lose on the river.

- ❑ Open-ended draws using only one card in your hand are not nearly as strong as straight draws using both cards in your hand.
  - • You could already be beat by a flopped straight.
  - • If you hit your straight, you will have to split the pot with an opponent holding the same card as you.
  - • When you hit your straight, you will not get a lot of action since the board will be too scary for your opponents.
- ❑ When you decide to draw using only one card with a three-connected flop, you almost always want to be drawing to the high end.
- ❑ The following are some general guidelines for playing gut-shot straight draws when you don't have other outs such as pairs or overcards and there are no semi-bluffing opportunities:
  - • Generally you are not getting sufficient pot odds to draw unless the pot has been raised before the flop. The only exception is when there are a lot of callers on the flop.
  - • You should almost always fold if there is a risk of someone raising behind you.
  - • You should almost always fold when the flop is two-suited, unless the pot is exceptionally large.
  - • You should almost always fold if you are using only one card in your hand.
  - • One exception to these guidelines is when the pot is extremely large.
- ❑ You can sometimes bet or raise straight draws as a semi-bluff, especially against one or two opponents and/or you have other elements to your hand such as pairs or overcards.

Test Your Skills

1/ **$20-$40.** You call with Q♣ J♣ in early position. Two middle players call. Four players see the flop of K♥ T♣ 2♠. The big blind checks. There is $90 in the pot. What do you do?

Answer: Bet. The big blind has indicated weakness by checking. You only need to beat two players, and even if they call, you have outs. In the actual hand, the player bet and hit the straight on the turn against a lone opponent holding AQ.

2/ **$15-$30.** You hold Q♠ J♠ in the big blind. A middle player raises, the small blind calls, and you call. Three players see the flop of T♠ 9♦ 6♦. The small blind bets. There is $105 in the pot. What do you do?

Answer: Raise. You have a good straight draw *plus* two overcards with a decent size pot. You should raise to drive out the preflop raiser in case he holds hands like AQ or AJ. Raising may also allow you to take a free card on the turn. In the actual hand, the player raised and his opponent folded on the turn.

3/ $15-$30. You hold J♦ 8♣ in the small blind. An early player, three middle players, and the button call. You call and seven players see the flop of T♣ 9♦ 4♠. It is checked to the second middle player who bets and the next middle player raises. There is $150 in the pot. What do you do?

Answer: Call. You are 5 to 1 against improving to a straight on the next card and you are getting 5 to 1 pot odds on your call. You should expect to win additional bets if you improve.

4/ $20-$40. You post $20 in the cutoff and are dealt J♠ T♠. A middle player raises, another middle player calls, and you call. The big blind calls and four players see the flop of K♥ 9♠ 8♣. The preflop raiser bets and the middle player folds. There is $190 in the pot. What do you do?

Answer: Raise. One opponent has already folded. This is a large pot, so go ahead and try to win the pot on a semi-bluff. You could also possibly take a free card on the turn. In the actual hand, the preflop raiser check-raised the turn card of the 2♠ with A♣ A♦, but the player hit the straight on the river.

5/ $20-$40. You hold J♦ T♦ in middle position. An early player calls, you call, and the button calls. Four players see the flop of Q♣ 9♠ 5♥. It is checked to you. There is $90 in the pot. What do you do?

Answer: Bet. Two of your three opponents have indicated weakness, so go ahead and bet to try and win the pot outright. In the actual hand, the player bet and all three opponents called! Oh well…Not exactly the result he expected, but still a good one since he was getting good odds on the straight draw with three opponents in the hand.

6/ $15-$30. You make a weak call first in from middle position with 7♥ 6♥ and only the small blind calls. Three players see the flop of Q♥ 9♦ 8♠ and the small blinds bets. There is $60 in the pot. What do you do?

Answer: Fold. Calling and raising are close options to folding. Drawing to an open-ended straight is not always correct. When the pot is very small, you are confident your opponent has a pair, and you do not have overcards, then folding is correct. You are 5 to 1 to improve to a straight on the next card, which means you need to win at least one more big bet from your opponent to *break even* on your draw since there is only $60 in the pot. You might not win this bet if your opponent holds a weak pair.

The other problem with this hand is that you have to discount your outs to the ten since your opponent could have a jack. If your opponent is capable of folding a weak pair, you could raise as a semi-bluff or call with the plan of raising the turn. In the actual hand, the player raised and a ten came on the turn. He ended up losing to J2.

7/ $20-$40. You hold J♦ T♦ in the big blind. A middle player raises and you call. The flop is K♦ Q♠ 4♥. There is $90 in the pot. What do you do?

Answer: Bet, with check-raising a close second. Note that the situation in this hand is different than the previous problem. The pot has been raised giving you good pot odds to play to the river. You also might be able to get your opponent to fold a weak pair like JJ and lower. Check and call is not a good play in this situation. With a good draw against a lone opponent, you need to try and win the pot outright if possible. Check-raising indicates more strength than betting out but could cost a lot if your opponent has a strong pair.

In the actual hand, the player check-raised and was reraised. His opponent showed KJ. Although his strategy did not work here, you should always try and win the pot outright if possible with good draws against a lone opponent.

8/ $15-$30. You hold J♦ 8♦ in middle position. An early player calls and you make a weak call. The button and small blind call. Five players see the flop of Q♠ T♦ 3♣. The early player bets. There is $90 in the pot. What do you do?

Answer: Fold. The pot is small and someone might raise behind you. You don't have any overcards and a 9 wouldn't even give you the nuts.

9/ $1-$2. You hold 6♣ 5♣ on the button. Everyone folds and you decide to limp in. Note that you should usually fold in this situation, but if you do play you should usually raise. The small blind calls and three players see the flop of Q♦ 4♠ 2♣. Both blinds check. There is $3 in the pot. What do you do?

Answer: Bet. Both blinds have indicated weakness. If you are only called, you most likely have 10 outs. In the actual hand, the player checked. The small blind bet the turn of 7♦, and the player won with 65 high when his opponent showed 53 on the river!

10/ $15-$30. You hold K♦ T♣ in the big blind. An early player calls and two middle players call. The cutoff raises, the small blind calls, and you call. Six players see the flop of A♦ Q♥ 4♣. The early player bets and a middle player calls. There is $210 in the pot. What do you do?

Answer: Call. This is a perfect situation for a gut-shot draw. The flop is a rainbow and your call will close the betting. A gut-shot draw is 11 to 1 against improving and you are getting 14 to 1 pot odds.

11/ $15-$30. You hold A♣ 3♣ in the small blind. An early and middle player call and the button raises. You call and the big blind calls. Five players see the flop of K♥ Q♦ J♠. The big blind bets. The early player, middle player, and button all call. There is $210 in the pot. What do you do?

Answer: Fold. Similar to the last hand, your pot odds are 14 to 1. The big problem with this hand is that there is a decent chance you will have to split the pot with another opponent if you hit your straight, significantly decreasing your pot odds. The player folded and the big blind showed TT, hitting a straight when a 9 came on the turn.

12/ $1-$2. You hold A♥ T♣ in the cutoff. Two early players and a very weak middle player call. You call and the small blind calls. Six players see the flop of J♦ 8♥ 7♥. The middle player bets. There is $7 in the pot. What do you do?

Answer: Fold. You have a gut-shot draw, an overcard, and a backdoor flush draw. A ten might even be good against this opponent who would bet any pair; however, there are a lot of problems with this hand. There still are several opponents left to act who might check-raise. Your weak opponent might actually have a good hand such as a set or two pair. The ace overcard is not any good against AJ, A8, or A7. There are two suits on the flop that weakens all of your draws. You may have to split the pot if you hit your straight. In the actual hand, the player called and lost when a 7 and a 2 came on the board. An opponent in the blinds showed KJ and the weak player showed 9♣ 3♣.

Overcards

Drawing to overcards too often is a common mistake made by many players. Overcard draws have six outs, which is approximately 7 to 1 against improving when drawing one more card. The big problem with these types of draws is that you are drawing to a relatively weak hand that might not win. You could be drawing practically dead to opponents with sets, two pair, or an overpair to your overcards.

In addition, there are many ways your outs could be counterfeited. If the flop is two-suited, two of your six outs are vulnerable to flush draws. For example, you hold the K♣ Q♦ with a flop of 9♣ 8♥5♥. The K♥ or Q♥ could give you a pair while giving someone else a flush. You could also be vulnerable to straight draws. In the same example, if a queen comes, you would lose to JT. You are also vulnerable to two pair. Many opponents play a pair with an overcard. If someone holds a hand like K9 or K8, your out is counterfeited.

Advanced Concept: Drawing to overcards with an ace in your hand is even more risky than drawing to a hand with a king or queen. Many opponents play hands such as Ax, so there is an increased chance that your overcard ace could be counterfeited.

In the example above, hands like K9 and K8 are not too common unless played out of the blinds; however, many opponents play A9, A8, and A5, especially if they are suited. In most cases, your hand should be thrown away when you are drawing to overcards and one of them is an ace, unless you have a specific reason to believe that an opponent does not hold an ace. The only time an ace overcard adds some value is in heads-up situations, or possibly against two opponents, when there is the possibility that you could win with just ace high depending on the board.

When you hit your overcard, you can also lose to opponents who have a better kicker. For example, if you hold KJ and an opponent holds KQ, you only have three outs to the jack. Although rare, sometimes you could be drawing dead when two opponents counterfeit all of your outs. For example, with KJ, you are drawing dead if your opponents hold KQ and AJ. Finally, overcards can lose to an opponent hitting a set, backdoor flush, or backdoor straight.

Let's summarize why overcard draws are especially weak and vulnerable draws:

♠ Your odds are only 7 to 1 against improving when drawing one more card, and you are drawing to a relatively weak hand.

♠ You could be drawing practically dead to opponents with sets, two pair, or an overpair to your overcards.

♠ Your out could give an opponent a flush or straight.

♠ Your out could give an opponent two pair, especially when you are holding an ace.

♠ Your out could give an opponent a pair with a better kicker.

♠ You could lose to an opponent hitting a set, backdoor flush, or back-door straight.

As bad as all this sounds, there are times when drawing to overcards is OK, but you must remember that these are not very strong draws. At best, drawing to overcards is usually a marginal decision. In other words, folding or calling would be acceptable. If you always folded overcards when you suspect an opponent has at least a pair, you would not be giving up much at all.

Advanced concept: Drawing to overcards is a marginal decision at best, even when almost all the conditions are perfect.

Most beginning players will save money by never drawing to overcards. For those players who want to consider drawing to overcards, the conditions should be just right. At a basic level, you need to be reasonably confident that you are drawing to a winning hand and are getting sufficient pot odds to justify the draw. The problem is that for both these criteria to be met, you need an almost perfect scenario to be able to call.

The following discussion will look at the conditions needed to meet these two basic criteria. The discussion assumes an opponent has bet out and you feel he has at least a pair. It is also assumed that you have no other type of draw like a gut-shot straight draw. There are situations when you can call or semi-bluff with overcards against opponents who may not have anything, but these will be discussed later.

You should almost always be against a few opponents. The fewer opponents you are against, the better chance you have to win if you improve. When you are playing overcards against a field of four or five opponents, all the risks we discussed about drawing to a weak hand are increased.

There is an increased chance that an opponent holds a set or two pair, or that your outs are counterfeited.

Of course there are exceptions to when you might draw. If the pot is extremely large, such as in a capped pot with many opponents, you can sometimes draw to your hand. With a large pot, backdoor flush and straight opportunities might make a call profitable.

For example, if you hold the K♥ Q♥ with a flop of T♦ 7♥ 5♣, you have a chance at a backdoor flush and backdoor straight, while *also* having over-cards as potential outs. Another heart, K, Q, or J will allow you to draw to the river. A backdoor flush draw only has a 1 in 24 chance in succeeding (about 4% of the time), so you need a very large pot to justify these types of draws with weak overcard outs. Adding a backdoor straight will improve these odds slightly.

Be wary of playing when the preflop raiser is now the flop bettor or either calling a flop bet. Remember that you need to be reasonably sure that your overcards will win if you hit. Preflop raisers often are holding AA, KK, QQ, AK, and AQ. When there are several opponents and the preflop raiser is bet-ting the flop, you should almost always fold your overcards. You are likely playing against a premium hand and there is a good chance that you are drawing dead. If someone bets into the raiser and he calls, there still is a chance that the preflop raiser counterfeits your overcards. Remember, all these scenarios assume that the bettor probably has a hand. In heads-up sit-uations, your strategies can be very different, which we will discuss later.

The pot should be large. You have to be getting sufficient pot odds to jus-tify calling a draw that is 7 to 1 against improving. Unfortunately, this is somewhat contradictory to the first two conditions we discussed above. It is hard to have a large pot with only a few opponents, without a preflop raise, or with a preflop raise but the raiser folds. However, there are two scenarios when this might occur. Sometimes a player will raise preflop and then fold against a flop bet. This might happen when the preflop raiser had a medium pocket pair and now folds to a bet on the flop. In this case, the pot might be large enough to justify a call to your overcards.

The other scenario when the pot could be large enough to call is when there are several players who call preflop with no raise, and then two or three play-ers call the flop. For example, three players limp in along with the small blind and big blind. The small blind bets, an early player calls, the cutoff calls, and you are acting last on the button. There are now eight bets in the pot that might justify calling; however, this is still a marginal call since you need to discount your outs.

Generally only play for one bet. You should almost never call raises or face the risk of a raise unless the pot is exceptionally large. Generally this means that your call will close the betting or you are acting next to last.

The flop should be favorable so that there is less risk that your outs are counterfeited. Generally fold when the flop type increases the risk that your outs are counterfeited. For example, three-suited, two-suited, three-connected, two connected high cards, a high pair, or all high cards are all dangerous flops for overcard draws.

Let's look at which types of flops can sometimes be played with overcard draws under the right conditions.

Dangerous Flops

Almost never draw to overcards with flop types of a high pair, three-suited, three-connected, or all high cards. The exception of course is when you have a flush or straight draw also; however, be careful drawing with an all-high card flop since the only value of your hand is probably the straight draw.

For example, when you hold AK and the flop is QJ9, your hand is especially vulnerable. The ace or king could easily give someone two pair or a straight, so your only out may be the gut-shot ten, especially against several opponents.

Two-Suited

When the flop is two-suited, you may only be drawing to four outs if an opponent has a flush draw. This draw has the same odds as a gut-shot draw, except your draw is only to a pair and you have the risk of running into a flush on the river.

If one of your overcards is one of the two suits on the flop, this increases the value of your hand a little. For example, if you have the K♣ Q♠ and the flop is T♥ 6♣ 4♣, all three of your outs to a king are good. You would have five outs in this case, the three kings and two queens, in addition to your backdoor flush draw.

These draws however are still very weak. You should almost always be folding with a two-suited flop. The only times you might consider calling is when the pot is exceptionally large or you are only against one or two opponents with a large pot and the risk of a flush draw is not very high.

Two-Connected

When there are two connected high cards, you should usually fold against several opponents unless you have a straight draw also. With several opponents, there is a good chance you are against a set, two pair, or that your outs are counterfeited if they have straights or two pair draws. Against one or two opponents, you might play if there is a large pot. If the connected cards are low, you do not need to worry so much about the straights, unless your opponents played out of the blinds or from late position.

Three of a Kind

Three of a kind flops are sometimes playable since an opponent will most likely need a pocket pair to have a decent hand. This is the one type of flop where holding an ace overcard is advantageous compared to a king or queen since you could possibly win with ace high. Tend to fold these hands against a preflop raiser since the likelihood of a pocket pair is higher.

Low Pair

The number and position of your opponents is important when playing overcards to a flop with a low pair. If you are playing against the blinds or against many opponents, you should probably fold with a low pair on the flop; however, you could possibly play against one or two opponents depending on the situation. For example, two early players are unlikely to be playing low cards.

Rainbow with One High Card

You can sometimes play a rainbow flop with only one high card under the right conditions. The problem with these flops is that your out could give an opponent two pair since your opponents usually play high cards. For example, if the flop is T65, the most likely hands of your opponents are AT, KT, QT, JT, and finally T9. If you hold KQ, your hand is vulnerable to an opponent holding KT or QT. This does not mean that you should always fold, but you need to discount your outs for this possibility.

Sometimes you can pin down your opponents on more specific hands. For example, if a solid player playing out of early position comes out betting on this flop, he probably does not hold KT or QT since most strong players do not play these hands from early position. ATs or JTs are more likely; therefore, you should be reluctant to play overcards in this situation unless you have specifically KQ.

Advanced Concept: Be careful when playing overcards when one of your overcards is exactly one card above the highest card. Many opponents like to play connected cards, so your out could be counterfeited.

Rainbow of All Rags

The best type of flop for overcard draws is a rainbow flop of all rags. Of course, against many opponents you still have to worry about two pair and straights, but against just a few this risk is reduced. Again, be careful with an ace overcard, as many opponents will play Ax and your out could be counterfeited.

Betting Strategies

Whenever the conditions are right to play your hand, you need to decide what betting strategies you will use. Realize however, that most of the time you should be folding.

Semi-bluffing against three or more opponents generally is not profitable; therefore, your general strategy in these cases is to check and call if the conditions are right. There are times when you might bet from late position if everyone checks, hoping for a free card on the turn. This strategy generally depends on the risk of a check-raise. You can also try raising for a free card, but you are paying a high cost for a relatively weak draw. This play works best when you were the preflop raiser and the conditions are just right, such as a large pot against a few opponents with a favorable flop. Be careful in trying this play against aggressive opponents who will sometimes reraise their top pair.

Against one or two opponents, there is always the possibility that the flop has not helped anyone, so you can sometimes semi-bluff by either betting or raising. This is especially true if you were the preflop raiser. Betting after a preflop raise is usually justified, because your opponents will sometimes fold and you still have outs if they call. Ace high might even be the best hand.

A semi-bluff raise however is more risky since an opponent has already indicated strength. On the other hand, sometimes you can get strong players to fold middle or bottom pair, or even top pair with weak kickers. When they do call, you still have your overcard outs and possibly the chance for a free card on the turn.

Knowing when a semi-bluff has a decent chance at success takes time and experience. You need to look at the betting sequences preflop, the position of your opponents, the type of opponent, and the type of flop, to help determine the possible holdings of your opponents and the chances that a bluff will be successful.

Chapter Review

❑ Overcard draws are especially weak and vulnerable draws:
- ♠ Your odds are only 7 to 1 against improving when drawing one more card, and you are drawing to a relatively weak hand.
- ♠ You could be drawing practically dead to opponents with sets, two pair, or an overpair to your overcards.
- ♠ Your out could give an opponent a flush or straight.
- ♠ Your out could give an opponent two pair, especially when you are holding an ace.
- ♠ Your out could give an opponent a pair with a better kicker.
- ♠ You could lose on the river to an opponent hitting a set, backdoor flush, or backdoor straight.

❑ Drawing to overcards is a marginal decision at best, even when almost all the conditions are perfect. Most beginning players will save money by never calling to overcards.

❑ The conditions should be just right to consider drawing to overcards:
- You should almost always be against a few opponents.
- Be wary of playing when the preflop raiser is now the flop bettor or either calling a flop bet.
- The pot should be large.
- Generally only play for one bet.
- The flop should be favorable so that there is less risk that your outs are counterfeited.
  - Favorable flops include three of a kind and a rainbow flop of all rags.
  - Low pairs or two connected low cards are generally favorable, unless you are playing against opponents in late position or the blinds.
  - One high card and two rags can sometimes be played against a few opponents.
  - Almost never draw with flop types of a high pair, three-suited, two-suited, three-connected, two connected high cards, or all

high cards. Generally you need added value to your overcards such as flush or straight draws to be able to play (see other exceptions noted in text).

- Be less inclined to play overcards when one of them is an ace or one of your cards is exactly one card above the highest card on the table.

❑ Overcards can sometimes be played as semi-bluffs against one or two opponents, especially if you were the preflop raiser.

Test Your Skills

1/ $20-$40. You hold K♦ J♠ on the button. Two middle players call and you call. The small blind calls and five players see the flop of 9♦ 4♣ 3♥. The big blind bets and the cutoff calls. There is $140 in the pot. What do you do?

Answer: Fold. You have six outs, which is 7 to 1 and the pot odds are offering exactly 7 to 1. The problem with this hand is that your hand may not be any good even if you improve. Your opponents could have a set, two pair, a pair with a kicker that matches one of your hole cards, or two overcards such as AK, AQ, AJ, or KQ. Once you discount your outs for these possibilities, you are no longer receiving the pot odds required. In the actual hand, the player called and folded on the turn.

2/ $15-$30. You raise in the cutoff with A♠ T♣. A strong player calls in the small blind and the big blind folds. The flop is 7♥ 4♥ 3♦. The small blind bets. There is $90 in the pot. What do you do?

Answer: Fold. The strong player probably has a medium pair or ace high with a better kicker than yours. He might be betting a flush draw, but you will have to pay bets on three streets to find out if he is semi-bluffing, and he still can hit a hand to beat you. Drawing one more card to try and improve is risky if your opponent holds Ax or a flush draw. The pot is not big enough to justify calling.

Note that we are evaluating what you should do on one particular hand. In a long session, you cannot always fold overcards when the flop is all rags, or your opponents will take advantage of this and always bet out; therefore, you will sometimes need to either call or raise to mix up your play.

3/ $20-$40. You raise in middle position with K♠ Q♠. A middle player and the big blind call. Three players see the flop of 6♦ 5♠ 3♥. The big blind checks. There is $130 in the pot. What do you do?

Answer: Bet. This is not a great flop and one that is difficult to drive out opponents since there are no scare cards; however, you were the preflop raiser and nobody reraised, so keep betting to put pressure on your opponents to hit something. In the actual hand, the player bet, and both players called. The Q♥ came on the turn. The big blind check-raised and the player made it three bets. His opponent showed Q♣ 2♠.

4/ $20-$40. You hold A♣ J♥ in the small blind. A middle player raises and another middle player calls. You make a questionable call and three players see the flop of T♠ 4♣ 3♣. The preflop raiser bets and the other player folds. There is $160 in the pot. What do you do?

Answer: Fold. You need to discount your outs against a preflop raiser. If a jack comes, you would lose to AA, KK, QQ, JJ, and TT. If an ace comes, you would lose to AA, TT, AK, AQ, and AT. Even with the backdoor flush that adds a little value to your hand, the pot is not big enough to justify a call. In the actual hand, the player called and a jack came on the turn. The player check-raised and won against KQ. Calling won the hand, but in the long run this is not very profitable. The player was fortunate that his opponent had a hand that did not counterfeit his outs.

5/ $15-$30. You hold K♣ Q♣ on the button and the cutoff posts $20. A middle player calls and you raise. Both blinds, the middle player, and the cutoff call. Five players see the flop of J♦ 7♥ 5♣. The big blind bets and the middle player calls. There is $180 in the pot. What do you do?

Answer: Call. The pot is quite large. You need to discount your outs for the possibilities of sets, two pair, and the chance that your opponents counterfeit your outs. It is unlikely however that you are against a premium pocket pair. The backdoor flush and straight possibilities add a little to your hand. If you discount your six outs to four, you are now 11 to 1 and the pot odds are still sufficient to take another card. In the actual hand, the player called and everyone checked the turn card of 3♠. The K♠ came on the river and the player bet with one caller showing 8♠ 7♣.

6/ $20-$40. You hold K♥ Q♠ in the big blind. An early player calls, a middle player raises, and the button calls. You call and four players see the flop of T♣ 9♣ 9♠. The middle player bets and the button raises. There is $230 in the pot. What do you do?

Answer: Fold. Whenever you are drawing to overcards, you need almost a perfect situation. In this hand, the gut-shot draw adds some value to your hand, but the overcards are very weak with a pair on the flop. You almost need to play this hand like a gut-shot draw; however, gut-shot draws are weak draws whenever the flop is paired, suited, or you must pay two bets to play. In this case, you have all three working against you. In the actual hand, the player folded, and the T♦ came on the turn. The middle player showed A♥ T♥ and the button A♠ 9♦.

7/ $20-$40. You hold A♦ Q♣ in middle position. A weak early player calls and you raise. Both blinds call and four players see the flop of 8♥ 8♣ 2♠. It is checked to you and you bet. The small blind calls and the early player raises. There is $240 in the pot. What do you do?

Answer: Fold. If you were only against the weak early player, you might call if he tends to be a maniac; however, this is one of those dangerous flop types where you need to back off whenever two opponents decide to play. The small blind has called and a weak player who plays many hands has check-raised. They are indicating strength even though you raised preflop. It is likely at least one of them has the 8. Even if they don't, they probably have a pair and you would have a weak draw. In the actual hand, the small blind showed 2♦ 2♥ and the early player J♦ 8♦.

8/ $20-$40. You hold A♠ K♣ in middle position. An early player calls and you raise. The cutoff and big blind call. Four players see the flop of Q♠ 9♥ 8♣. Everybody checks to the cutoff who bets and only the big blind calls. There is $210 in the pot. What do you do?

Answer: Fold. There are many ways for your opponents to hold sets, two pair, or even a straight with this flop. There are also many ways your two opponents could be counterfeiting your outs with hands AQ, A9, A8, KQ, K9, or K8. Against one opponent, you might draw to your overcards, but against two opponents drawing is risky. In the actual hand, the player called and the cutoff won the pot on the turn.

9/ $20-$40. You raise with Q♠ J♠ in the cutoff. The small blind reraises and the big blind calls. You decide to cap the betting. Three players see the flop of 7♣ 7♥ 4♥. The small blind bets and the big blind calls. There is $280 in the pot. What do you do?

Answer: Call. You need to be worried that an opponent holds a high pocket pair or possibly AQ or AJ; however, they might also have hands like AK or a middle pair and your two overcards would be good. Even with only three outs, the pot is big enough to take one more card. You can sometimes justify a weak draw with the good pot odds a capped pot preflop is offering. In the actual hand, the player called and folded the turn.

10/ $15-$30. You hold A♦ Q♦ in middle position. An early player calls and you raise. The following middle player reraises, the button calls, the small blind caps, and everyone calls. Five players see the flop of J♠ 6♥ 4♠. The middle player bets, the button calls, the small blind raises, and the early player calls. There is $405 in the pot. What do you do?

Answer: Fold. This is a very large pot giving you 13.5 to 1 pot odds; however, there is a good chance that you are drawing dead. The small blind is playing like he holds a premium pair QQ or higher. In this case, you can only hope that he holds KK or QQ, giving you three outs to the ace. However, the middle player could be holding AK, AJ, or a high pair, also making it possible that you are drawing dead.

There are two other concerns in this hand. Your call would not close the betting as the middle player might reraise and the small blind could cap. Finally, there are two other players in the hand who may have sets or either a flush draw, making two of your outs no good. This is a hand where calling can get you in a lot of trouble since you are probably drawing to a second-best hand.

In the actual hand, the player folded. The turn was the A♠. Everyone checked. The river was the 3♥ and everyone checked. The middle player showed QJ and the small blind QQ. Even though the player would have won the hand, note that he only had three outs to the ace, which is 15 to 1 against improving, and the pot odds were only 13.5 to 1. Also, even if he did call, it would have been a difficult hand to play given the flush possibilities on the turn.

11/ $20-$40. You raise in middle position with K♥ Q♥. A middle player calls and an aggressive player on the button raises. Three players see the flop of J♥ 7♣ 2♠. It is checked to the button who bets. There is $230 in the pot. What do you do?

Answer: Call. This is not the ideal overcard situation, as there is a decent chance that your outs are counterfeited; however, you have a backdoor flush *and* straight draw that adds value to your overcard draw. Calling is justified with such a large pot. Your hand will be helped on the turn with any K, Q, T, or heart, which gives you 18 cards to improve your chances of winning a large pot. Note that if the pot had not been reraised preflop, folding would be the best decision. In the actual hand, the player called and the 9♥ came on the turn giving the player a flush, gut-shot straight, and overcard draw. The T♣ on the river gave the player a straight.

12/ $1-$2. You hold K♥ Q♠ on the button. Two middle players call and you call. The small blind calls and five players see the flop of 7♣ 5♥ 2♠. The small blind bets. The big blind and one middle player call. There is $8 in the pot. What do you do?

Answer: Call, with folding a very close second. The flop is a rainbow, so you don't need to worry about flush draws. Your call closes the betting, so you don't need to worry about raises. Your two overcards are good overcards since most opponents generally won't play K7, K5, K2, Q7, Q5, or Q2, unless they are in the blinds. However, since the bettor is in the blinds, you still need to discount your outs for the possibility of an opponent holding two pair or that he counterfeits your outs. The middle player might be slow-playing a set. If you discount your six outs to five outs, you are 8 to 1 against improving and there is $8 in the pot making it a borderline decision. In the actual hand, the player called and everyone checked the turn card of the 8♦. The Q♥ came on the river and the player won against A♣ 2♦.

Trash Hands

I define a trash hand as a hand that has no pairs, no straight or flush draws, and does not have two overcards. For example A♣ 7♣, 7♥ 4♥, or K♠ 8♦ with a Q♦ T♥ 5♠ flop. The only time when trash hands are playable is when you are against one or two opponents and you believe a bluff can be successful. Sometimes ace high is the best hand, which might even justify a bet.

Let's look at some examples of when playing trash hands might be profitable. Sometimes bluffing out of the blinds can be profitable with an all rag flop, or when there is a rainbow flop with only one high card. For example, you are in the big blind with an 864 flop against two early position callers. Betting out might win the pot, as it is unlikely this flop helped your opponents.

Another example is with a Q53 flop and you are in early position with AT. You might bet out into one or two opponents representing a pair of queens hoping that they fold. When the flop is two-suited, two-connected, or has two high cards, be less inclined to make these types of bluffs, as it is more likely that your opponents either have a hand or have a draw. The exception to this is when you are acting last and both of your opponents have checked. In this case, bluffing may be successful since your opponents have indicated weakness and they might suspect that *you* were the one helped by the flop.

Internet Tip

You will find yourself in small blind versus big blind situations a lot more on the Internet than you would in a live game since in a live game you often "chop." Bluffing with trash hands in these situations can often be profitable. If neither player raised preflop, you only have to win once every three hands for bluffing to break even; therefore, betting out the flop from either the small blind or big blind can often be successful.

There are many different scenarios when bluffs might work, but be careful in playing these trash hands. Remember, bluffing is risky when you don't have many outs. Also, bluffs against three or more opponents are rarely profitable with these types of hands.

Hopefully, these chapters on the flop have covered most of the common situations you will find yourself in. Although it is impossible to cover every situation, you should now have a good background to be able to evaluate any situation that might arise.

One thing to remember is that there are always a wide variety of strategies available to you. Sometimes two strategies could have an equal expectation. For example, sometimes calling has a break-even expectation, so this is the same as folding. Remember to vary your play so that your observant opponents aren't able to read you like a book, and pay close attention to your opponents so that you can begin to learn their betting patterns. The more you understand the betting strategies of your opponents, the better decisions you can make when you play against them.

If you have the discipline to play good starting hands and you have a good understanding of how to play the flop, you should be a profitable player. Now we move to the turn and river where mistakes become more costly, but if you have played well up to this point, you should be getting the best of it!

Test Your Skills

1/ $20-$40. You hold 6♦ 3♠ in the big blind. Everyone folds to the button who decides to just limp in. The small blind calls and three players see the flop of J♥ 4♦ 2♥. The small blind checks. There is $60 in the pot. What do you do?

Answer: Bet. By definition, this really isn't a trash hand since you have a gut-shot draw, but 63 isn't exactly a stellar hand either with no pair. However, even if an opponent calls, you might win even with another 6 so you probably have seven outs. The small blind has checked, so you probably only have to beat the button player who limped in. The jack gives you a scare card and makes it less likely that your opponents hold overcards. The small pot also gives your opponents incentive to fold. Go ahead and bet to try and win the pot. If you are raised, you should fold. In the actual hand, the player bet and his opponents folded.

2/ $20-$40. You hold 8♦ 4♠ in the big blind. An early player and the small blind call. Three players see the flop of 6♥ 3♣ 3♠. The small blind checks. There is $60 in the pot. What do you do?

Answer: Bet. This flop does not have a high card to protect against your opponents playing overcards; however, the low pair on the flop provides this protection. A rainbow flop protects you against opponents on a flush draw. Bet the flop and if only the early player calls, go ahead and bet the turn on any card. In the actual hand, the player bet and only the early player called. The turn was the 2♥ and his opponent folded.

3/ $20-$40. You hold 5♦ 2♣ in the big blind. An early, middle, and late player call. The small blind calls and five players see the flop of Q♥ 6♣ 3♠. The small blind checks. There is $100 in the pot. What do you do?

Answer: Check and fold if three opponents do not play the flop. You actually have four outs to the straight draw, which gives you some value to the hand; however, you are against four opponents and three have not yet acted. A queen is a likely card for three opponents who did not raise preflop. It would be very difficult to get all of your opponents to fold this flop. You should check and only call if several opponents play the flop to justify the odds for your draw. In the actual hand, the player checked, the button bet, and the small blind raised. Both showed a pair of queens on the river.

The Turn

The turn is one of the more difficult rounds to play in Hold'em. The bets are doubled, so the true strength of everyone's hands is usually communicated. Many players will often call a cheap bet on the flop hoping to hit overcards, gut-shot straights, two pair, etc., but will often fold these hands on the turn when the betting becomes more expensive. Since bets are doubled, any mistakes on this round of betting can become very costly.

Staying the Aggressor with Strong Hands

A common situation in Hold'em is that you raise preflop and then either bet or raise on the flop. Generally, you should continue to be the aggressor on the turn with a strong hand, although there are a few exceptions. For purposes of this section, a strong hand is one that you are relatively confident is currently the best hand.

When acting early with a strong hand, your two options are betting out or trying for a check-raise. Generally continue to bet when you are unsure that an opponent will bet and giving a free card would be dangerous. Against several opponents with a large pot, you might consider checking, hoping that a late position opponent will bet so that you can check-raise to drive out your remaining opponents.

If a free card would not be too dangerous, a check-raise can sometimes be a good strategy to gain extra bets against your opponents. You gain extra bets by either inducing your opponents to bet a weak hand that they would have folded or by them calling a check-raise. If they don't bet, you might gain a crying call on the river when you come out betting.

Checking also gives you equity in future hands. If your more observant opponents notice that you *always* bet out your strong hands, they will steal many pots when you check. On the other hand, if you check-raise a lot, they may tend to steal less in fear that you might check-raise. This could give you a free card, which might improve your weaker hands to the winning hand.

Let's look now at your options when acting after your opponents. Whenever your opponents check, you should almost always bet your strong hand. You want to earn bets! You need to continue to put pressure on your opponents and make them pay a price for their draws. Giving free cards can be dangerous, as opponents can sometimes hit a miracle card to beat your hand. If you are check-raised, you can then evaluate how strong your hand is compared to your opponent's possible holdings (see Calling Raises).

When you are worried that an opponent may have hit a draw and he checks, tend to check hands with outs and bet hands with few or no outs. If you are check-raised when you have few outs, you can safely fold. For example, you hold A♣ K♠ with a K♦ Q♦ 5♣ 9♦ board against two opponents. If your opponents check, you should usually bet since you do not want to give a free card. If an opponent then check-raises, you are most likely beat and can safely fold. However, if you hold K♣ Q♣ with the same board, you might consider checking since you have four outs that could beat either a flush or straight.

There is another scenario when you might consider checking the turn in late position rather than continuing to be the aggressor. If you are relatively confident that your opponents will fold, and the risk of a free card hurting you is minimal, you might check when the pot is relatively small. This kind of play could gain you an extra bet in three different ways:
- You might induce an opponent into making a bluff on the river.
- An opponent might improve to a second-best hand and will now either bet or call on the river.
- You might induce a crying call on the river. For example, an opponent might call with ace high or a weak pair if he thinks your check on the turn indicated weakness.

Internet Tip

On the Internet, players tend to be a little more aggressive than in live play, so this kind of play works even better online than in a live game since many opponents can't resist trying a bluff at the pot.

This type of play should not be used too often. It is often difficult to know when your opponents will fold, and most hands are not strong enough to be able to give a free card. In addition, sometimes an opponent might be slow-playing a strong hand weaker than yours and you could lose the opportunity to gain a few bets on the turn.

For example, you raise preflop with KK and bet the flop with a K♣ 8♥ 2♦ 5♣ board. What should you do if your opponent checks? A free card could only hurt you if your opponent has a runner-runner flush opportunity. However, what could your opponent have been calling with on the flop? He might have the last king or possibly 88 or 22, in which case you would lose a lot of bets by slowplaying your set on the turn. If your opponent calls on the flop with this type of board, there is a decent chance he will call the turn also, so usually go ahead and bet. What if the board is K♣ 9♣ 2♦ 5♥? Giving a free card in this case is dangerous, because your opponent could be on either a flush or gut-shot straight draw.

Let's look at an example when you might consider checking. You hold T♣ T♦ with a T♥ 6♦ 2♣ 3♠ board. You *might* consider checking this hand on the turn against a strong opponent if the pot is small and it is unlikely he holds a small set based on your opponent's position and betting on previous rounds. Your opponent might be playing two overcards and would probably fold if you bet. Note that I specifically referred to your opponent as a strong opponent. Never give up betting opportunities against *weak* opponents who will call with all kinds of hands.

Staying the Aggressor with Weak Hands

There are many situations when your hand is not very strong and you have to decide whether to continue betting as a semi-bluff or to back off your hand. For example, a common situation is raising preflop with AK only to miss your hand on the flop and turn. Some of your considerations include:

- **Number of opponents:** Generally only *consider* a semi-bluff against one or two opponents. A semi-bluff is rarely successful against three or more opponents on the turn.
- **Type of board:** The type of board, along with the position and previous betting of your opponents, should give an indication of the type of hand you are against. Could your opponents be on a draw, or do they already have a made hand? Do they have a strong draw or a weak draw? Betting out can sometimes win the pot against weak draws or when a scare card comes such as an ace.
- **Type of opponent:** Avoid bluffing a lot against weak opponents who will call to the river with many types of hands. On the other hand, you have a better chance of success if you are against a strong opponent who

will respect your turn bet and fold either weak draws or medium pairs. For example, a strong opponent might fold middle pair or even top pair with a weak kicker while weak opponents will almost always call with these hands.

- **Your position:** Acting early can sometimes communicate a strong hand by your willingness to bet into one or two opponents; however, this may be risky depending on the board. If you plan on calling a turn bet in any case, you must weigh the possibility of winning the pot immediately by betting versus the risk that an opponent will raise making your draw more expensive.

When acting in late position and your opponents check to you, a bet might win the pot since your opponents have indicated weakness; however, you still have the risk that an opponent might check-raise. In marginal situations where you are not sure if a bluff will be successful, tend to check hands with outs and bet hands that don't have many outs. You can safely fold to a check-raise with only a few outs, while checking with several outs allows you to draw for free rather than risk paying two bets for your draw. Sometimes you might bet a marginal holding with the intention of checking the river for a "free" showdown. This strategy is usually better than checking the turn and calling the river since you don't give your opponents a free card.

In summary, you can *sometimes* continue to be the aggressor with weak hands against one or two opponents; however, this type of aggression should only be used in the right situations. In many cases, you will need to back off your hand even against a lone opponent, depending on the type of board, opponent, and betting sequences. Review the chapter "Bluffing" for further insights into making successful bluffs and semi-bluffs.

Betting the Turn

In the previous two sections, we discussed what you should do when you were the aggressor before the turn. Sometimes you have the opportunity to become the aggressor by either betting out or raising a strong hand or as a bluff.

Let's look at when you must act first and have a big hand from either slowplaying the flop or hitting a draw on the turn. The two most common options available to you are betting out or trying a check-raise (in rare cases you might simply check and call as a possible slowplay to the river).

An important consideration between the two options is whether or not you expect an opponent to bet behind you. As discussed previously, it can be disastrous to give a free card on the turn; however, check-raises can be an effective strategy, especially against aggressive opponents who you are relatively confident will bet the turn. On the other hand, sometimes you might bet out hoping to be raised so that you can reraise.

Let's look at a couple of examples. You hold 7♦ 7♣ in both of them. In the first example, the board is A♦ T♦ 7♥ 2♣. You called preflop from early position and were raised by a middle position player. You checked and called on the flop as a slowplay. Check-raising the turn in this type of situation can be a good play since there is a decent chance that your opponent will bet again with this board. Even if he doesn't bet with a hand like KK or QQ, a free card is not too risky. Another option is to bet out hoping that your opponent raises with a hand like AK or AQ so that you can reraise.

Let's say you have the same hand, but this time the board is A♦ T♦ 7♥ 2♦. The board is now three-suited. If your opponent has K♦ K♣ or Q♦ Q♣, he may be more inclined to check the turn and take a free card with his draw to the flush; therefore, betting out is probably the best option against most opponents.

If you are acting behind your opponents and it is checked to you, it is almost mandatory to bet a strong hand. You generally don't want to give a free card to your opponents and you want to gain bets with your good hands. Again, there are some rare times when checking may be considered as a slowplay with a small pot (see Staying the Aggressor with Strong Hands section), but in most cases you should bet out your hand.

The other time you might bet the turn is as a bluff or semi-bluff. Sometimes you can bet out if you sense there is a decent chance your opponents will fold. If your opponents check, a bet could win the pot since they have indicated weakness. Sometimes a scary turn card will allow a bet to be successful. For example, whenever an ace comes, the board pairs, or a third suited card comes, you might bet out hoping that your opponents will fold. Remember that semi-bluffs are more successful against a lone opponent than several.

Raising the Turn

There are three main reasons to raise the turn:
- You have a strong hand and want to get more money in the pot.
- You have a semi-bluff opportunity.
- You want to protect a vulnerable hand.

Whenever you have a strong hand, the turn is a good round to show your strength by raising. You should rarely slowplay all the way to the river. Sometimes you might just call a turn bet when your hand is exceptionally strong so that the remaining opponents behind you will call. Another example where you might slowplay to the river is against an aggressive opponent who you believe is bluffing. Allowing him to continue a bluff and then waiting to raise the river can sometimes be a good strategy.

A semi-bluff raise can also be a successful strategy sometimes. As we have discussed before, when you have a good draw against one or two opponents, you usually want to make at least one attempt at winning the pot either on the flop or turn. Raising the turn with a strong draw can be a profitable strategy under the right circumstances. For the cost of one more bet, you have the chance of winning the pot immediately, and when you are called you still have a lot of outs. The biggest risk to this strategy is that you are reraised.

For example, you have A♦ 9♦ with a board of Q♦ 9♥ 5♣ 2♦. A semi-bluff raise could be a good strategy here. You might be able to get hands such as JJ or TT to fold, as well as overcards to your pair of 9's. Another example of a semi-bluff raising opportunity might be K♦ Q♥ with a T♦ 7♥ 5♣ J♦ board. Be careful in trying these raises against weak opponents who are not capable of folding a hand like second or third pair.

The final reason to raise on the turn is to drive out your opponents to protect a vulnerable hand. For example, you hold TT with a J954 board with several players seeing the turn card. You might raise hoping that you hold the best hand (you would not do this against a rock) and to drive the remaining opponents out of the hand. You probably would just check the river if an opponent calls your turn raise. Notice how this strategy cost the same as calling a turn and river bet. The benefit is that it drives out the other opponents to protect your hand if it is the best.

Calling Bets

The preferred strategy in poker is generally to raise or to fold, but there are times when calling is correct, especially with your strong draws and little chance of winning the pot on a semi-bluff raise.

Calling bets on the turn is much different than calling bets on the flop. Because flop bets are small, you are generally getting decent odds to see one more card to try and improve your hand. However, you rarely are getting good odds to draw on the turn, except for the premium draws to flushes and open-ended straights. Exceptions to this are when the pot is very large.

Let's look at strategy when an opponent bets and you are unsure whether or not you hold the best hand. There are four considerations in your decision to call or fold, assuming you have determined that raising is not a good option:
- The probability that you currently have the best hand
- The probability that your hand will improve to the best hand
- The probability that your opponent will improve to the best hand if you currently have the best hand
- The pot odds

The three top bullet points combined is the probability that you will win the hand. This probability does not always need to be very high if you are getting good pot odds. For example, if you feel you have a 25% chance of winning the hand, you need at least 3 to 1 implied pot odds on your calls. In summary, to call a turn bet, you need to compare the overall probability that you will have the best hand on the river versus the implied pot odds on your call.

Calling Raises

Calling raises too often on the turn is another common mistake made by many players. One problem with calling raises on the turn is that you often end up calling the river. Since your goal is to win a big bet an hour, making the mistake of calling the turn and river when you shouldn't would wipe out two hours of earnings. When calling a raise on the turn, think about whether or not you will call the river if you don't improve. Paying two big bets significantly decreases the pot odds you are receiving to see if you will win the hand.

Many opponents wait until the turn to raise their really strong hands. A lot of players are also reluctant to make semi-bluff raises on the turn, especially at the lower limits. For these reasons, you need to be very careful about when you call raises on the turn. Most opponents who raise the turn almost always have *at least* top pair with a good kicker, and they often have two pair or better; therefore, you should often fold pairs when raised on the turn. The main exception to this is in tight aggressive games where some opponents will raise the turn on a semi-bluff, especially in heads-up situations, so you *sometimes* need to call with a mediocre holding such as a pair depending on the circumstances.

Let's look first at a couple of situations where folding to a raise is quite straightforward. Many opponents are very predictable on the turn and you can use this to your advantage to make correct decisions. For example, some opponents will *never* raise or check-raise on the turn as a bluff or semi-bluff. If this type of player raises, you can safely fold unless you have a very strong hand.

Another situation where you can safely fold marginal hands is when an opponent raises after two players have already called the turn. It is very rare for a player to raise two players on the turn without a very strong hand. For example, if you bet out, are called by one opponent, and then raised by another, you should generally fold unless you have a very strong hand or are getting good odds on a draw.

Advanced Concept: There are two situations when folding to raises on the turn with a mediocre holding such as a top pair is relatively straightforward:
1. *Your opponent is the type who never raises the turn on a bluff or semi-bluff.*
2. *An opponent has raised after two players have already called the turn.*

In these two situations, I would need at least top pair with top kicker to call, and often an even better hand depending on the type of opponents I am against.

Unfortunately, in tight aggressive games, turn play is not this straightforward most of the time. You will find yourself in a lot of heads-up situations where it is difficult to get a good read on your opponent's hand. In heads-up situations, some players will raise the turn with many types of hands such as top pair, middle or bottom pair, flush and straight draws, and of course two pair or better. When these types of players raise, sometimes you should fold top pair with top kicker, while other times you might be reraising. You might even need to call with bottom pair and possibly even ace high in some situations. Calling in these types of situations often depends on the type of board and how your particular opponent might play that board.

Let's look at a common example. You raise in early position with AK and a middle position player calls. The flop is all rags such as 642. You bet and are called. The turn is another rag such as a 4. You bet and your opponent raises. What do you do? Against most opponents you should almost always fold; however, you sometimes need to call in some of the tight aggressive high-limit games where some opponents will raise with Ax. Realize however that most players will not raise in this situation as a semi-bluff. The type of opponent you are playing often has an impact on these type of borderline decisions.

Always evaluate the type of board to guide your decision. If the board is three-suited such as A♦ T♦ 5♣ 2♦, consider what types of hands your opponent could be holding. For example, a raise on the turn with this board could mean your opponent hit a flush, *or* it could mean he holds the K♦ or Q♦ and is raising on a semi-bluff, *or* maybe he has Ax and is protecting his hand against an opponent with a draw. Note how the number of players in the hand makes a difference on the possible holdings. If two players have called a turn bet and an opponent raises, you can generally assume that he is not raising on a flush draw. However, in a heads-up situation some aggressive players might raise with K♦ T♣ hoping that you might fold a hand such as KK, QQ, or JJ.

Also note how high the board cards are. It is less likely for opponents to make draws on a flop like A♦ 9♦ 5♥ than they are with a flop of T♣ 5♦ 2♥. If your opponent waits to raise the turn with an A♣ 9♦ 5♥ 3♠ board, you should ask yourself, "What kind of hand would my opponent call the flop with and then raise the turn?" You should be concerned about a set, two pair, or a pair of aces with a good kicker. Against most opponents in this heads-up situation, you could safely throw away KK, AJ, and maybe even AQ. Against tight rocks who wouldn't raise with two pair or less, you could even throw away AK, as it is likely that your opponent has a set.

On the other hand, what if your opponent raises the turn with a T♣ 5♦ 2♥ 8♦ board? Since the cards are relatively low, it is more difficult to determine your opponent's strength. He could be raising with a set, a pair of tens, or maybe even a hand such as 77 hoping that you are holding a hand like AK. A tricky opponent might even raise with a hand like QJ or a diamond draw. With this type of board against certain opponents, you should be more likely to call with an overpair or top pair.

One final situation to discuss is when you need to call a raise cold, forcing you to pay two big bets to see the river. In almost all cases, one of your opponents has a very strong hand, unless he is trying to protect a vulnerable medium holding. The other problem with calling in this situation is that the original bettor could reraise. To call a raise cold, you almost always need a *very* strong hand or draw. For draws, the pot will need to be quite large to justify calling a raise cold.

For example, if you have the nut-flush draw on the turn, you are 4 to 1 against improving. In a $10-$20 game, you will need at least $160 in the pot to justify calling a raise to $40. In reality, you probably need more in the pot to call, as one of your opponents could have a set reducing your outs to seven, which is 6 to 1 against improving. This is an even bigger problem if the original bettor has the set, as he will likely reraise.

Chapter Review

❑ **Staying the Aggressor with Strong Hands**
- When acting early, generally continue to bet when you are unsure that an opponent will bet and giving a free card would be dangerous.
- When acting early against several opponents with a large pot, you might consider checking, hoping that a late position opponent will bet so that you can check-raise to drive out your remaining opponents.
- If a free card would not be too dangerous, a check-raise can sometimes be a good strategy to gain extra bets against your opponents.
- Almost always bet when acting last and your opponents check (see exceptions below).
- When you are worried that an opponent may have hit a draw and he checks, tend to check hands with outs and bet hands with few or no outs.
- Consider checking in late position when you are relatively confident that your opponents will fold, the risk of a free card hurting you is minimal, and the pot is relatively small.

❏ **Staying the Aggressor with Weak Hands**
- Generally only *consider* a semi-bluff against one or two opponents. A semi-bluff is rarely successful against three or more opponents on the turn.
- The type of board, along with the position and previous betting of your opponents, should give an indication of the type of hand you are against to help determine whether a bluff can be successful.
- Avoid bluffing a lot against weak opponents.
- Acting early can sometimes communicate a strong hand by your willingness to bet into one or two opponents.
- When acting late and your opponents check to you, a bet might win the pot since your opponents have indicated weakness.

❏ **Betting the Turn**
- When acting first with a strong hand, tend to check-raise if there is a good chance that an opponent will bet. Tend to bet out when a free card can be dangerous.
- If you are acting behind your opponents and it is checked to you, it is almost mandatory to bet a strong hand.
- Sometimes you might bet the turn as a bluff or semi-bluff. These generally are more successful when an opponent suddenly indicates weakness by checking, or a scare card comes.

❏ **Raising the Turn**
- There are three main reasons to raise the turn:
  - You have a very strong hand and want to get more money in the pot.
  - You have a semi-bluff opportunity.
  - You want to protect a vulnerable hand.

❏ **Calling Bets**
- The preferred strategy in poker is generally to raise or to fold, but there are times when calling is correct, especially with your strong draws and little chance of winning the pot on a semi-bluff raise.
- You rarely are getting good odds to draw on the turn, except for the premium draws to flushes and open-ended straights. Exceptions to this are when the pot is very large.
- Whenever an opponent bets and you are unsure whether or not you hold the best hand, there are four considerations in your decision to call or fold, assuming you have determined that raising is not a good option:
  - The probability that you currently have the best hand
  - The probability that your hand will improve to the best hand
  - The probability that your opponent will improve to the best hand if you currently have the best hand
  - The pot odds

❏ **Calling Raises**
- Most opponents who raise the turn almost always have *at least* top pair with a good kicker, and they often have two pair or better; therefore, you should often fold pairs when raised on the turn.
- In tight aggressive games, some opponents will raise the turn on a semi-bluff, especially in heads-up situations, so you *sometimes* need to call with a mediocre holding such as a pair depending on the circumstances.
- There are two situations when folding to raises on the turn with a mediocre holding such as top pair is relatively straightforward:
  - Your opponent is the type who never raises the turn on a bluff or semi-bluff.
  - An opponent has raised after two players have already called the turn.
- To call a raise cold, you almost always need a *very* strong hand or draw.

Test Your Skills

1/ $5-$10. You hold J♦ T♦ on the button. A middle player posts $7. An early player calls, the middle player checks, and you call. Four players see the flop of J♣ 7♥ 5♠. The early player bets, the middle player folds, you raise, and only the early player calls. The turn is the A♦. The early player checks. There is $44 in the pot. What do you do?

Answer: Bet, with the intention of checking the river. Your kicker may not be good and your opponent may have hit a good hand on the turn; however, a bet will protect your hand against a king, queen, or straight draw. You can safely fold if you are check-raised. An opponent who check-raises in this situation probably has either a set or two pair, such as AJ, A7, or A5. Note how betting and checking the river, or betting and folding to a check-raise, cost the same as checking the turn and calling a river bet. In the actual hand, the player checked and then called his opponent's bet on the river, who showed K7.

2/ $20-$40. You hold K♥ J♥ in the cutoff. A middle player calls and you raise. Two players see the flop of 8♣ 7♦ 5♥. The middle player checks and calls your bet. The turn is the Q♠. Your opponent checks. There is $150 in the pot. What do you do?

Answer: Bet. Stay the aggressor. Your opponent so far has indicated weakness on every street. Bet and hope your opponent folds. If your opponent check-raises, you can safely fold with only three weak outs. In the actual hand, the player bet and his opponent called. The A♣ fell on the river. The player bet a bluff with this scare card and his opponent folded.

3/ $1-$2. You are in the small blind with 10♥ 8♥. Five players see the flop of 9♣ 7♦ 6♣. You bet out and there are three callers. The turn is the 3♣. You bet, an early player raises and a late player reraises. There is $21 in the pot. What do you do?

Answer: Fold. Against several opponents who call a two-suited flop, there is a good chance that you are against a flush draw. Once an opponent raises and another reraises, the probability of a flush is very high. Although you can't be sure an opponent has a flush, it will cost you at least $6 to call the turn and a river bet. You also face the risk that the early player will cap the pot. Even in those rare cases where you do have the best hand, you could still lose on the river card. In the actual hand, the player called only to lose to Q♣ 8♣.

4/ $15-$30. You hold A♠ A♦ on the button. An early position player calls, a middle player raises, the cutoff calls, and you reraise. Four players see the flop of T♥ 8♣ 4♣. The middle player bets and the cutoff calls. You raise and everybody calls to see the turn of the 6♥. It is checked to the cutoff who bets. There is $355 in the pot. What do you do?

Answer: Raise. In the first section of the chapter, Staying the Aggressor, we discussed a concept that you should tend to check hands with outs and bet hands with no outs whenever you are worried that your opponent has hit a big hand. This hand is an extension of that concept, in that you should tend to raise with few outs and call with several outs. It is doubtful that the bettor has two pair as he would not call a raise preflop with T8 or 86. A straight with 97 is also unlikely.

Your opponent either has a set, where you have only two outs, or he has a pair or draw, in which case you are currently winning. If you are ahead of this opponent, raising should drive out the remaining opponents to give you a better chance of winning the hand. If your opponent reraises, you can safely fold your hand with only two outs. Note how raising and folding to a reraise cost the same as simply calling the turn and river, but a raise gives you a better chance of winning by driving out the remaining opponents. In the actual hand, the player raised, the early player called, and the cutoff reraised. The player folded his aces and the cutoff showed 88.

5/ $15-$30. You are in middle position seated with only $103. You are dealt A♦ A♠. An early player calls and you decide to slowplay and only call. The small blind calls and four players see the flop of K♣ T♦ 6♠. It is checked to you and you bet. The small blind raises, the early player calls, you reraise, and everybody calls. The turn is the T♣ and it is checked to you. You have $43 remaining and there is $195 in the pot. What do you do?

Answer: Bet. The small blind indicated he had top pair by check-raising the flop, and the early player may have a straight draw. If you check the turn, you will most likely call a river bet, so go ahead and bet to protect your hand. In the actual hand, the player checked. The Q♠ fell on the river, the small blind bet, the early player raised, and the player went all-in with his last $43. The small blind reraised and showed QQ while the early player showed J9! Both of your opponents would probably have folded to a turn bet. Author's note: I particularly liked this hand as I was the player with QQ...woohoo!

6/ $20-$40. You hold Q♠ 3♦ in the small blind. Everyone folds to you and you call. The flop is K♣ T♦ 2♥. You bet and the big blind calls. The turn is the J♣. There is $80 in the pot. What do you do?

Answer: Bet. You bet the flop on a bluff hoping that your opponent had two rag cards. If you bet the turn, you might be able to get your opponent to fold Ax, a pair of tens, or a pair of 2's. If you are called, you still have outs to the straight, possibly to another queen, and maybe even with a 3. You would call a bet, so go ahead and stay the aggressor by betting.

7/ $20-$40. Continuing with problem #6. You bet and the big blind raises. There is $200 in the pot. What do you do?

Answer: Reraise, with calling a close second. This is really dependent on your opponent. In small blind versus big blind situations, strategies become very aggressive. Your opponent could be raising with any pair. A reraise might get your opponent to fold a weak pair such as tens or 2's . On the other hand, some opponents will never fold a pair in a heads-up situation between the blinds. I like reraising against most opponents, as this cost you only one more bet to try and immediately win a decent size pot, and you still have a lot of outs if called. In the actual hand, the player reraised and his opponent folded.

8/ $15-$30. You hold 4♦ 4♣ in the big blind. An early player raises and another early player calls. The cutoff calls and you call. Four players see the flop of 9♦ 4♠ 3♥. You bet and the preflop raiser and the cutoff call. The turn is the A♥. There is $175 in the pot. What do you do?

Answer: Check-raise. This is a perfect turn card for you. You bet out on the flop representing a pair. When an ace comes on the turn, there is a good chance that one of your opponents has hit a pair of aces giving you the chance to check-raise. Even if they check, a free card is not too dangerous and they might make a crying call on the river. Another option is to bet, hoping that an opponent will raise, but some opponents may not be so aggressive. In the actual hand, the player check-raised the cutoff who showed A♠ 2♦.

9/ $20-$40. You hold A♣ 6♣ in middle position. An early player calls and you call. A solid conservative player on the button raises and the big blind calls. Four players see the flop of Q♣ 7♦ 4♣. The early player bets, you raise, and the button reraises. The big blind calls $60 cold and the early player caps the betting. Everyone calls and the turn card is the 9♣. It is checked to you. There is $350 in the pot. What do you do?

Answer: Bet. Trying to check-raise here would be a big mistake. The preflop raiser most likely has a premium pair since he made it three bets on the flop; however, with so much action, he might check with the three-suited board. You need to bet to collect more bets and charge your opponents for drawing to full houses. In the actual hand, the player bet. The big blind raised and the early player got stuck in the middle, as the player reraised and the big blind capped. The big blind bet the river and the player raised, collecting a pot of $1170. The big blind showed K♣ T♣.

10/ $15-$30. You raise in early position with K♠ K♣. The small blind and big blind call. Three players see the flop of 9♣ 5♦ 4♦. The big blind bets, you raise, and both blinds call. The turn is the 6♥. The big blind bets. There is $210 in the pot. What do you do?

Answer: Raise. The big blind did not reraise the flop, indicating his hand was not super strong. His bet on the turn probably means he is worried about giving a free card. He could have a set, but the betting patterns do not indicate this to be the case. You should raise to drive the remaining opponent out of the pot, especially with so many straight possibilities on the board. In the actual hand, the player only called and the small blind called. The river card was a 5 but fortunately did not help out his opponents. The bettor showed K♦ 9♦.

11/ $20-$40. You hold K♥ T♦ on the button. Everyone folds and you raise. The big blind reraises and you call. The flop is 9♥ 8♦ 3♠. The big blind bets and you call. The turn is the J♣. The big blind bets. There is $230 in the pot. What do you do?

Answer: Raise. An opponent in the big blind might reraise against a button raise with any pocket pair or Ax. You have an open-ended straight draw with an overcard for a total of 11 outs and 14 possible outs. You are going to at least call, but for one more bet you might be able to win the pot immediately by raising. In the actual hand, the player raised and his opponent folded.

12/ $15-$30. You hold T♦ 8♣ in the big blind. An early player, middle player, and the small blind call. Four players see the flop of A♣ J♦ 9♥. Everyone checks. The turn is the 7♦ and the small blind bets. There is $90 in the pot. What do you do?

Answer: Raise. The 7♦ probably has not helped the remaining opponents unless they have a flush draw, so it will be difficult to keep them in the pot. Your straight is also vulnerable to a split pot, so raise and charge your opponents a higher price for drawing. In the actual hand, the player only called and his opponent checked and called the river with KJ.

13/ $15-$30. You call in early position with A♠ 8♠. Three players and the small blind call. Six players see the flop of K♠ 7♣ 5♠ and everyone checks. The turn is the 6♠. The small blind bets and the big blind calls. There is $150 in the pot. What do you do?

Answer: Call, with raising a close second. There still are three opponents to act behind you who could have straight draws and weak flush draws. Only calling gives them a chance to contribute some more money to the pot. If you are lucky, one of them will raise. If you raise, you might drive out the remaining opponents and possibly the blinds since they will be worried about the flush. The risk in just calling is that the remaining opponents fold and another spade comes on the river drying up your action. In the actual hand, the player called and the remaining opponents folded. The big blind bet out the river of 3♣ and called the player's raise showing 8♦ 4♥.

14/ $20-$40. You hold K♦ K♥ in the cutoff. A weak early player raises and you reraise. The small blind and a strong player in the big blind call. Four players see the flop of 8♥ 7♣ 5♠. The early player bets, you raise, the small blind folds, and the big blind reraises. Everybody calls. The turn is the A♠.

The big blind checks and the early player bets. There is $460 in the pot. What do you do?

Answer: Fold. The early player raised preflop indicating a premium hand. To win you need to hope that the early player is bluffing *and* the big blind is not slowplaying a real strong hand like a set. This is a large pot but it will cost you $80 to finish out the hand, which is a little better than 6 to 1 pot odds. In the actual hand, the early player showed A8 and the big blind JJ.

15/ $20-$40. You hold J♥ 9♥ in middle position. An early player calls, you call, a late player calls, and the small blinds calls. Five players see the flop of J♠ 8♣ 3♦. The early player bets, you raise, and only the early player calls. The turn is the J♦. Your opponent checks, you bet, and your opponent raises. There is $300 in the pot. What do you do?

Answer: Make a crying call. You are probably losing this hand, except against a very weak or wild player. What hand could you beat that your opponent would play from early position and check-raise the turn? It is very doubtful he is playing J7 or lower. Your opponent most likely has a jack with a better kicker, 88, or 33; however, you are getting 7.5 to 1 pot odds to draw.

If your opponent has Jx, you have three outs to the 9 for a win, and six outs to an 8 or 3 for a split. The six outs need to be discounted to three outs since you will split. Six total outs is 7 to 1 against improving, so you are getting sufficient pot odds if he holds Jx. If he holds 88, then you have seven outs for a win, the last jack, a 9, or a 3. Seven outs is 6 to 1 against improving, which again is profitable. In the actual hand, a 9 fell on the river and the betting was capped. His opponent showed 88.

16/ $15-$30. You raise in the cutoff with A♠ A♦. The button and big blind call. Three players see the flop of J♣ 6♣ 5♦. You bet and both opponents call. The turn is the 7♣. You bet, the button raises, and the big blind calls. There is $295 in the pot. What do you do?

Answer: Fold. Whenever opponents wait to raise the turn, you need to be worried about strong hands. This is especially true when you are against two opponents. With this type of board, you need to be worried that one of your opponents has a flush, straight, set, or two pair. Even if you are lucky enough to currently have the best hand, your opponents still have strong draws to beat you on the river.

In the actual hand, the player folded. The button showed Q♣ Q♥ and the big blind J♠ 5♠. The player would have won the hand when the 7♦ fell on the river. Given his opponents' hands, the player actually had good pot odds to justify calling to eight outs; however, this situation was a best-case scenario given that neither player had a flush, straight, or set. Folding is still the best play in the long run.

17/ $1-$2. You hold K♠ T♣ in the big blind. An early and middle player call. Three players see the flop of K♣ 6♠ 5♣. You bet and both players call. The turn is the J♣. You bet, the early player folds, and the middle player raises. There is $12.50 in the pot. What do you do?

Answer: Fold. A flush or a set is a distinct possibility, especially since your opponent waited to raise on the turn. Even if he doesn't have a premium hand, your kicker is not very good. Most opponents at this limit will not try semi-bluff raises on the turn. In the actual hand, the player lost an additional $4 calling the turn and river when his opponent showed a flush.

18/ $20-$40. You hold K♠ Q♠ in middle position. An early player calls and you raise. The big blind calls and three players see the flop of K♦ J♥ 2♣. You bet and the early player calls. The turn is the Q♦. You bet and your opponent raises. There is $290 in the pot. What do you do?

Answer: Call. Your opponent probably would have raised or reraised the following hands from early position preflop: AA, KK, QQ, JJ, AK, and AQ. The likely hands that an opponent might play from early position and check-raise the turn include: AT, KQ, KJ, KT, QJ, T9s, and possibly 22. You win against three of these hands, split against one of them, and lose against two of them.

Unfortunately, AT and T9s are the more likely hands since you already hold a king and queen. However, you might be winning, and even if he has you beat, you have outs to a full house. With outs, I prefer just calling in this situation rather than reraising and face the risk of a capped pot. In the actual hand, the player called and his opponent showed T♣ 9♣.

19/ $10-$20. You hold K♠ J♠ in the cutoff. A middle player calls, you call, and the button calls. Four players see the flop of K♥ 5♦ 2♥. It is checked to you and you bet. The button raises, the big blind calls, and you reraise.

Both players call. The turn is the 9♠. The big blind checks, you bet, the button calls, and the big blind raises. There is $215 in the pot. What do you do?

Answer: Fold. With this board, the most likely hand of the big blind is a set. He called a raise cold on the flop indicating a strong hand. Most players will not check-raise the turn against two opponents without a very strong hand. In the actual hand, the player folded. The big blind showed 43 and the button KJ. Although you would have split the pot in this hand, calling in this situation in the long run would be unprofitable.

20/ $20-$40. You hold A♥ K♣ on the button. A player posts $20 in middle position. An early player raises, the poster folds, and the cutoff calls. You decide to only call. The small blind calls and four players see the flop of A♦ 3♥ 9♣. The early player bets and you raise. The small blind calls and the early player reraises. You decide to just call and the small blind calls. The turn is the 6♣. The early player bets, you call, and the small blind raises. The early player calls. There is $580 in the pot. What do you do?

Answer: Fold. You probably have the early position player beat or you both might split the pot. What should concern you is the check-raise by the small blind. Remember the advanced concept discussed earlier: Whenever a player raises *two* players on the turn, especially two players showing a lot of strength, he most likely has at least two pair. With this board your opponent probably has a set.

The other warning sign on this hand was the cold call by the small blind on the flop. This flop had no straight or flush opportunities and you have one of the aces, so you should immediately be concerned that a cold call indicates a strong hand like a set of 9's or 3's. In the actual hand, the player called and the small blind showed 99 and the early player AK.

21/ $20-$40. You raise with K♥ Q♥ in middle position. Both blinds call and three players see the flop of Q♦ 5♠ 3♠. You bet and both players call. The turn is the 8♥. You bet, the small blind raises, and the big blind calls. There is $380 in the pot. What do you do?

Answer: Call, with folding a close second. Whenever an opponent waits to check-raise the turn, you need to be careful. Possible hands of the small blind that have you beat include AQ, 88, 55, and 33; however, the pot is quite large and he could also be raising with a medium holding to protect his hand, hoping that the queen did not help you.

Possible hands where you are winning or splitting include KQ, QJ, QT, JJ, TT, or 99. He may also be raising with a semi-bluff flush draw or possibly A8, A5, or A3. There are many hands that you beat and only a few that will beat you. The cold call by the big blind indicates a flush draw. With such a large pot, I would call. Reraising with only one pair would be risky, especially since you will probably not drive any opponents out of the pot. In the actual hand, the player called and his opponent won with a flush showing A♠ Q♠.

22/ $15-$30. You hold A♦ K♦ in the small blind. An early player calls, a strong middle player raises, and a weak late player calls. You only call and the big blind folds. Four players see the flop of A♣ 5♦ 4♠. You check, the middle player bets, the late player calls, you raise, and they both call. The turn is the Q♣. You bet, the preflop raiser folds, and the late player raises. There is $315 in the pot. What do you do?

Answer: Fold. When an opponent waits to raise the turn, you usually need to be worried about sets and two pair, especially when they did not raise the flop. Possible hands of your opponent include 55, 44, AQ, A5, and A4. This opponent probably would have raised the flop with AQ and probably would have reraised A5 and A4, so these hands are the least likely. The hands most likely to slowplay are 55 and 44.

On the other hand, this is a weak opponent who might feel that AJ and AT are strong hands (although you would think he would have raised the flop with this hand). You will have to invest $60 to win $345, so the pot odds are almost 6 to 1. It is difficult to fold AK, but folding is probably the best decision. Reraising is definitely not correct. In the actual hand, the player called and his opponent showed AQ.

Note that your decision would probably be different if you were heads up on the flop. His raise on the turn indicates a lot of strength since he is raising an opponent who check-raised two opponents on the flop. Most players respect these types of check-raises. In a heads-up situation, you might check-raise with many hands, so your opponent may feel that AJ, AT, or A9 are strong hands. It is very hard to throw away AK against a lone opponent, but when there are several opponents in the hand, a raise on the turn usually indicates a lot of strength.

23/ $15-$30. You hold A♦ Q♠ in middle position. An early position player raises and you call. A strong player calls on the button as well as the big blind. The big blind is one of the top players at the site. Four players see the flop of A♣ J♥ 2♦. The early player bets and you raise. The button folds and the big blind and early player call. The turn is the 8♦ and it is checked to you. There is $220 in the pot. What do you do?

Answer: Check, with bet and fold to a raise being a close second. There are two worries in this hand. First, the big blind who is a very strong player called a raise cold on the flop. What hands could you expect to beat from a strong player in this situation? Maybe AT, but a strong player would probably fold AT either preflop or on the flop. Probable hands of the big blind include AQ, AJ, JJ, A2s, and 22, and you can't beat any of these.

A secondary concern is the preflop raiser who only called your flop raise. He could have several hands including a gut-shot draw, AK, AQ, KK, or is possibly slowplaying a set or AJ. Since you probably can't beat the big blind, go ahead and take a free card hoping for a queen.

You need to be confident in your read of your opponents to make this play. In a low-limit game, you should probably bet. If you bet and are raised, you can fold against most opponents, unless he is the type of opponent who thinks Ax is a great hand. In the actual hand, the player checked the turn. The river was the 7♠. The big blind bet out, the early player raised, and the player folded saving a bet on the turn. The big blind showed A♥ J♦ and the preflop raiser showed 8♣ 8♠.

The River

The river is a much different type of betting round, as now all cards have been shown. You either have a really strong hand, a busted draw, a medium holding, or a decent hand with worries that an opponent hit a draw. Most players make quick decisions on the river without thinking through the various possibilities. For example, should you always bet out when you think you have the best hand? The answer is no. Should you check and call a set when the board has four suited cards or four connected cards? Sometimes you should bet out, yet most players make the quick, most obvious decision, which is sometimes incorrect.

Betting correctly on the river is important as these are big bets and each bet made or saved can significantly add to your earnings rate. Some players tend to back off and lose betting opportunities when they are afraid someone has the nuts. Other players call too often on the river, just so they can see their opponent's winning hand. There are times when you can win the entire pot with a good bluff, or lose the entire pot if you fold the winning hand. These types of mistakes can be very costly. Think through each situation to be sure you have evaluated each possibility.

Don't Fold the Winning Hand

One of the most costly mistakes you can make in limit Hold'em is folding the winning hand on the river. You should always realize that you are getting significant pot odds to call. If there is $24 in the pot and you face a $4 bet, you only need to win once every seven times for calling to be correct. With the good pot odds, calling on the river is usually correct if you feel you have some chance of winning the hand.

The river is not the time to show your great hand reading skills and attempt to make a great fold, unless you are extremely confident in your reading ability and knowledge of your opponent. On the other hand, don't waste bets just to see your opponent's hand when it is obvious that you are beat.

Let's look at some general considerations to help you determine if calling is correct. One important consideration is the type of opponent you are against. You can fold your weak hands with more confidence against a tight player who never bluffs than if you are against a tricky player who is not so straightforward. Against these tricky players, evaluate all of the betting sequences in the hand to help determine if you have some chance of winning.

Another important consideration is whether or not the bettor could have been on a draw. An opponent playing a board of A♣ 9♦ 4♥ 2♠ is likely to have a decent hand; however, opponents might be playing a draw with flops that are two- or three-suited or contain two connected or even two gapped cards. A weak hand can win if your opponent is betting a busted draw.

For example, in a $10-$20 game you get a free play in the big blind against two early callers with 6♣ 2♣ and a T♣ 9♣ 3♦ flop. You decide to bet out as a semi-bluff into your two opponents and one of them calls. The turn card is the 4♦. You decide to bet again and your opponent calls. The river card is the 2♥. You check and your opponent bets.

You will lose if your opponent has any pair, but you should call against most types of opponents since they could have played an overcard, flush, or straight draw such as K♥ J♠, Q♦ J♦, or A♣ 7♣. You only need to win once every six times in this particular example for calling to be profitable.

When there are no obvious flush or straight draws on the board, you need to try to determine the strength of your opponent's hand. Does he have top pair or better? Is it possible that he was betting only overcards? Is it possible that he was betting a low pair?

Evaluate all the betting sequences in the hand preflop, flop, and on the turn to help you determine his possible hands. Once you have narrowed down the possibilities, you can evaluate the probability that your hand will win. Even with a small probability of winning, you might be justified in calling if you are receiving the proper pot odds. Do not outsmart yourself and throw away the winning hand on the river. Folding the winning hand on the river is one of the most costly mistakes you can make as you lose the *entire* pot!

Folding to Save Bets

The above section showed that it is often correct to call on the river rather than losing the entire pot for one more bet; however, sometimes you need to fold to save bets when it is obvious that you have a losing hand. Many players have a natural curiosity and want to *see* their opponent's winning hand just to know how they got beat. Don't just call because you want to know whether he hit a set or the flush!

Curiosity is a good poker player's worst enemy when it starts costing you a full bet on the river. Remember, a good player expects to make about one big bet an hour. If you call on the river one time per hour when you shouldn't, you are wiping out your entire win rate.

The tricky part is determining when you should fold. Use the same reasoning presented in the "Don't Fold the Winning Hand" section to determine whether or not calling is justified. Again, the type of opponent, type of board, and betting sequences should help you in your decision. If all of these considerations indicate with a high degree of certainty that your opponent has a better hand, you need to fold to save that bet; however, always consider the pot odds before deciding.

One important consideration when deciding whether to call or fold is the number of opponents involved in the hand. The more opponents you are against, the more likely it is that you need a strong hand to win. This is especially true when there has been a bet *and* a call on the river. You must have a much stronger holding calling the river against two opponents than you would need against only one.

If there were several opponents on the flop or turn with lots of raises, this also indicates that someone has a strong hand. Also, generally fold against an opponent who bets out into several players on the river with a scary board. In heads-up situations, opponents might try a bluff, but against two or more players, bluffing is not very common on the river.

Let's look at a common example when folding on the river is correct. You hold A♠ K♥ in early position and raise. A middle player and the button call while the blinds fold. The flop is A♣ 9♣ 5♦. You bet, the middle player raises, the button calls, and you reraise with everybody calling. The turn is the 2♥. You bet and everybody calls. The river is the 6♣. You bet, the middle player calls, and now the button player raises. What should you do? The most likely holding for this player is a flush, or maybe a small chance of either two pair or a set, but in either case you should fold since he has at least a pair beat.

Advanced Concept: Whenever the flop is two-suited and there is more than one opponent playing to the river, there is a decent probability that one of them is on a flush draw. This is especially true when they couldn't be drawing to overcards or a straight.

In the example above, the button player called a raise preflop and then called a raise on the flop. What are his likely holdings? A bet and a raise on the flop clearly indicate that one of his opponents has at least a pair of aces. If the button player has an ace, the middle player probably has the flush draw. Even if all three players have an ace, it is doubtful a button player would try a raise on the river with only a pair of aces against two opponents.

Let's look at another common example. You hold A♥ A♠ and raise in early position. The middle player and button call again. The flop is the A♣ T♣ 5♣. You bet and both players call. The turn is the 6♥. You are worried about a made flush, but you bet because you do not want to give a free card. Both opponents call. The river is the 2♣. You are beat. You might think, "I can't fold a set of aces," but you can! Save the bet! If you were heads up, you would need to call against some opponents and fold against others. Some lone opponents might try a bluff with this scare card, while others would only bet with the flush. Against two opponents with this type of flop, at least one of them had a flush draw.

Other examples that might give a strong indication that you are beat are when four parts to a straight appear or if a card is paired on the river. The previous betting sequences may indicate that you have the losing hand with these types of boards. For example, let's say four players call to the river and you were betting on every street with AK. The board on the river is KT52T and the small blind bets out. A player betting into three opponents will almost always have trip tens. If he bets into two opponents, you probably should still fold. If he bets into you heads up, you might need to call, unless you have a great read on your opponent and know he would only bet trip tens.

Be sure not to fold a winning hand, but don't make silly calls when you know you are beat. Save those bets!

Betting or Raising to Gain Bets

A common mistake made by many players is betting or raising the river whenever they think they have the best hand. Do not make this same mistake!

Advanced Concept: Only bet or raise a good hand on the river against a lone opponent when you have at least a 50% chance of winning when your opponent calls.

The key part of this advanced concept is when your opponent *calls*. Many times you will bet the river and your opponent folds. That bet hasn't gained you anything.

Let's look quickly at an example. You hold Q♥ Q♠ with a K♣ 5♣ 2♥ 4♠ 8♦ board. You bet out on the flop and are called. You bet out on the turn and are called. You determine that the most likely holding for this opponent is a flush draw. Should you bet the river? The answer is no, since your opponent will fold if he was on a flush draw. Betting will gain you nothing. A better option would be to induce a bluff by checking.

Many opponents with a busted draw may see your check as a sign of weakness and won't be able to resist betting as a last chance bluff to win the pot. In this case, checking gains you a bet while betting out probably gains you nothing.

On the other hand, if you are against an aggressive player who tends to call too often with weak pairs, then it is probably correct to bet. It is unlikely your opponent holds a pair of kings since an aggressive opponent probably would have raised either the flop or turn. He most likely would have raised a flush draw also at some point. In this situation, betting could be correct since you will win over 50% of the time when your opponent calls with a weak pair. The reasoning however is different. You check if you believe your opponent was on a draw, and you bet if you are reasonably confident that your opponent will call with a hand weaker than a pair of kings.

You need more than a 50% chance of winning when there is the risk that your opponent could raise with a better hand and you would call. In this case, you might lose two big bets against a very good hand and only win one bet against a weak hand, so you need more than a 50% chance of winning to justify this risk. For example, if you have roughly a 50% chance of winning a showdown but there is a 5% chance your opponent would raise and a 70% chance he would win when raising, you should just check and call rather than betting out.

For example, you hold KQ with a K548T board. You believe there is a 10% chance your opponent holds KQ, a 30% chance of KJ, a 20% chance of KT, and a 40% chance he would fold his other hands if you bet. You rarely would have a read this specific, but it is shown for example. Should you check or bet?

Let's play this hand 10 times and look at the scenarios. If you bet first, four times you will win when he folds but gain nothing, once you will split and gain nothing, three times you will win a big bet, and twice you will lose two big bets when your opponent raises two pair. Your net result is minus one big bet for an overall negative expectation. Remember, the money in the pot is already yours if you have the best hand, so you don't include this in your analysis.

Now let's look at the results when you check, assuming that your opponent will bet any pair of kings and check anything else. Four times you gain nothing when he checks, you split once, you win a bet three times against KJ, and you lose a bet two times against KT. The overall result is plus one bet for a positive expectation. It is actually more profitable to check this hand. It would be even more profitable if you induce some bluffs by getting your opponent to bet an inferior hand that he would have folded if you had bet.

You had a 50% chance of winning a bet in a showdown, but because of the risk that your opponent might raise, you were better off just checking and calling in this example. Things get more complicated if you take away the assumption that your opponent would bet any pair of kings. Some opponents may not bet a hand that they would call with. In the example, some opponents might not bet KJ if you check. In this case, you are better off betting out even though you have a negative expectation on the bet. Do you see why? You actually lose more by checking and calling if your opponent will only bet two pair.

To summarize, there are several considerations you must make when betting into a lone opponent on the river with a good hand:
- Probability that you will win in a showdown (should be at least 50%)
- Probability that your opponent would raise and you would call
- Probability that your opponent would bet a weaker hand if you check but fold this hand if you come out betting
- Probability that your opponent would check a losing hand that he would call with if you bet

Expanding on the second point, sometimes your opponent will raise and you will fold. This doesn't necessarily make your river bet incorrect. For example, you hold AA against a known opponent and a board of AKQ5T. Betting in this situation would be correct if you know that your opponent would only raise with the jack but would call with two pair and you are unsure if he would bet two pair if you check. If you bet and he raises, you can safely fold, losing the same amount as checking and calling. If you bet and he calls with two pair, you gain a bet. Your expectation is the same when he has the jack, but you gain a bet when he doesn't.

Advanced Concept: Sometimes it is correct to bet into a scary board on the river with a strong hand if you can safely fold when you are raised.

This rule does not apply against tricky opponents. If you are against an opponent who will bluff raise or do other things to try to win the pot, the decision process is a little more complicated. In this case, you need to compare the various probabilities of all of the possible scenarios:
- The probability of him calling and you winning the bet
- The probability that he will raise and you will lose two bets
- The probability that he will raise and you will win two bets
- The probability that if you check he would bet a hand he would not have originally called with

I realize that this can get quite complicated, so you just have to use your best judgment in the heat of the action.

Another option when acting first on the river is to check-raise. There are two reasons to try a check-raise with a strong hand on the river:
- To induce a bluff.
- To gain more bets when you are confident that an opponent will bet *and* call your raise.

For example, you hold Q♦ J♦ with a board of K♦ T♣ 5♥ 7♦ 2♦. Your opponent raised your flop bet and bet the turn, so you are fairly certain he will bet the river. This would be a good time for a check-raise to try and gain two bets.

This scenario would be different however if the board was K♦ T♣ 7♦ 5♥ 2♦. Do you see why? In this case, the bettor may be worried that you were on a flush draw since the *flop* was two-suited. A check-raise in this case might backfire if your opponent decides to check. You lose a bet if he would have called. Check-raises also gain you nothing if your opponent doesn't call your raise but would have called your bet.

Let's look at another situation quite similar. Most opponents are reluctant to bet when a scare card falls on the river that makes the board four-suited or four-connected, or pairs a key card, especially top pair; therefore, it is usually best to go ahead and bet into your opponent with a strong hand to try and gain at least one bet. Most opponents will call a bet to ensure you are not bluffing but are reluctant to bet and risk a check-raise.

Advanced Concept: Check-raising is risky when the board would scare your opponents from betting; therefore, usually bet out to gain at least one bet.

For example, check-raising is risky when holding A♦ T♥ and a board of K♦ T♣ 7♦ 5♦ 2♦. You should probably not try a check-raise in this scenario except against an extremely aggressive and maniac opponent. Most opponents would never bet this board on the river unless they have the A♦ or Q♦; however, most opponents would call a bet to make sure you aren't bluffing.

One more situation that occurs on the river is when you are against several opponents and are faced with a bet and you have a very strong hand. Sometimes consider just calling rather than raising your strong hands to get the remaining opponents to call. This is especially true if there is even a small chance that the bettor has the nuts and will reraise or there is a good chance you might split the pot with the bettor.

For example, if you hold Q♣ T♦ with a J♥ T♠ 9♦ 8♣ 5♦ board, you should just call if there are opponents behind you. You probably are going to split the pot with the bettor, so it is best to give your remaining opponents a chance to call. In addition, there is the possibility that your opponent holds KQ and would reraise costing you money.

Betting or Raising as a Bluff

As we discussed earlier, one of the worst mistakes you can make on the river is folding the best hand. On the other hand, getting an opponent to fold the best hand is a great achievement since you win the entire pot. The most common example of a bluff bet on the river is when you are on a draw and you bet hoping that your opponent is on a busted draw also or will fold a weak pair.

For example, you raise in late position with the 9♣ 8♣ and the big blind calls. The flop is J♦ T♦ 5♣. The big blind checks and calls to you on both the flop and turn and now checks again on the river. A bet here is correct against most opponents. Your opponent could be on a flush draw or a straight draw with AQ, KQ, K9, or Q9. You are probably getting sufficient pot odds that your opponent will fold.

Be careful on who you try to bluff on the river. Bluffs are generally more successful against strong opponents who are capable of folding a weak hand such as middle or bottom pair. Most weak players tend to call with anything. Determining whether to try a bluff on the river is simply an exercise of comparing the pot odds versus the probability that your opponents will fold.

Bluff raises on the river are generally not profitable, as it is difficult to get an opponent to fold who has already bet on the river, and you have reduced pot odds on your raise.

Internet Tip

On the Internet, bluff raises on the river are even less successful than in a live game. Your opponents have a tremendous curiosity to see your cards. They also realize that opponents on the Internet try a lot of tricky plays, so they are more willing to call. Bluff raises usually are only successful if you catch a player trying a bluff also, or you are against a very strong player who has the ability to throw away a good hand. Weak players will almost always call a raise on the end with any kind of hand, unless they were bluffing also.

However, there are times when you can identify an opportunity to successfully bluff raise on the river. Here is a hand in a $20-$40 game where I was fortunate that my opponent did not try a bluff raise. I had AA in the big blind. An early player called, a middle player raised, the button called, I reraised, the early player called, the middle player capped, and everyone called. There was $330 in the pot.

The flop was 5♥ 3♦ 6♥. I decided to check the flop and wait until the turn to try a raise so that I would have a better chance of driving out some opponents. The middle player bet and everyone called. The turn card was the 9♠. I checked to the middle player who bet, the button called, and I raised. Everybody called and the button was all-in at that point. There was $730 in the pot. The river was the dreaded J♥. This card was terrible for me, as now a flush was likely, or possibly the middle player hit a set. I checked. The early position player bet and the middle player decided to call.

I was fairly confident that the early player had a flush since he called a raise cold on the turn, but I still called since I was getting over 20 to 1 pot odds. The early player showed A♦ 7♦ and the middle player QQ.

I only bring up this example because the middle position player saved the pot for me. If he had raised the river, I would have folded since my pot odds would have only been 10 to 1 and all the action indicated a flush or possibly a set. The middle position player could have risked $40 more by raising to drive me out of the pot, hoping that the early position player did not have the flush.

A scare card on the river can improve your chances for a successful bluff. For example, a suited card falls, or the board pairs and you represent trips, or an ace comes on the river and you represent the ace. These kinds of plays can work against strong opponents because they have the ability to throw away hands on the river when they think they are beat; however, these types of plays rarely work against weak opponents as they almost always call.

The Worst Bet in Poker

Let's close out the chapter with one of the worst bets in limit poker: betting into a lone opponent on the river when there is a made hand on the board that is not the nuts. For example, the board shows 87654 and you decide to bet without a 9 in your hand. Another example would be betting into a board with five suits without another suit in your hand. This bet gains nothing because a lone opponent will almost never fold in this situation. The best thing that can happen is that you split the pot; however, if your opponent has a higher straight or flush and raises, you lose two bets.

I can't tell you how many times I see players make this mistake even at $20-$40, only to lose two big bets. I doubt that anyone who buys a poker book would make this kind of mistake, but I have seen it enough times that I thought it was worth mentioning. Note that this scenario is different if there are several players in the hand. In this case, sometimes you can get one or two players to fold if they are worried that someone might have the nuts.

Chapter Review

❑ **Don't fold the winning hand**
  • One of the most costly mistakes you can make in limit Hold'em is folding the winning hand on the river.
  • With the good pot odds, calling on the river is usually correct if you feel you have some chance of winning the hand.
  • An important consideration in determining whether calling is correct is the type of opponent you are against. You can fold your weak hands with more confidence against a tight player who never bluffs than if you are against a tricky player who is not so straightforward.
  • Another important consideration is whether or not the bettor could have been on a draw. A weak hand can win if your opponent is betting a busted draw.

❑ **Folding to Save Bets**
  • Sometimes you need to fold to save bets when it is obvious that you have a losing hand. The type of opponent, type of board, and betting sequences should help you in your decision.
  • The more opponents you are against, the more likely it is that you need a strong hand to win. This is especially true when there has been a bet *and* a call on the river.
  • Whenever the flop is two-suited and there is more than one opponent playing to the river, there is a decent probability that one of them is on a flush draw. This is especially true when they couldn't be drawing to overcards or a straight.
  • Generally fold against an opponent who bets out into several players on the river with a scary board.

❑ **Betting or Raising to Gain Bets**
  • Only bet or raise a good hand on the river against a lone opponent when you have at least a 50% chance of winning when your opponent *calls*. This should be even higher if there is a risk that your opponent could raise with a better hand and you would call.
  • Considerations when betting into a lone opponent on the river with a good hand include:
    ▪ Probability that you will win in a showdown (should be at least 50%)
    ▪ Probability that your opponent would raise and you would call
    ▪ Probability that your opponent would bet a weaker hand if you check but fold this hand if you come out betting
    ▪ Probability that your opponent would check a losing hand that he would call with if you bet

- Sometimes it is correct to bet into a scary board on the river with a strong hand if you can safely fold when you are raised. This rule does not apply against tricky opponents.
- Check-raising can be a good strategy with a strong hand to either induce a bluff or gain more bets when you are confident that an opponent will bet *and* call your raise.
- Check-raising is risky when the board would scare your opponents from betting; therefore, usually bet out to gain at least one bet.
- Sometimes consider just calling rather than raising your strong hands when there are still opponents to act behind you. This is especially true if there is even a small chance that the bettor has the nuts and will reraise or there is a good chance you might split the pot with the bettor.

❑ **Betting or Raising as a Bluff**
- Getting an opponent to fold the best hand is a great achievement since you win the entire pot.
- The most common example is when you are on a draw and you bet hoping that your opponent is on a busted draw also or will fold a weak pair.
- Bluffs are generally more successful against strong opponents who are capable of folding a weak hand such as middle or bottom pair. Most weak players tend to call with anything.
- Bluff raises on the river are generally not profitable, as it is difficult to get an opponent to fold who has already bet on the river, and you have reduced pot odds on your raise.
- A scare card on the river can improve your chances for a successful bluff.

Test Your Skills

1/ **$20-$40.** You hold Q♦ J♦ on the button. The cutoff raises and you call. The big blind calls and three players see the flop of 8♦ 4♣ 3♦. The cutoff bets, you call, and the big blind calls. The turn is the Q♥. The cutoff bets and you raise. The big blind reraises, the cutoff calls, and you call. The river is the 7♣. The big blind bets and the cutoff raises. There is $670 in the pot. What do you do?

Answer: Fold. You were beat on the turn and only called because of your draw. Even though the pot is very large, you cannot call $80 more on the river. The cutoff showed Q♠ 7♠ and the big blind K♣ K♥.

2/ $15-$30. You post $15 in the cutoff and are dealt A♣ A♦. An early player raises, a middle player calls and you reraise. Three players see the flop of K♣ Q♦ 4♦. The early player bets out, the next player calls, you raise, and they both call. The turn is the 6♦. They check to you and you bet. They both call and the river is the 3♣. They both check. There is $340 in the pot. What do you do?

Answer: Bet. If an opponent had two pair or better, they most likely would have check-raised the turn. In the actual hand, the player checked and his opponents showed K♥ T♠ and A♥ Q♣.

3/ $1-$2. You hold K♠ J♥ in the cutoff. A middle player calls and you call. The button and small blind calls. Five players see the flop of K♣ 6♠ 3♠. The big blind bets. The middle player calls, you call, and the button calls. The turn is the A♥. The big blind bets, you call, and the button calls. The river is the 5♠. It is checked to the button who bets. The big blind calls. There is $19 in the pot. What do you do?

Answer: Fold. Sometimes you can call a river bet against a lone opponent hoping that they are bluffing or betting a weak hand; however, whenever you are against a bettor *and* a caller, you usually need a very strong hand to call. In the actual hand, the button showed Q♠ 7♠ for a flush and the big blind showed A♦ K♦.

4/ $20-$40. You hold A♣ J♦ on the button. A middle player calls and you raise. Two players see the flop of 7♣ 5♠ 2♣. You bet and the middle player calls. The turn is the K♣. You bet and the middle player calls. The river is the 3♠. The middle player bets out. There is $270 in the pot. What do you do?

Answer: Call. It is difficult to know what hand this player is holding; however, this bet on the end is quite suspicious. He is calling all the way and then all of a sudden he bets out on a very innocent card of 3♠. Maybe he called with two overcards on the flop and then got a flush draw on the turn. Call and make sure he is not bluffing. Your call only has to be correct once every seven times to be profitable. In the actual hand, his opponent was bluffing with Q♣ J♥.

5/ $15-$30. You hold A♠ Q♦ in early position. An early player calls and you raise. The big blind calls and three players see the flop of 8♥ 4♠ 2♠. You bet and the big blind calls. The turn is the K♥. You bet and the big blind calls. The river is the J♠ and the big blind checks. There is $190 in the pot. What do you do?

Answer: Bet. When your opponent called on the flop, he most likely has a flush draw, a small pair, or two overcards. If your opponent hit the king on the turn, he probably would have check-raised. It is doubtful that he would call a turn bet with a hand like AJ or JT, so it is doubtful that the jack was helpful. Most opponents would bet out the river with a flush, afraid that you would not bet; therefore, the betting sequences seem to indicate that he has a small pair.

There are two high cards on the board, making it very difficult for an opponent to call a bet on the river with only a small pair. You only have to be right once every seven times for bluffing to be profitable. In the actual hand, the player bet and his opponent folded.

6/ $20-$40. You hold A♠ K♠ in middle position. An early player raises, a middle player calls, and you reraise. Three players see the flop of J♣ 3♠ 2♠. The early player bets, the middle player calls, and you raise. The early player reraises and the middle player folds. You cap the betting. The turn is the 4♣ and you both check. The river is the 3♦ and the early player checks. There is $390 in the pot. What do you do?

Answer: Check. Your opponent will call with any pair, so you will lose whenever your opponent calls, unless he calls with a hand like AQ. Check and hope your AK is good. In the actual hand, the player checked and his opponent showed T♥ T♦.

7/ $15-$30. You call in early position with A♣ 4♣. A middle player calls, another middle player raises, and the small blind calls. Four players see the flop of K♠ 2♥ 2♣. Everybody checks. The turn is the 8♣. You bet and only the first middle player calls. The river is the J♣. You bet and are raised. There is $285 in the pot. What do you do?

Answer: Reraise. Some players have a tendency to back off on the river when they see the pot in their grasps. Sometimes you should still take risks to gain more bets even though you might not have the nuts. The only feasible hand that your opponent could beat you with is 88 and maybe JJ or 22; however, these hands are unlikely based on the betting sequences of your opponent. The chances that you are reraised and lose are worth the risk of gaining another bet. His probable hands are KJ or maybe a small flush. In the actual hand, the player only called and his opponent showed a queen high flush.

8/ $15-$30. You hold K♣ K♦ in the cutoff and post $15. A middle player posts also. An early player calls and another early player raises. The middle player folds and you reraise. Only the raiser calls. Two players see the flop of T♥ T♣ 5♦. The early player checks and calls. The turn is the 6♦ and your opponent checks and calls. The river is the 7♣ and the early player checks. There is $235 in the pot. What do you do?

Answer: Bet. If your opponent had the ten, he most likely would have check-raised either the flop or turn. Don't be afraid to bet and gain another bet. In the actual hand, the player bet and his opponent called with AJ.

9/ $20-$40. You raise with K♠ Q♣ in the cutoff. Only the big blind calls. The flop is A♦ Q♦ 5♠. You bet and your opponent calls. The turn is the 4♣. You both check. The river is the 3♣ and your opponent bets. There is $170 in the pot. What do you do?

Answer: Call. Your opponent could have been on a flush draw or a gut-shot draw. He might also have a pair of queens or even a pair of 5's. When you check the turn in this situation, you should almost always call a river bet. You only need to be right 1 in 5 times for calling to be correct. In the actual hand, the player called and his opponent showed A♣ 9♥.

10/ $20-$40. You hold A♣ K♣ in early position. An early player calls and you raise. Two players see the flop of Q♠ 8♣ 6♦. You bet and your opponent calls. The turn is the K♥. You bet and your opponent calls. The river is the Q♣. Your opponent checks. There is $230 in the pot. What do you do?

Answer: Bet. Your opponent has shown weakness on every street. Many opponents are afraid to check trips on the river because they are afraid you will not bet. Go ahead and bet to try and collect one more big bet. In the actual hand, the player bet and his opponent showed 9♦ 8♠.

11/ $20-$40. You hold A♠ J♥ in the small blind. An early player calls and you call. Three players see the flop of A♥ T♣ 3♣. The early player bets, you call, and the big blind calls. The turn is the 7♠. You bet, the big blind folds, the early player raises, and you call. The river is the J♠. There is $280 in the pot. What do you do?

Answer: Bet. Check-raising is risky for two reasons. First, if your opponent's hand is not too strong, he may only check the river. Second, if your opponent holds a set, you will lose three bets by check-raising and then calling a reraise. It is doubtful that he has a pair of aces with a high kicker since he did not raise preflop. If he only has one pair, he will probably check and you lose a bet. If you bet and he raises, you earn two bets against two pair and lose two bets against a set. In the actual hand, both players checked and his opponent showed A♣ 8♥. Don't lose bets on the river with your strong hands.

12/ $20-$40. You hold 6♥ 2♥ in the big blind. An early player and the button call. Three players see the flop of A♣ 6♦ 5♥. You bet and the early player calls. The turn is the K♥. You check, the early player bets, and you call. The river is the 3♥. There is $190 in the pot. What do you do?

Answer: Check-raise. You bet the flop hoping that your opponent did not hold an ace. Once he calls the flop, you can be relatively confident that he holds an ace, unless he has a hand like 76, which is unlikely from early position. Your opponent bet the turn indicating strength. You only checked and called the turn indicating to your opponent that you hold a weak hand like a pair of 6's or 5's. There is a good chance your opponent will bet the river given the innocent river card. Check-raising ought to work most of the time. In the actual hand, the player check-raised and his opponent showed A♦ Q♥.

13/ $20-$40. You hold A♥ 7♥ in the small blind. The cutoff posts $20. The button raises and you reraise. The cutoff folds and only two players see the flop of K♦ 4♦ 4♠. You bet and the button calls. The turn is the K♥. You both check. The river is the 6♥. There is $200 in the pot. What do you do?

Answer: Check. If you bet, your opponent will only call with a hand that either beats you or you both split the pot. You have nothing to win by betting, and you risk that your opponent might raise with a hand that he was either slowplaying or a hand like middle pair. Checking might induce some opponents to try a bluff. In the actual hand, both players checked and his opponent showed 3♠ 3♥.

14/ $15-$30. You hold J♥ 9♥ in the cutoff. An early player and a middle player call. You call and the small blind calls. Five players see the flop of 9♣ 8♦ 5♦. The small blind bets, you raise, the small blind reraises, and you cap the betting. The turn is the J♣. You bet and your opponent calls. The river is the 6♥. The small blind checks. There is $255 in the pot. What do you do?

Answer: Bet. Most opponents are afraid to check-raise a straight with a scary board like this because they are worried that you will not bet; therefore, go ahead and bet to try and collect another big bet. If you are check-raised, you can safely fold unless your opponent is a very tricky player. In the actual hand, the player bet and his opponent showed A9.

15/ $20-$40. You hold A♣ A♥ on the button. A middle player raises and you reraise. Two players see the flop of 9♦ 7♦ 2♣. You bet, the middle player raises, and you reraise. The turn is the T♦. You bet, your opponent raises, and you just call. The river is the J♦. Your opponent bets. There is $470 in the pot. What do you do?

Answer: Fold. The only likely hands you can beat are KK and QQ and only if they don't have a diamond in them. Your opponent check-raised both the flop and turn indicating a very strong hand. Meanwhile, you need to ask yourself what your opponent thinks you have. You reraised preflop, reraised the flop, and called a check-raise on the turn, indicating a very strong hand also. Would your opponent bet out the river with KK or QQ without a diamond, hoping that you would fold AA with such a large pot? If he thought you had AA, why would he check-raise the turn?

You are getting tremendous pot odds, but there is no way you can win this hand unless your opponent is a total maniac. I suspect your opponent has either an ace high flush or KK with a diamond. In the actual hand, the player folded.

Playing Your Opponent

Throughout the book, we have talked about strategies to use against typical opponents. We have also discussed how you should alter your play depending on the type of opponent you are against. To raise your play to an advanced level, it is critical that you recognize opportunities to take advantage of each opponent's strengths and weaknesses.

What do I mean by playing your opponent? Some of the things to consider:
- Play more hands against players with loose starting hand requirements and fewer hands against tight players.
- Play more hands against players who play poorly after the flop.
- Don't bluff very often against loose players and play aggressively against tight players.
- Induce bluffs against loose aggressive players. Induce calls against tight players.
- After the flop, tend to call, raise, and reraise your borderline hands against aggressive, tricky opponents and fold against rocks who never bet or raise without a strong hand.
- Note that the playing style of your opponent preflop is sometimes different than after the flop.
- Generally try to sit to the left of maniacs and to the right of tight players.
- Mix up your strategies based on the flow of the game to keep your opponents off balance.

These are only some of the things you might consider. Let's discuss each of them in a little more detail.

Tight vs. Loose Players

One of the most important things you can do at the table is distinguish between the good players and the weak players. To take this further, you should distinguish between tight/loose and aggressive/conservative.

When a tight player enters the pot preflop, you should call less often, especially if they have raised. On the other hand, you can play more hands against loose opponents. For example, if a loose player raises in early position, I might be more inclined to play AQ than I would against a tight player. When your opponents play poorly after the flop, you can also play more hands since they will pay you off more when you hit a good hand.

After the flop, be very selective when you try to bluff loose players. They tend to call a lot even with weak hands, so it is difficult to get them to fold a hand. If they are also aggressive, you can try to induce bluffs from them since they are always trying to bet and win the pot. On the other hand, tight players will fold their weak hands and sometimes even top pair with a weak kicker, so bluffs and semi-bluffs have a better chance of success. Inducing calls is also a good strategy against tight opponents since they will probably fold to a bet with any kind of weak hand.

Aggressive vs. Conservative Players

Another important characteristic to look for in your opponents is whether they are aggressive or conservative. Aggressive players tend to raise a lot and will try a lot of deceptive plays. These players will often bluff whenever they are given an opportunity. On the other hand, rocks and conservative players tend to only raise with their very strong hands. You usually do not need to worry about them bluffing very often. For example, a check-raise on the turn from a rock is very dangerous! Tend to call or raise your borderline hands against the aggressive tricky players and fold these hands against the rocks or conservative players.

A good general strategy to employ after the flop is to play aggressively against tight opponents and conservatively against loose opponents. Try to bluff your tight opponents out of the pot. When you have a very strong hand and an aggressive loose player is betting, sometimes you should just let them continue betting rather than drive them out of the pot. Waiting to raise the turn or even the river is especially effective against these players. With medium hands against these opponents, sometimes you should raise when you feel you have the best hand to ensure they pay a higher price for their draws. *Observe your opponents and choose the best strategy that counteracts each opponent's playing style.*

Contrasting Playing Styles

One important note about tight versus loose players. A player's style can be different after the flop than it is preflop. For example, some advanced players play a lot of hands, but their post-flop play is excellent. Also, some tight players fall in love with their starting hands and tend to play too loosely after the flop. Be sure to identify each opponent's tendencies.

Position Relative to Your Opponent

One important tactic to help you in playing your opponent is your position at the table relative to your opponent. For example, you want to play more hands against poor players or maniacs; therefore, it is to your advantage to be sitting to their left. When they enter the pot, you can play a few more hands. When you are sitting to their right, you never know when they are going to play or raise, so you'll have to generally use your same tight starting hand criteria as normal. Another advantage of sitting to their left is that you can raise or reraise to try and isolate yourself against the poor player.

Generally it is also good to sit to the right of tight players, especially when the overall game is relatively tight. You should have more opportunities to steal the blinds. Your raises will tend to drive these opponents out of most of the pots. On the flop, you can often bet out and get these types of opponents to fold. Sometimes, however, it can be an advantage to have these types of players sitting in front of you. If they are so tight that they only bet the very premium hands, you can easily fold your borderline hands whenever they enter the pot.

There is one player who I love to play against for just this reason. He is a top player who wins a lot of money; however, this player practically never check-raises or slowplays. He always bets out his strong hands; therefore, when he bets, I can easily fold unless I have a super strong hand also. On the other hand, if he checks, I can try to steal the pot since I never have to worry about him check-raising. If he were sitting on my left, I would not be able to use this valuable information nearly as much since I would always have to act before him.

As a side note, one interesting thing about this player is that he is still able to win a lot of money because most of his opponents are not very observant and do not recognize this part of his game. My PokerStat software (discussed in a future chapter) was a great help when I saw that he had only check-raised five hands out of 5000!

Internet Tip

If you are on the Internet and want to change seats, view the lobby and see if there is a waiting list for the game. If there is a list, there is nothing you can do. However, if no one is waiting to enter the game, simply leave the game and then come back in so that you can select your new seat. Sometimes missing a few hands, even if you already posted the blinds, is worth the new seat, so don't always wait until you have to post again before moving.

Flow of the Game

You should also mix up your strategies based on the flow of the game to keep your opponents off balance. For example, if you have check-raised the same opponent a few times in a row with a strong hand, you might try betting out the next time. He might then suspect that you are on a bluff and may play back at you. On the other hand, if you have bet out a few strong hands several times in a row, you might want to check-raise.

Another thing to be aware of is the different moods of your opponents. An opponent's mood can change his playing style so always be looking for changes, this is especially true against regular opponents you play often.

Playing your opponent is an important skill to raise your game to an advanced level. Poker is not meant to be played using a formula. Observe your opponents and recognize their strengths and weaknesses so that you can use this knowledge against them. Knowledge equals opportunity!

Chapter Review

❑ To raise your play to an advanced level, it is critical that you recognize opportunities to take advantage of each opponent's strengths and weaknesses.
❑ Some things to consider when playing your opponent include:
  • Play more hands against players with loose starting hand requirements and fewer hands against tight players.
  • Play more hands against players who play poorly after the flop.

- Don't bluff very often against loose players and play aggressively against tight players.
- Induce bluffs against loose aggressive players. Induce calls against tight players.
- After the flop, tend to call, raise, and reraise your borderline hands against aggressive, tricky opponents and fold against rocks who never bet or raise without a strong hand.
- Note the playing style of your opponent preflop is sometimes different than after the flop.
- Generally try to sit to the left of maniacs and to the right of tight players.
- Mix up your strategies based on the flow of the game to keep your opponents off balance.

Bankroll Management

Let's go back to a statement I made in "The Skill of Poker" chapter: "If a good poker player plays 100 hours of $20-$40, he could win as much as $20,000, but once in a blue moon he might lose $10,000. A good poker player could only *break even* after 1400 hours of play. Given any time below that, he could possibly lose."

Does this statement surprise you? A good understanding of the fluctuations that will occur playing Hold'em should help you manage your emotions and bankroll; otherwise, this game can be extremely frustrating, and if you are not careful, you could lose your entire bankroll in a short period of time.

I'll be the first to admit that bankroll management is not the most exciting subject when talking about poker; however, I cannot emphasize enough the importance of having some basic understanding of bankroll management, earn rate, and the fluctuations that will occur in Hold'em. If you have an unlimited bankroll, feel free to skip this chapter. For the rest of us, your bankroll is your lifeline and needs to be protected. At the very least, this subject should help you understand better the significant fluctuations you will incur playing Hold'em.

Earn Rate

Your *earn rate* is simply the amount of money you have earned or lost divided by the number of hours you have played. A very good poker player earns about one big bet an hour in a full ring game; therefore, if you are playing $5-$10, you should make about $10 an hour. At $20-$40, a good player should make about $40 an hour. In short-handed games and heads up, you could even earn more since you have more hands per hour to benefit from your good play.

You should record your results by each game and limit that you play. For example, I record results for Texas Hold'em, Omaha Hi-Lo, and 7-card stud separately. I also distinguish between full ring games, short-handed play, and heads up, since each requires different skills. Finally, record your results for each limit such as $1-$2, $3-$6, $10-$20, $1-$2 pot limit, etcetera.

There is a software tool called StatKing offered by ConJelCo that is very helpful in recording and tracking results. This tool is discussed later in the "Record Keeping" chapter.

For players who play more than one table at a time, it is important to keep statistics for *each* table. If I play two tables at the same time, I will record the time played for both tables. For example, if I play for one hour on two tables of $15-$30 and win $200, I will record two hours played with a win of $200 for the session. This may not give you an actual hourly earn rate, but it allows you to evaluate your playing on an even scale.

Your *expected* earn rate could differ from your historical *actual* earn rate. If you have only been playing for 500 hours, you could have very different results in the future than what you have been earning so far. For example, if you have had relatively unlucky cards on average, your expected rate will be higher than your actual. You need to play a tremendous number of hours before you can feel confident that your historical actual rate is close to what you can expect to earn in the future.

For example, I have recorded over 3500 hours in my main game of $20-$40, but from a statistical perspective, I am still only 70% confident that my expected earn rate is within $10 of the actual. Statistically, I might expect in the future to earn either $10 more or $10 less an hour, depending on whether or not I was "lucky" over those previous 3500 hours. It takes a tremendous amount of hours before the cards start to break even. You can often run good or bad for hundreds of hours, which can significantly impact the earn rate you are achieving. For example, let's look at the possible range of earnings for a good player who ought to earn $40 on average playing $20-$40:

After 100 hours:	-$11,000	to	$19,000
After 300 hours:	-$14,000	to	$29,500
After 500 hours:	-$12,500	to	$52,500
After 1000 hours:	-$ 6,800	to	$87,000
After 1400 hours:	0	to	$112,000

These ranges show why it takes a long time before you can feel confident in expecting the same actual results to continue in the future. This is one of the reasons Hold'em is so popular. Losing players often have good runs, giving them the impression that they are good players.

For example, a poor player who normally loses $40 an hour could actually earn up to $10,000 over a 100 hour period by getting lucky! Once they experience a lucky streak, they keep coming back thinking they can win again at the same rate. Unfortunately for them, the law of averages will eventually catch up and they will lose back their winnings and even more, as long as they keep playing poorly.

Standard Deviation

Another important measure is your standard deviation. Without getting too technical, this measures the fluctuations you can expect in your play. Aggressive players who play a lot of hands can expect greater variances than a tight player does. The aggressive loose player will lose a lot most of the time and occasionally experience a big win, while a tight conservative player will not have huge swings either way. The higher your standard deviation, the more bankroll you need to handle the fluctuations in your results.

Calculating your standard deviation is outside the scope of this book. If you use StatKing to track your results, the software will calculate your standard deviation for you. For those who want more information on earn rate and standard deviation, Mason Malmuth provides all of the formulas in his book *Gambling Theory and Other Topics*.

The Bankroll

Using your earn rate and standard deviation, StatKing can calculate how much bankroll you would need to ensure never going broke and how many hours you would need to play to at least break even. For a player who earns $40 an hour playing $20-$40 with a standard deviation of $500, you could play up to 1400 hours and only break even. You would need about $14,000 to ensure never going broke. If you play $10-$20 with an earn rate of $20 an hour, you would need $7,000 and still 1400 hours to ensure you break even. At $5-$10 you will need $3500, and so forth.

Many players often ask how much money they need to play at a given limit. A good player who earns one big bet an hour needs about 350 times the big bet to ensure never going broke; however, most players need more since their earn rate is less.

If you are slightly more aggressive with your money, you can play at limits higher than your bankroll dictates; however, you just need to be sure to drop down a limit if things begin to turn bad. For example, let's say you have $1600 to play with. If you don't want to go broke, you should just play $2-$4. However, another strategy could be to play $3-$6, and if your bankroll drops to $1200, switch to $2-$4 and then if your bankroll drops to $800, switch to $1-$2.

People are different when it comes to managing their bankroll. Some players may want to "gamble" a little with their money. If you don't mind going broke, then you can take more chances. But if you want to play poker for the years to come, you must ensure that you manage your bankroll effectively.

A Sample Bankroll Strategy

Let's develop a bankroll strategy for the average player who wants to start playing Hold'em but can't afford to lose a great deal of money. This player would eventually like to earn a second income playing poker on the Internet, but can't risk any hard-earned savings or their spouse will quickly put an end to their playing days, lol. For example purposes, let's say this player has $500 to risk.

We assume that since this player is just starting out, he is not at an expert level; however, he has read and studied this book and therefore has the potential to be a solid player, :). The first goal for this player is to demonstrate that he can win. $500 ought to be enough to win at $.50-$1 limits. If you lose $500 at these limits, then Hold'em is probably not for you. You should demonstrate that you can win at least 100 big bets before moving on to another limit; therefore, this player should build his bankroll to $600 to demonstrate to himself that he can win.

For some people it may be difficult to play at these low limits. You can only expect to earn about $1 an hour on average if you play well, and for many people this may seem insignificant. However, it is better to gain experience at the lower limits before you start risking your bankroll at the higher limits. You could lose $500 very quickly at $1-$2 if you have a bad run of cards and/or you are still learning the basic concepts of the game. Hold'em is a game of patience and if you want to succeed within the confines of your bankroll, you must demonstrate patience before reaping rewards. This is no different than if you were investing in the stock market or trying to grow a business.

It should take about 100 hours of play to build this player's bankroll up to $600. Later we will talk about deposit bonuses in the "Promotions" chapter, but these bonuses might increase his bankroll up to $800. Now that the player has demonstrated success, he can begin to move up to higher limits. He can now play $1-$2, and if his bankroll drops down to $500 again, he should drop back down to $.50-$1 and start all over again. Once he earns another 100 big bets an hour at $1-$2 or $200, he should have a bankroll around $1000. Add another $200 for deposit bonuses for a total of $1200. With $1200 he can move up to $2-$4 limits. If he drops down to $800, then again he should drop down a limit.

Once he earns another 100 big bets at the new limit, he can move up another limit and so forth. You need about $2500 to begin playing $5-$10. You will probably experience a distinct increase in the level of competition at this limit, so I suggest playing a little more time at this level to demonstrate you can win against better players. Once you reach $5000, you will have demonstrated that you can beat the game at the lower limits.

Keep following the same process until you reach a limit that you are comfortable with. The following chart shows recommended bankrolls needed for moving up and down limits:

	Bankroll*	Avg. Hours of Play
$.50-$1	$500	100
$1-$2	$800	100
$2-$4	$1200	100
$3-$6	$1800	100
$5-$10	$2500	225
$10-$20	$5000	125
$15-$30	$7500	100
$20-$40	$10,000	

*Includes deposit bonuses opportunities

Please note that this strategy is for someone who doesn't want to risk losing his entire bankroll, while also allowing you to move up limits rather quickly if you are doing well. If things start to go bad, you need to be sure to drop down to the limit indicated.

Each person has different levels of risk they are willing to assume. For example, some people could not handle losing $500 in a day. If this is the case, you should never play above $2-$4. It is possible, although rare if you are a good player, to lose up to 100 times the big bet in any given session; therefore, be sure you are comfortable with the limit you are playing. Once you reach a limit you are comfortable with and have a bankroll of about 350 times the big bet, you should be able to play forever without going broke, assuming you are a player who earns one big bet an hour on average.

Some players might also have higher bankrolls to start with. If this is the case, you can start where the table suggests, but realize that you still need to build some experience. If you begin losing, you should probably drop down a limit quicker than the chart indicates. Some people may be more willing to risk everything and say, "I only have $1000 to lose, but I can't play for $25 pots; therefore, I am going to risk it and play $10-$20. If I lose it all, that is OK with me." If you are that person, that is fine. Just realize that if you hit a bad run of cards, you could lose your entire bankroll in one session and be finished.

Like anything in life, to be successful you need to make a plan. What are your goals playing poker? How much would you like to earn per week? Once you know your bankroll and the hours you expect to play, you can estimate how long it will take to reach your goals.

The sample plan above suggests that you will need to play 800 hours on average before you can begin to play $20-$40 when starting out with a $500 bankroll. If you have a $2500 bankroll, you could begin playing $20-$40 within 500 hours. Once you reach $20-$40, you could add over $1600 a month to your income playing as little as 10 hours a week.

Each person will have different goals. Just be sure to make a plan that is realistic given your bankroll, the limits you are comfortable playing, and the time you are willing to invest.

Chapter Review

❑ It is important to have a basic understanding of bankroll management, earn rate, and the fluctuations that will occur in Hold'em.

❑ A very good poker player earns about one big bet an hour in a full ring game. You need to play a tremendous number of hours before you can feel confident that your historical actual rate is close to what you can expect to earn in the future.

❑ A good player who earns one big bet an hour needs about 350 times the big bet to ensure never going broke.

❑ The following chart shows recommended bankrolls needed for moving up and down limits assuming you are a winning player:

	Bankroll*	Avg. Play Hours
$.50-$1	$500	100
$1-$2	$800	100
$2-$4	$1200	100
$3-$6	$1800	100
$5-$10	$2500	225
$10-$20	$5000	125
$15-$30	$7500	100
$20-$40	$10,000	

*Includes deposit bonuses opportunities

More on Internet Poker

Site and Game Selection

One of the unique features of the Internet is the tremendous selection of different sites and games. This gives an experienced player a great advantage, as you can evaluate all the games and decide which site and which game has the best action at the moment.

Site Selection

There are a tremendous amount of poker sites to choose from. Some of them are very large and some very small and they all have different things to offer. Let's look at some of the criteria you should evaluate in choosing a site.

- Financial Security: The most important criteria in choosing any site is the financial stability of the company. You need to be sure that you will be paid, and in a timely manner. A few sites have gone bankrupt and left their customers out in the cold. Traffic is a good indication in how a site is doing. PokerPulse.com is an excellent site to compare traffic for all of the different poker sites. The smaller sites could be under financial pressure if they are having difficulty attracting players to the site.
- Site Security: We discuss cheating and collusion in a later chapter, but it is important that the site does an effective job of monitoring the site for cheating and collusion.
- Software: To enjoy playing, it is nice to play at a site with user-friendly software. The most important criteria in evaluating the software is the speed of the game. Speed has improved dramatically at many of the sites, but some of the smaller sites still have issues with speed. Look and feel is also important since you will be spending a lot of time looking at the computer. Each site has different color schemes, presentation, and sound effects. Some sites use 3-D characters, just your name, or provide the ability to post a picture to represent yourself at the table.
- Games: This book is about Texas Hold'em, but there are many types of games available on the Internet. The most popular games that almost every site offers include: Omaha, Omaha Hi-Lo, 7-card stud, and 7-card stud Hi-Lo. Some sites also offer other games such as 5-card stud, Pineapple, Draw, and Razz. Although the sites *offer* the games, it is sometimes difficult to find active games other than Hold'em, especially at the higher limits.

- Limits: Related to game offerings, you need to choose a site that offers games at the limits you want to play. The most common limits range from $.25-$.50 up to $30-$60, although you can find limits as low as $.01-$.02 and some limits higher than $30-$60. Pot-limit and no-limit games are also very popular. Again, although the site *offers* a particular limit, sometimes it is difficult to find an active game going.
- Traffic/Number of Players: A site can offer a lot of games with a lot of different limits, but if no one is playing them it does not do you any good. The larger sites have a big advantage since it is easier to find the game you are looking for at any time of day.
- Tournaments: Almost all of the sites offer single-table tournaments and most multi-table tournaments. A new breed of player is developing which is the sit-n-go specialist, a player who primarily plays the single-table tournaments.
- Type of Players/Game: Some sites have games that are typically tight and aggressive, while other sites have loose conservative games. Some players don't like very loose or very tight games and prefer something inbetween. Choosing a site with the most profitable games is essential to increase your earn rate.
- Customer Support: When you have a problem, it is nice to get a quick response from the site. Some sites offer 24-hour online customer support and toll free telephone numbers, while others require that you send an email.
- Promotions: Deposit bonuses are a great way to add to your bankroll and are a good incentive to try new sites. Other types of promotions such as bad beat jackpots and freeroll tournaments can also give you good incentive to play at a particular site.
- Rake: As of the publishing of this book, there still has not been a tremendous push to differentiate in regards to rake, although there are some small differences, especially at the lower limits and for short-handed play.

My website, www.InternetTexasHoldem.com, reviews all of the major sites to help guide you in your selection process of a good poker site. The website is also a good resource to keep up-to-date with site promotions, deposit bonuses, tournament schedules, and online news.

Game Selection

Choosing a good game to play can dramatically increase your win rate. A popular poker saying is, "You could be the tenth best player in the world, but if you are playing in a game against the best nine, you are in trouble." It only makes sense to play in games with the weaker players. Good poker players are good fishermen. Find the fish, but avoid the sharks!

I generally use four criteria in choosing a game:
- Percentage of players playing the flop
- Average size of the pot
- Number of small stacks and large stacks
- Knowledge of opponents

One of the easiest ways to spot a good game is by the percentage of players playing the flop. Most sites indicate this percentage in the lobby next to each game. The higher the percentage is, the looser the game. This is usually a good indication of the overall quality of the players. Generally you find better players at the higher limits which is why you will usually see lower flop percentages at the high limits compared to the low limits.

How do you use this information? If I see a full ring game of $20-$40 where 35% of the players are playing the flop, my eyes light up. I should have a tremendous advantage if I only play about 20% of my hands. On the other hand, if 22% of the players are playing the flop, my advantage is very slight. I would expect to earn more money in the loose game where 35% of the players play the flop than I would in the tight game.

Another indication of the type of action is the average size of the pot. The size of the pot gives an indication on how aggressive or conservative the game is. If you see a really high average compared to the other games at the same limit, it might indicate that there is a maniac or two raising with a lot of hands.

I also take a look at the stack sizes of the players. Although another generalization, a small stack is generally an indication of a weak player; therefore, if I see several small stacks sitting at the table I will be encouraged to sit down. On the other hand, if there are a lot of average stacks and a few big stacks I will try to find a better game.

Finally, after a high level review of the games, I will look to see which players are playing in each game. If I spot a couple of weak players I have played before, I will jump in. On the other hand, I will avoid the game whenever I see a bunch of regulars who I know are consistent winners.

I also like playing against unknown players. This might indicate that they are new to the game or are possibly stepping up from lower limits. Maybe they lost a lot of money a year ago and are trying their luck again. Of course, they could be really good players who are new to the site, but it is better playing against opponents who could be weak rather than players you already know play well. If you are unsure about the quality of the players, simply watch the game for a few minutes before sitting down.

It is also important to be flexible in the limits you are playing. For example, if you normally play $5-$10 and see that all the games look really tough, it might be better to just drop down to one of the loose games at $3-$6. You might only be able to manage a $5 earn rate in a tough $5-$10 game, while you might be able to win $8 in a really loose $3-$6 game.

One note about jumping up a limit. I generally play $15-$30 and $20-$40, although I occasionally play $30-$60 when the game looks especially good. If I don't see any weak players in the big game, I will just play my regular game of $15-$30 or $20-$40 since I probably can earn more. When you want to start moving up limits, do so gradually and try to choose good times to move up to improve your chances of success.

The world of Internet poker is a huge ocean filled with many fish. If you don't find any fish at your regular poker site, start exploring some of the others. I play up to five different sites a week. I am constantly looking for the best action. If I can't find a good game at my regular site, I'll look somewhere else. I realize that if you only play a few hours a week, you may not want to spread your bankroll too thin. But if you have a bankroll at several sites, it only makes sense to "shop" around for the best game.

Hold'em Variations

This book focuses on *limit* Texas Hold'em in a full ring game of nine or ten players; however, there are other variations of the game that players like to play. These include:
- No-limit and Pot-limit
- Short-handed games (six players or less)
- Heads up

You could write a separate book for each of these different variations. They all have special considerations and strategies that you won't find in a full ring game. Generally you need to be an advanced player to be successful at any of these variations.

In no-limit and pot-limit poker, you can lose your entire stack on any one hand. This drastically changes the value of hands. Bluffing is a key component of strategy since most pots do not go to the river. You also need an excellent understanding of odds so that you bet the proper amount on each street to prevent your opponents from getting good pot odds to draw. Players who tend to go on tilt should definitely avoid this form of poker. On the Internet, these are played mostly at very low limits since collusion and cheating would give a player a tremendous advantage in this form of poker. The overall quality of players on the Internet in these games is not too good, so an advanced player could do quite well.

Short-handed games are very aggressive games with usually only two or three players contesting each pot. Suited connectors go down in value and high cards go up in value since there are not a lot of players who see the flop. Bluffing and semi-bluffing are again very important to strategy. To play well, you generally need to have an advanced level of play since a lot of the action is determined by *playing your opponent.*

Good players can win a lot of money playing short-handed since there are more hands dealt per hour to take advantage of each opponent's weaknesses; however, not all good ring players are good short-handed players and vice versa. Players who tend to play too many hands in a full ring game can sometimes do quite well in a short-handed game if they play well after the flop. I do not recommend playing short-handed games until you have a lot of experience playing the game. Your winnings will also fluctuate a lot with this form of poker, so be prepared for big losses occasionally.

An even more aggressive game is heads-up play. To be successful, you need a very aggressive style and ability to play your opponent. Most of your success comes from studying your opponent's tendencies to identify when he has a weak or strong hand. Advanced heads-up players have a tremendous advantage over their less experienced opponents and can win a lot of money; however, the fluctuations are brutal, so be prepared if you want to try heads-up play. To get an idea on some of the considerations for heads-up strategies, refer to the sections on big blind versus small blind play discussed in the two starting hand chapters.

All of these different variations of Hold'em are a lot of fun; however, I generally don't recommend trying these forms until you become a consistent winner at ring games. The short-term fluctuations in these games can be very discouraging to a beginning player.

Online Tells

A *tell* is an act or gesture that might give an indication to how strong or weak your opponent's hand might be. For example, in a live game, you might notice that every time your opponent throws his chips that he is actually bluffing. There are two types of tells. General tells indicate the significance of certain actions for most players. An individual tell is an action specific to a certain player.

Tells are only generalizations. This means that the majority of the time your opponent will follow the tell. For example, generally most players act strong with weak hands and act weak with strong hands; however, some players like to use reverse psychology if they realize you are the type of player who knows that "strong means weak." General tells serve as a good guideline until you learn more about each individual opponent. Once you begin to know your opponent, you should be able to identify that player's individual tells.

In live games, there are many different tells since you can see how your opponent acts during a hand. Players shake, look away, turn red, scratch their nose, slam their chips, or even say things that might indicate the strength of their hand. *Internet tells all relate to the speed at which an opponent bets.*

Before we discuss each of the online tells, let's look at the two ways you can act on the Internet to bet, raise, check, call, or fold. The most common way is selecting one of the several buttons that appears on your screen when it is your turn to act. The other way is to pre-select your action using the "act in turn" buttons. For example, you can select check/fold or bet/raise before the action ever gets to you. When you use these "act in turn" buttons, your action will occur almost *instantaneously* when it is your turn.

One note of caution when using these types of tells. If you look at the game list and notice your opponent is playing two tables, a lot of these tells do not work since the timing of his actions could be thrown off. Let's look now at some of the tells you can find depending on how fast or slow your opponent acts.

A delay followed by a check often indicates weakness

Most opponents who "think" or wait a longer time *than normal* and then check, are trying to suggest they have a decent hand. They are trying to indicate strength by "thinking" about betting, but they really want you to check so that they can get a free card. If your opponent was going to check-raise, he would generally check at a normal speed and then raise.

Note that tells are always given in relative terms. A check in poker usually indicates weakness, but it is the delay that your opponent takes to check that makes it even more likely that your opponent has a weak holding.

A delay followed by a bet often indicates strength

An opponent who "thinks" a long time and then bets usually has a strong hand. In this case, he is trying to indicate weakness by "thinking" a long time to lure you into calling.

An instantaneous bet/raise on the *turn* or *river* usually indicates strength

Most players who bet or raise *instantaneously* using the "act in turn" buttons on the turn or river generally have strong hands. Normally strong means weak when discussing tells, but I generally find that my opponents have strong hands in these cases. Your opponent thinks that you think he would never raise so fast with a strong hand; therefore, he uses reverse psychology and raises instantaneously to make you think that he is weak.

I believe these types of plays are meant to bully you into calling, so he *dares* you to call with his instantaneous raise. Don't let this bullying strategy work against you. If you don't know your opponent, generally an instantaneous action on the turn or river indicates a very strong hand.

This tell has varying degrees of reliability depending on the street. On the river, an instantaneous raise almost always means the nuts or a hand close to it. On the turn, it generally indicates a very strong hand, although some players will occasionally raise instantaneously with the intention of checking the river. An instantaneous raise preflop also generally indicates a strong hand, especially from early to middle position; however, if they are in late position and are raising a late position player, it is difficult to make generalizations since they might just be bullying their opponent.

I have found it difficult to generalize about players who bet or raise instantaneously on the *flop*. Some players raise with good hands, while others raise with weak hands trying to buy a free card. This is especially true with preflop raisers who try to buy a free card with overcards.

An instantaneous check usually indicates weakness

Many players use the check/fold button when they plan on folding their hand to any bet. This is especially true with players who are playing two tables. There are two situations where you can use this information to your advantage. Let's say you are in last position. The first player checks and the next two players instantaneously check. Since the two middle players probably don't have anything, a bluff might be successful against the lone opponent who checked early.

Another situation occurs when you are the player who checks early. If your opponents instantaneously check behind you, you might have a bluffing opportunity on the next card. These tells work best at the larger sites where use of this button is common. Many players at these sites play two games at once and use the check/fold button to quickly move back and forth between hands.

Two notes of caution related to this tell. Although not very common, be careful against some tricky players who might use the check/*call* button to slowplay their hands. Second, *there is a fine line between instantaneous checking and checking quickly.* Use of the *auto* check/fold button before another player has acted means that they would have folded their hand if their opponent had bet. This is very different than someone who checks very quickly once it is his turn to act. This leads us into our next tell.

A quick check usually indicates weakness, but beware if the player check-raises

A quick check can indicate weakness also, especially when there are several players playing the hand; however, if a player checks quickly and then raises, be very careful! When a player check-raises, the quick check was probably an attempt to indicate weakness so that you would bet into his strong hand.

Remember that all of these tells are generalizations. They work best against unknown opponents since you don't have any other information to go by. Once you have played with a player for a while, observe their betting patterns and then record what happens when they don't follow their usual pattern. Does his betting pattern follow the general tell or does he use reverse psychology? Some opponents use the "act in turn" buttons with both good hands and as bluffs, so an instantaneous bet from these types of players does not mean anything. Record notes on each player's tendencies or "tells" for future reference.

As a final note, try not to give tells about your own play to your opponents. There are two ways to do this. One way is to simply bet at the same speed throughout every hand. Another way is to *randomly* change the speed of your betting. For example, if the last card shown is a red card, you act after two seconds, and if it is a black card, you act after four seconds. This strategy will confuse your more observant opponents who are looking for tells and can't find any.

High vs. Low Limits

I refer to high-limit games on the Internet as $10-$20 and up, while low limits are $5-$10 and down. The following discussion is a generalization of the type of game you should expect to find at high limits versus low limits and some high-level implications on strategy. Again, as all generalizations are never correct 100% of the time, be sure to evaluate your game to know what type it is.

High-limit games are generally tight and aggressive. Many of the players have decent starting hand requirements and a raise preflop is common. They still will play more hands than they should, but they are usually good enough to not play hands like A7 or Q8s from early position.

In a tough $20-$40 game, you may only have about 20% of the players seeing the flop. A normal $20-$40 game is around 25% or 30%. In tough high limit games, full ring games with more than 30% of the players seeing the flop are not too common. In these tight aggressive games, a lot of your profit comes from bluffs and semi-bluffs, as many hands do not go down to a showdown. In general, your overall strategy of play will include:
- Raising preflop from good position to gain control over the hand
- Raising preflop with high cards and medium pairs to drive out opponents
- Folding middle suited connectors and small pairs most of the time
- Using semi-bluffs as a main arsenal of your play on the flop and turn

Low-limit games are generally loose and passive without a lot of preflop raising. Many players play a lot of starting hands with the attitude that any two cards can win. Once they win one time with a weak hand like 75s, they will keep playing the hand waiting for that next big win. Generally, more than 30% of the players see the flop and sometimes more than 40%. At limits such as $.50-$1.00 and $1-$2, 40% to 50% is not uncommon. These players will also tend to see the turn and river more, as they will draw to weak hands hoping for the miracle card. Many of these players don't realize that even when they improve their hand, they still might lose.

How does this change your overall strategy? Since many players will see the flop and make weak draws, you generally need to have the best hand to win in a showdown. It is rare to get all of your opponents to fold; therefore, your strategy of play is quite different than in a high-limit game. Strategies include:

- Raising preflop with premium hands that stand up well against multiple opponents
- Raising less often with borderline hands when you are first in preflop since it is more difficult to drive out opponents behind you and steal the blinds. For example, middle pairs such as 88 and 77 should only be called in early or middle position, whereas in a high-limit game you might raise to drive out your opponents
- Playing suited connectors and pairs more often, especially from late position since you are generally getting better pot odds with more callers
- Playing a straightforward game with little bluffing since you are generally against several opponents, and many players will call too often to the river with weak hands

Of course, these are generalizations. Some high-limit games are very loose while some low-limit games are very tight. Be sure to evaluate the type of game you are in and adjust your strategies accordingly.

Stack Sizes

Just like in live ring games, stack sizes can sometimes tell you something about your opponents. In general, the better players have larger stacks and the weaker players have smaller stacks for several reasons:

- The better players generally win, so they tend to have a large bankroll.
- The weaker players generally lose, so it is natural that their bankrolls are often small.
- Many weak players who play small limits will sometimes jump up a limit to try their luck, and usually don't have an adequate bankroll for the limit they are playing.

Of course these are all generalizations. Good players have bad runs and poor players have good runs. But you can get a quick generalization about new opponents by looking at their stack size when you first sit down at the table. This is especially true at the higher limits, which require more bankroll to play. Of course, after a few minutes of playing an opponent your impression may change, but at least you have something to go by when you first sit down.

There are generally two different playing styles for players with small stacks. The first type is someone who plays a lot of hands, which is probably why his stack is so low. The other type of player is one who just moved up from a lower limit game. This player probably is playing very tight since he is scared of losing a lot of money. With either type of player, you can use this information to your advantage. Play aggressively against the scared player and don't try to bluff the loose player.

The one exception to this rule is when their stack becomes so low that they will go broke with just a few more bets. In this case, both types of players generally tighten up a lot waiting for that big hand. Now you can be aggressive both preflop and flop. Be inclined to try and steal their blinds. On the flop, try to be the aggressor and then back off if your opponent either bets first or raises. Since he is playing survival poker, it is doubtful that he is bluffing. I love playing against very small stacks! An aggressive style against these opponents will usually reap good rewards, and the risk is small since you can back off if your opponent shows any signs of strength.

Regarding your own stack, avoid playing with a stack so small that you cannot get full value out of a big hand. If you are playing $10-$20 and your stack gets down to $100, you could easily run out of chips by the end of the hand. If you are playing a tight aggressive strategy recommended in this book, you do not want this to happen. If at all possible, always re-buy chips to add to your stack before you get too low. This means a minimum stack of 10 times the big bet. So in a $10-$20 game, you need at least $200 in your stack before any given hand.

You never know when you will hit a monster hand against a maniac who keeps raising you back. Although 10 times the big bet is the minimum I recommend, I prefer to sit down with at least 40 times the big bet to minimize the chance that I might have to add chips later.

Multiple Tables

Internet poker has two advantages in regards to speed when compared to live games. First, Internet games go much quicker than live games. You don't have to wait for dealers to shuffle, you can use the "act in turn" buttons, there are never any misdeals, there are no mistakes with chips, and there is a set time limit to act. Second, you can play two, three, or even four tables at the same time! Playing one hour of Internet poker at two tables is the equivalent of playing three to four hours in a live game.

Playing multiple tables is a great advantage for good players who are able to increase their overall hourly earn rate; however, there are also several disadvantages that can sometimes destroy your earn rate.

How to Play Multiple Tables

There are several ways to play multiple tables. You can play two tables simultaneously at the same poker site. Most poker sites allow this, although there are a few exceptions. The other way is to play one table at two different poker sites.

From a technical perspective, there are two ways to play two tables on your computer screen. Most players simply sit down at two tables and then switch back and forth between the two tables. Another option is to reduce the screen size for each table, so that you can see both tables on the screen at the same time. To do this, right click on your desktop and select properties, then settings, and then adjust the screen area. You will need to increase the pixels to reduce the size of each table. For those with poor eyesight, beware! The screens will be very small. Also, some older monitors may not be able to handle changes in pixels, so only try this with newer models. For those who don't mind the small screens, this method has a few benefits since you can follow the action better at both tables. I prefer switching back and forth between the screens since the small screens are not very good on my eyes for long periods of time.

It is also possible to play three or more tables at the same time; however, this is not recommended. It requires a great deal of concentration that makes you prone to make errors. If you do play three sites, it is easier when you play a couple of games at a site with slow software, and then the third game with fast software. A few sites will allow you to play three tables simultaneously, but this can get quite confusing at times.

Advantages and Disadvantages

There are advantages and disadvantages in playing more than one table. Of course, only try multiple tables if you are a winning player, otherwise you will lose your money twice as fast! If you are a winning player, there are still some downsides that must be considered.

First, you can sometimes make mistakes by hitting the wrong button. For example, you might call when you actually meant to fold, decreasing your earn rate for that table. Most importantly, because you are playing two tables, it is more difficult to evaluate your opponents. You will not be able to follow all of the betting sequences and see all of the showdowns.

It takes a great deal of concentration to try to learn the playing styles of 18 players at the same time. I only try playing two tables when I am fresh and alert, and am already familiar with many of the players I am playing with. For example, I might play a game where I am familiar with almost all the players, and then play another game at another site. I'll concentrate more on the action and players at the second site to learn their styles.

Your earning rate per table will inevitably decrease since you are unable to fully concentrate on every hand at each table. For example, you may not notice that a player has gone on tilt and is betting and raising every hand. You then might fold a hand that you would have called or raised had you known this opponent was playing so loose. Therefore, if you normally earn one big blind an hour at one table, do not expect to earn the same rate at two tables simultaneously.

You will also experience greater variances by playing two tables at the same time. Sometimes you will lose at both and lose a lot of money in a short time. This is a big problem if you tend to go on tilt. When playing at two tables, there are more opportunities for something to go wrong. If you lose two bad beats pretty close together and then go on tilt, you are jeopardizing your bankroll at two tables. If you are like many players who get too upset when something goes wrong, I would not recommend playing at two tables.

Although there are downsides, there is a great advantage to playing more than one table. You can increase your *overall* hourly earning rate. For example, let's assume that you average one big bet an hour playing one table. If you are playing two tables simultaneously, you should expect your earning rate to decrease per table. If it decreases to 1/2 a big bet per hour, you will be earning the same per hour at two tables but with greater fluctuations. However, if your earn rate only decreases to 3/4 a big bet per hour, your overall hourly rate will increase to 1.5 big bets per hour.

For example, you usually earn $40 an hour playing $20-$40. By playing two tables, your earn rate might drop to $30 per table, but now you are making $60 an hour!

The ability to play multiple tables is a great advantage over live poker games. For good players, this can add to your earning rate per hour and is more fun since there is more action. However, playing multiple tables is not recommended until you are a very solid player, and should only be done when you are at your full concentration potential.

Record Keeping/ Player Analysis

One great advantage to playing on the Internet is the ease in being able to take notes while playing. I have seen some players take a notebook to a live poker game, but this is a tedious exercise and communicates to the other players that you are a serious player. There are three types of record keeping that I find helpful:

1. **Earnings results:** At a minimum, you should record your gain/loss and time played for each poker session.
2. **Player analysis:** Since you will be playing hundreds and even thousands of different opponents, it is to your advantage to record notes on your opponents and their various playing styles.
3. **Hand analysis:** Recording the results of various hands and the strategies you employed can help you better evaluate your individual play.

Let's discuss each of these in more detail and some of the tools available to make this an easier task.

Earnings Results

Every player should record the gain/loss, time, site, game, and limit for each session. With this information, you can calculate your earnings rate at each game to track how you are doing. This helps you to constantly evaluate your game and benchmark yourself to other players.

In general, a very good to advanced player can expect to earn about one big bet an hour at a full table Hold'em game. If you are averaging below one big bet an hour, then you know there is something in your game that needs improvement (given enough hours to have a statistically viable sample).

One of the great tools on the market is StatKing offered by ConJelCo. StatKing is basically a statistical database where you are able to record your results for each session and then evaluate them in many different ways. You simply input the date, site, game, limit, hours, and gain/loss for each playing session. StatKing will then calculate your earn rate and standard deviation by month, year, or any other time period. You can also sort by game, limit, site, or any combination of the three.

There is also a helpful function that tells you how much bankroll you need, what your earning rate is within a certain probability, and how much you could win or lose in a 10-hour or 100-hour time period. You could just use a spreadsheet to do all of this yourself, but for a small price I find StatKing invaluable.

Player Analysis

Your opponents have many different playing styles. Some players are rocks who never bluff and only raise with the nuts, while others are loose attacking every pot. You can save and earn bets when you know what type of player you are playing. Since you cannot see faces, it is difficult to just "know" all of your opponents by name alone. Taking notes on your opponents helps a lot if you play with a player and then don't see him for several weeks or months later.

Most sites allow you to record notes about the players on the site. You simply right click on the opponent and you are able to record notes on that player that are easily accessible. You should record general notes on their play as well as specific notes on how hands were played. An example of a general note might be, "weak player, loose starting hands, calls too much to the river, and likes check raise bluffs on the turn." In addition, I developed a short hand notation to record how they have played various hands. For example, "cR66BB" means that the player called a raise in the big blind with 66.

After recording many of the hands that your opponents play, you can begin to get a feel for the quality of their starting hands and the strategies they use after the flop. When does he raise the flop? Does he ever semi-bluff? Does a check-raise always mean a very strong hand? Answers to these questions can save and earn you bets.

If the site doesn't have a feature where you can record notes, another way is to simply record notes in a spreadsheet while you are playing. Simply sort the players you are playing to the top of the spreadsheet, and then toggle back and forth between the game and the spreadsheet.

In addition to taking notes while you are playing, I highly recommended that you take advantage of the hand histories that you can request from the site. This is a great tool to evaluate each opponent's play away from the game so that you are not distracted.

Advanced Concept: One great advantage to using hand histories is that you are allowed to see your opponents' cards if they call the river, even though they might not show their cards in actual play when they lose. This can help you learn more about each opponent quicker.

There are a couple of software tools, Poker Tracker and PokerStat, which make it even easier to evaluate your opponents. Both products will automatically download your hand histories into the software so that you can evaluate a variety of things about your play and that of your opponents.

The software also calculates your earning rate for your play, although I still recommend using StatKing to track earnings. However, both software programs will calculate the earnings results of your opponents! You can easily see exactly how much each of your opponents has earned or lost while playing at a table with you. In addition to their earn rate, you can see a great deal of information about your opponent:

- How often they call preflop
- How often they raise
- What percentage of the time they play to a showdown
- How often they defend their blinds against a raise from late position
- How often they will try to steal the blinds from late position
- What percentage of showdowns do they win

This is just a sample of the information you can evaluate. You can also ask the software to list all of the hands you have played with a particular opponent. Of course, you still can't see their hand if they folded, but you will be able to go through their hands pretty quickly to get a feel for their play. For those opponents I play against a lot, I will sort their hands to look for specific tendencies. For example, you can ask for all the hands where the player check-raises. You can then see if this opponent will only check-raise with very strong hands or sometimes will semi-bluff.

The software also allows you to evaluate all of the hands that you play, which is discussed more in the next section of the chapter.

Both of these products are evolving quickly with new features added each month. I suggest evaluating both products online for their most up-to-date features and pricing information. PokerStat can be found at http://www.thsoftware.com and Poker Tracker at www.pokertracker.com. Both sites offer a free download of a demo database to try out the software.

Hand Analysis

It is also very important to constantly evaluate your game and see which strategies and hands are most profitable. For example, how profitable is 33 when played in late position? What about KT? AK? I read about a poker professional who kept a notebook for over a year and a half in a live game recording notes on every single hand that he played. He then returned home and recorded his notes into a database in his computer to evaluate the results for every single hand. This gave him a great tool to evaluate what is profitable and what is not!

However, this is a tremendous amount of work. Poker Tracker and PokerStat allow you to do this almost automatically. With these tools, you can evaluate every hand you have played and use filters to look at almost every type of situation you can imagine. You can sort by number of players at the table, position, and hands where you raised preflop, etc. For example, this tool can help you determine how many callers you need for various hands to be profitable from each position.

There is no better way to evaluate your play and look for leaks in your game. If you are playing hands that are unprofitable, these software programs can quickly identify the problem. You can also use the software to identify other leaks in your game after the flop. If you are serious about improving your game, these products are an indispensable tool.

Promotions

Promotions are a great way to add to your bankroll every month. I earn a little over $100 a month on average by taking advantage of the various promotions the sites offer. Some of the types of promotions include bad beat jackpots, high hand of the day, and bonuses for when a site reaches a certain milestone for hands dealt. My favorite promotion is the deposit bonus because it is free money deposited directly into my account!

The deposit bonus requires that you deposit money into your account, and in return you are awarded a bonus, generally between 20% and 25% of your deposit. To withdraw the bonus, you simply have to play a certain number of hands, which is usually five times the bonus amount. Each site has slightly different rules on how they work, but the concept is basically the same. Most sites also have a new member sign-up bonus, which usually can be up to $50.

Deposit bonuses are a great way for low-limit players to build a bankroll so that they can move to higher limits more quickly. Open an account in a new site to take advantage of the new member bonus. Once you have played enough hands, withdraw your money and start up an account at a new site. Keep doing this at six or seven reputable sites and your bankroll should build up quickly. Once you have exhausted the new member bonuses, the sites will still continue to offer other deposit bonuses from time to time that you can take advantage of.

One warning about deposit promotions from new sites. New sites try to build traffic by offering deposit bonuses to new players. Be very careful whenever depositing money into new sites that are not backed by a reputable company, as several have gone bankrupt and left with the players' money. I have been a victim twice and do not plan on becoming one again. If you do decide to play at a new site, keep your bankroll small. These bonuses are great, but only when backed by a reputable site where your money is safe.

Many sites now offer "points" for each hand that you play. You can use these points to purchase merchandise or enter various tournaments they offer. These tournaments are an excellent bargain since you are getting a chance to win a big prize without having to commit any of your own money. Some of these tournaments offer up to $25,000 in prize money. Almost all of the sites also have tournaments where you can win seats into special live tournaments such as the World Series of Poker or other tournaments offered in exotic locations such as Australia and Aruba. These are a great opportunity for players to get a chance at a major live event.

My website, www.InternetTexasHoldem.com, has a page summarizing all of the best promotions currently being offered by all of the major sites. The promotions are broken down by new member deposit bonuses, special deposit bonuses, and special promotions.

Tournaments

An exciting form of poker is tournaments, which continue to gain popularity on the Internet and in the live poker world. Tournaments are growing within the States and all over the world in places such as Europe, Russia, Costa Rica, and Australia. I developed a lot of my no-limit skills playing tournaments in Costa Rica and have been hooked ever since. In 2002, I was fortunate enough to win the New Zealand Poker Championship, which was an exciting break from my online endeavors. Tournaments are fun and exciting and quite an adrenaline rush when you are able to win a nice prize for just a small investment.

Of course, the biggest poker event of the year is the World Series of Poker held every year in Las Vegas where the champion of the main event in 2003 took home $2.5 million dollars! What was exciting about this year's winner, Chris Moneymaker, is that he won his 10K entry by playing a $40 satellite tournament online and had never played a live tournament before!

The scope of this book does not include tournament play. If you become a profitable ring player, the strategies you use can help you become an effective tournament player also; however, you will need to make many adjustments to your ring game in tournaments to consistently end up in the money. Just be aware that if you do play a lot of tournaments, there are several books that can help you on what kind of adjustments you ought to make in your play.

One excellent site to practice tournaments is at PokerSchoolOnline.com. The owner of PokerPages.com, a popular poker portal, runs this site. At Poker School Online, you pay either a monthly or annual fee for use of the services. Play money tournaments are run every single hour and the competition is quite good to hone your skills. The school offers prizes each month to the better players who can use the money to enter any live tournament they choose.

Practically every poker site now offers real money poker tournaments including heads-up tourneys, sit-n-go's or single table tourneys, and multi-table tournaments. Some tournaments can have literally thousands of participants. Many sites also offer the opportunity to participate in free tournaments or "freerolls," which are offered as promotions on occasion to their frequent players. Take advantage of these promotions to gain experience in this fun and exciting form of poker.

Collusion and Cheating

Many players are concerned about collusion and cheating on the Internet. Some avoid playing online for just this reason. There are conspiracy theories that the poker sites cheat their own customers. Some people don't trust computers and the Internet and believe other players can hack into the system to actually "see" the cards. Others simply believe that a lot of players collude online by either playing with two computers or talking to a buddy on the phone.

The first two concerns, conspiracy and hacking, are not very valid concerns. Poker sites have nothing to gain by cheating their own customers. It takes a significant amount of money to invest in software, marketing, and customer support to start-up a site. Sites are willing to invest this money for the tremendous income potential the site can earn from the rake. Why risk this income and their integrity by cheating their customers?

One popular theory is the "cash out curse." Some players believe that some sites will blacklist you once you have cashed out so that your cards start to run cold. What would the sites gain by doing this? They earn the rake in every game no matter who wins the pot. Good and bad runs are just an inherent part of the game, which explains why it often seems that you hit a bad run just after a nice run of the cards.

Another common worry is that computer hackers could somehow break into the system to "see" the cards of their opponents while they are playing. I am not a computer hacking expert; however, if this were possible, these sites would not be in business very long. Somehow I manage to make money, which would be very difficult if players could see my cards, :).

Collusion and cheating between players is a valid concern, just as it is in live games. It is quite easy for players to connect online with two different computers or call a buddy on the telephone. Being able to play two hands at the same table is an added advantage.

First, you have a better idea if your outs are counterfeited. For example, if one player holds KQ and another player QJ, both players would be better off folding since their queen is a weak out. On the other hand, if one player holds KQ and another JT, they have a good chance of hitting something on the flop between the two of them.

Second, two players can work together to build a larger pot when one of the players has a super strong hand. For example, if one player flops a set and bets out, the other player could raise even though he has absolutely nothing. This raise charges the other players more money for playing in a pot his partner is likely to win. Third, your partner can help you drive out the other opponents by raising and reraising.

Although players are able to collude, one great advantage to the Internet is that the poker site has access to everyone's cards. In a casino, the players' cards are often buried in the muck making it difficult to detect cheating. On the Internet, most sites have sophisticated detection programs that can look for unusual play or earnings that are unusually high.

If you suspect that two players are colluding together, contact the customer support team of the particular site to investigate. PokerStat software actually has a feature that will evaluate whether two players have potentially been colluding.

Another thing to realize about cheating is that good players don't need to cheat! The players who are most likely to cheat are the players who can't win otherwise. I know of a player who decided to connect two computers in his house so he could collude online. Unfortunately for him, he is not a very good player and lost several thousand dollars very quickly. Although it is an advantage to see the cards of two players, it still is not enough of an advantage to turn a losing player into a winning player. People might try to cheat, but if they aren't good players to start with, they still will find that winning is difficult.

Colluding and cheating occurs; however, the more important question is how much does this impact your earn rate. I believe the impact is quite negligible, especially when looking at the benefits of playing online versus a live casino. In a casino, you have to overcome the rake, parking, gas, meals, and most importantly tips, to make your session profitable. On the Internet, you have to overcome the rake and some collusion that might be taking place. I believe the tips you pay in a casino are far more than any money you might lose through collusion on the Internet.

Another form of cheating is abuse of the all-in feature. If a player gets disconnected, he still has a chance of winning the pot without investing any additional money. Some players abuse this feature and will intentionally disconnect themselves. Unfortunately, there is not much you can do when this happens. The only thing you can really do is contact customer support so that they will monitor the player and prevent him from playing if he abuses the all-in feature too often.

The bottom line is that I believe all of these are minor concerns when playing online. I have played for thousands of hours online and have demonstrated a good win rate. However, as discussed in the "Promotions" chapter, a more important concern is the site's reputation and financial stability. A few sites have gone bankrupt and have taken off with the players' deposits. This is not cheating but plain and simple robbery.

This risk can be mitigated quite easily. Try to play at reputable sites with a lot of traffic. Small sites with very little traffic are risky endeavors unless a well-known company backs them. If you decide to play at a small site, be sure to only keep a very small amount of money on deposit at any one time.

Playing Poker for a Living

I have been playing professional poker for over two years and thought I would share my experiences. There are some great benefits to playing poker on the Internet for a living:

- You can work your own hours.
- You are your own boss.
- You can take as much vacation as you like.
- You can work wherever you want in the world.
- You can work in your underwear, lol.

I quit a very good job as a Finance Director with a large pharmaceutical company to be able to take advantage of these benefits. I moved to New Zealand for a couple of years and enjoyed a nice relaxing life. I am now back in the states and have the flexibility to live wherever I want. The great thing about Internet poker is that I can work around my social life rather than plan my social life around work. It is a good life.

As with any job, playing poker for a living is not all fun and games. Playing 10 hours a week can be a lot of fun and be a great hobby; however, the fun and thrill of playing poker is not quite the same once you start playing 40 hours a week in front of a computer. I still have a passion for the game and enjoy playing *most* of the time, but this is definitely not something I will want to do for many years full-time. I am starting to look for other ways to add to my income (like writing this book and real estate), so that I can start reducing the hours of poker I play each week.

Let's look at some of the practical downsides to playing poker for a living. Although it is great to have as many vacation days as you want, these vacations days are not paid! I always enjoyed four weeks of vacation before with my finance job, but it is quite different when you know that no income is coming in while you are away. If you do decide to play for a living, I recommend setting aside some vacation pay each month just like a regular job. This way you can feel like you are being paid and enjoy your vacation without worrying about money.

There are also some additional expenses for being self-employed. American residents must pay full FICA and Medicare payments, which is 15.3% of your salary up to certain limits, rather than the 7.65% you pay when working for a company. You must also pay for medical and dental insurance.

Remember also that gambling income is taxable in the United States just like regular income, even if you play part-time. If you are an American citizen and move overseas, you are able to deduct over $80,000 a year from your income since you are not residing in the States. This effectively eliminates most income tax, but you still must pay the FICA and Medicare taxes.

Obviously, poker has some inherent risks that are part of the job. You will have an unstable income each month, with the risk of actually losing money during a month. If you recall from the "Bankroll Management" chapter, it is possible to play many hours and still lose as an expert player. To play professionally, you need to be the type of person that can handle these fluctuations. Although they shouldn't happen too frequently, they will occur, and believe me they are not much fun.

How much can you earn playing poker on the Internet? This all depends on the number of hours and tables you play in addition to the limit. You can also earn more in most short-handed games than you can in ring games. Of course, your hourly rate will depend on how good you are, :). When looking at hours, remember to account for lunch breaks and any other distractions that might occur during the day. Playing eight solid hours of poker a day can be quite tiring, especially when playing multiple tables.

Let's look at some possible scenarios. If you can work seven hours a day playing $10-$20 and earn one big bet an hour, you would earn $700 a week. If you work 48 weeks a year, you will earn $33,600 at $10-$20. If you are able to play two tables half the time you are playing, you could increase this to $50,400, assuming you maintain the same earn rate per hour at both tables. You would earn $25,200 playing $5-$10 or over $100,000 playing $20-$40. You could earn more if you can manage a win rate even better than one big bet per hour.

Once you estimate a projected income, remember to deduct the additional expenses such as Social Security and medical insurance to arrive at a net income estimate. I earned over $100,000 my first twelve months playing full-time at limits of mostly $20-$40 and $15-$30. A six-figure income is possible, but be sure to account for the downsides of the job.

Study of the Game

Poker is a fun game, but it is even more fun when you win. The more you study the game, the more you should win. Even if you only play a few hours a week, it makes sense to spend a little extra time *away* from the game to further improve your game each and every week. There are a lot of resources out there, some of which are free, which can help you improve your game.

Let's begin with other poker books. Every author has a different approach and style to the game that you can learn from. Most players who study the game consider the four books below "must" reading.

The Theory of Poker by David Sklansky. This classic poker book discusses overall poker theory and concepts. The book is suitable for beginning to advanced players and is useful for all forms of poker, not just Hold'em.

Winning Low-Limit Hold'em by Lee Jones. This is an excellent book for beginning players to learn successful Texas Hold'em strategies for the lower limits. The book does not include many hand examples to evaluate and practice.

Hold'em Poker for Advanced Players by David Sklansky and Mason Malmuth. This is an excellent book on Texas Hold'em strategies that targets the advanced player. The book focuses mostly on poker concepts and strategies rather than providing a lot of hand examples for practice.

Middle Limit Hold'em Poker by Bob Ciaffone and Jim Brier. This book provides over 400 actual *hand examples* of live games played at limits between $10-$20 and $40-$80. The discussion about poker concepts and specific Hold'em strategies is not as comprehensive as *Hold'em Poker for Advanced Players*, but the hand examples are excellent.

In addition to reading books, there is a lot of valuable information available on the Internet for free. Some of the best sites with specific information regarding strategies include:

- **CardPlayer.com:** Card Player magazine provides their entire database of articles for free at this site. There are many excellent articles focused on Texas Hold'em strategies written by some of the best poker authors in the business including David Sklansky, Mike Caro, Bob Ciaffone, Mason Malmuth, and many others.

- **PokerPages.com:** This poker portal is an excellent site to see results of tournaments from all around the world. The site also runs a series of articles that are sometimes focused on strategy. This site is also home to PokerSchoolOnline.com, which is a great site for players to develop their tournament skills.
- **Poker1.com:** Mike Caro, a well-known poker author, provides articles, statistical tables, and audio and video lessons that can all improve your game.
- **PokerRoom.com:** The Poker Room gives access to their database so that you can see the expected value of every starting hand. You can filter the results by position, limit, and the number of players playing. Note that these results are the average of players both good and bad.

My poker site is www.InternetTexasHoldem.com. The site is an excellent online resource to Internet poker. New articles on poker strategy will be posted. There is also a forum on Internet poker, where you can post questions to me and other users. In addition, the site will keep you up-to-date with the latest promotions and deposit bonuses, site reviews, and tournament schedules.

In addition to reading, it is also important to evaluate your own play and that of your opponents. As discussed before, the best way to do this is through the PokerStat or Poker Tracker software. If you don't purchase these tools, at the very least request hand histories from the site so that you can review your play afterwards.

Poker is a fun game, but it is even more fun when you win. Take the time to spend a little extra effort away from the table to improve your game. Hopefully this book is a great start and will serve as a reference for many years to come, but don't neglect some of these other great resources.

Internet Poker

Concepts Review

❏ Several characteristics unique to online games versus live games require that you make small adjustments to strategy:
  • **Short playing sessions:** Players move in and out of games a lot more than they do in a live game, so you are rarely playing the same opponents for a very long time.
  • **A virtual environment:** Players tend to be more deceptive and tricky on the Internet where there is no face-to-face interaction, and betting and raising is just a mouse click away.
  • **Internet distractions:** Opponents are not as observant playing on the Internet as they are in live games.

❏ Table image is not as important online as in a live poker game since players are easily distracted and move in and out of games a lot; therefore, generally play a more straightforward tight game online than you would in a live game.

❏ One of the unique features of the Internet is the tremendous selection of different sites and games.

❏ There are many criteria to evaluate when choosing a site: financial security, site security, software, games, limits, traffic, tournaments, type of players/games, customer support, promotions, and rake.

❏ There are three main criteria in choosing a game:
  • Percentage of players playing the flop
  • Average size of the pot
  • Knowledge of opponents

❏ Internet *tells* all relate to the speed at which an opponent bets:
  • A delay followed by a check often indicates weakness.
  • A delay followed by a bet often indicates strength.
  • An instantaneous bet/raise on the *turn* or *river* usually indicates strength.
  • An instantaneous check usually indicates weakness.
  • A quick check usually indicates weakness, but beware if the player check-raises.

❑ High-limit games are generally tight and aggressive. Strategies for these types of games include:
  • Raising preflop from good position to gain control over the hand
  • Raising preflop with high cards and medium pairs to drive out opponents
  • Folding middle suited connectors and small pairs most of the time
  • Using semi-bluffs as a main arsenal of your play on the flop and turn
❑ Low-limit games are generally loose and passive. Strategies include:
  • Raising preflop with premium hands that stand up well against multiple opponents
  • Raising less often with borderline hands when you are first in preflop
  • Playing suited connectors and pairs more often, especially from late position
  • Playing a straightforward game with few bluffs and semi-bluffs
❑ In general, the better players have larger stacks and the weaker players have smaller stacks for several reasons:
  • The better players generally win, so they tend to have a large bankroll.
  • The weaker players generally lose, so it is natural that their bankrolls are often small.
  • Many weak players who play small limits will sometimes jump up a limit to try their luck, and usually don't have an adequate bankroll for the limit they are playing.
❑ Avoid playing with a stack so small that you cannot get full value out of a big hand.
❑ Playing multiple tables is a great advantage for good players who are able to increase their overall hourly earn rate; however, there are also several disadvantages:
  • You can sometimes make mistakes by hitting the wrong button.
  • It is more difficult to evaluate your opponents.
  • You will experience greater variances by playing two tables at the same time.
❑ There are three types of record keeping that I find helpful:
  • **Earnings results:** At a minimum, you should record your gain/loss and time played for each poker session.
  • **Player analysis:** Since you will be playing hundreds and even thousands of different opponents, it is to your advantage to record notes on your opponents and their various playing styles.
  • **Hand analysis:** Recording the results of various hands and the strategies you employed can help you better evaluate your individual play.

❑ Deposit bonuses are a great way for low-limit players to build a bankroll so that they can move to higher limits more quickly.

❑ Tournament strategy requires that you make adjustments to your regular ring game.

❑ Collusion and cheating occurs on the Internet; however, it also occurs in live games. In a casino, you have to overcome the rake, parking, gas, meals, and most importantly tips, to make your session profitable. On the Internet, you have to overcome the rake and some collusion that might be taking place.

❑ A major concern in playing online is the reputation and financial stability of the site.

❑ Playing poker on the Internet for a living has some great benefits:
- You can work your own hours.
- You are your own boss.
- You can take as much vacation as you like.
- You can work wherever you want in the world.
- You can work in your underwear, lol.

❑ Downsides to playing professionally include:
- The fun and thrill of playing poker is not quite the same as when you play part-time.
- There are no paid vacations.
- American citizens must pay full FICA and Medicare.
- You must pay for medical and dental insurance.
- Gambling income is taxable in the United States just like regular income, even if you play part-time.
- You will have an unstable income each month, with the risk of actually losing money during a month.

❑ Poker is a fun game, but it is even more fun when you win. The more you study the game, the more you should win. Even if you only play a few hours a week, it makes sense to spend a little extra time *away* from the game to further improve your game. Additional resources include:
- Other poker books
- Online resources
- Self-evaluation: Poker Tracker and PokerStat are excellent tools to help you.

Glossary

Ace High: A hand with an ace but no pair.

Action: Frequency of betting. A game or hand with a lot of action is one where there is a lot of betting and raising.

Acting First: The player who must check or bet before the other players is *acting first*.

Acting Last: The last player to check, bet, call, or raise is *acting last*.

All-in: A player who bets the last amount of chips he has or is disconnected while playing a hand.

Arg: Internet jargon to indicate frustration.

Backdoor: A draw that requires both the turn *and* river card to improve. For example, the turn and river card are both suited, giving you a backdoor flush. Same as runner-runner.

Bad Beat: A hand that loses to an opponent who gets very lucky, especially when the opponent should not even have played his hand.

Bankroll: The money you have available to gamble.

Best of It: A game or bet where you have a long-term positive expectation.

Bet: The action of committing chips to the pot first in.

Bettor: The first person to commit chips to the pot on any given betting round.

Big Bet: The amount of the bet on the last two rounds of betting.

Blinds: In Hold'em, the blinds are the forced bets that the first two players to the left of the button must put in the pot. The big blind posts a small bet and the small blind usually posts a half small bet.

Bluff: A bet or raise when you have little chance of winning the pot if you are called.

Board: The community cards on the table.

Bottom Pair: A pair by matching one of your hole cards with the lowest card on the board or a pocket pair lower than all of the cards on the board.

Button: Also known as the dealer. The last player to receive cards and who acts last on the flop, turn, and river. The blinds sit to the immediate left of the button.

Call: To put money in the pot equal to an opponent's bet or raise.

Call a Raise Cold: To call a raise without having committed money previously on the same betting round. Note how this is different than betting or calling and then calling a raise by another opponent.

Caller: A player who puts money in the pot equal to the bet or raise.

Cap: The act of putting in the last raise allowable on any given betting round. A capped pot is one where the maximum number of raises has been reached.

Check: Declining to bet.

Check-raise: The act of checking and then raising after an opponent bets.

Close the Betting: Making the last call on any given betting round.

Cold Call: see Call a Raise Cold.

Counterfeited: A card that improves your hand but gives an opponent an even better hand.

Crying Call: Calling when you feel you have a very small chance of winning.

Cut-off: The player who acts right before the button or dealer.

Dealer: The dealer position is the same as the button position.

Discount: Reducing the odds for drawing to an out by the probability that the out is counterfeited or you are drawing dead.

Disregard: You should disregard an out when you are drawing dead to it.

Drawing Dead: Drawing with no chance of improving to the winning hand.

Early position: In a ten-handed game, the first three seats to the left of the blinds. After the flop, early position refers to players who must act first.

Expectation: The average result on any play in the long run.

Favorite: The hand that has the best chance of winning. Note that sometimes you could be the favorite without currently having the best hand. For example, an open-ended straight flush draw is the favorite over a pair.

First In: The first player who commits chips to the pot.

Fish: A poor player who usually loses money. Generally refers to players who draw to very weak hands and often play many poor starting hands.

Flop: The betting round where three cards have been dealt face up.

Fold: Giving up on a hand rather than calling a bet or raise.

Free Card: A card that you can see without having to call a bet.

Full Table: A game with nine or ten players.

Gut Shot: A draw to a straight where only one card can give you the straight.

Heads up: A pot contested against a lone opponent.

High Cards: Any card 9 or higher.

Implied Odds: The relationship between the current pot and the bets you expect to win to the current bet.

Induce a Bluff: Playing your hand weakly so that an opponent might try a bluff.

Induce a Call: Playing your hand weakly so that an opponent might make a crying call.

Kicker: The other card in your hand that has not matched the board.

Late Position: In a ten-handed game, the last two seats at the table generally known as the cutoff position in seat nine and the button in seat ten.

Limp: The act of calling first in before the flop.

Lol: Internet jargon for "laugh out loud."

Lone Opponent: When only one opponent is contesting the pot.

Loose: A player who plays many hands. After the flop, a loose player will often play to the river and will try bluffs a lot. A game is loose when there are a lot of players who see the flop.

Maniac: A super aggressive player who is constantly raising the pot and plays most of his hands.

Middle/Bottom Pair: A pair below the highest card on the table.

Middle Position: In a ten-handed game, seats six, seven, and eight.

Nuts: Holding the best possible hand on any given betting round.

Odds: The chance against an event happening.

Open: The first player to commit chips to the pot other than the blind money.

Open-ended Straight: A straight that can be made by two different cards.

Outs: A card that will improve your hand, preferably to the winning hand.

Overcard: A card higher than the highest card on the board.

Overpair: A pocket pair higher than the highest card on the board.

Pocket Pair: Holding a pair with the two cards dealt to you.

Position: The order in which you have to act. You are in early position if acting first and late position if acting last.

Pot Odds: The relationship between the total amount in the pot to the amount of the current bet.

Preflop: The first betting round when the players receive their two hole cards.

Probability: The chance that an event will occur, generally expressed in percentage terms.

Protect: Betting or raising so that your opponents must pay a price to try and draw to beat you.

Rag: A board card lower than a 9.

Rainbow: A flop with three different suits.

Raise: To increase the bet an additional amount.

Read: Determining the possible hands of your opponent.

Rebuy: The act of purchasing additional chips.

Reraise: To increase an opponent's raise an additional amount.

Ring Game: A full table cash game with nine to ten players.

River: The fifth board card.

Rock: A player who is very tight and rarely bluffs.

Running Pair: When the turn and river card are a pair.

Runner-runner: A draw that requires both the turn *and* river card to improve. For example, the turn and river card are both suited giving you a backdoor flush.

Scare Card: A card that is potentially dangerous either to you or your opponent.

Semi-bluff: A bet or raise, in which if called, you probably do not have the best hand, but you could improve to the best hand on the next card.

Set: Three of a kind when holding a pocket pair that matches one of the board cards.

Shark: A very good player.

Short-handed: Refers to games when only several players are playing. Some sites specifically offer short-handed games that only allow up to 5 or 6 players at the table.

Short-stacked: A player who does not have very many chips left to bet.

Slowplay: Checking or just calling a very strong hand on one round of betting to win more bets on later rounds of betting.

Small Bet: The amount of the bet on the first two rounds of betting.

Split the Pot: Dividing the pot equally between two or more opponents who have the same hand.

Steal: Raising to win the blinds preflop. Stealing the pot on later betting rounds is the same as a bluff.

Street: A betting round such as the flop, turn, or river.

Strong: Term to describe good poker players.

Table Image: How a player is perceived to play, generally relates to how tight or loose a player is.

Tell: An act or gesture that *might* indicate how strong or weak your opponent's hand might be.

Tight: A player who doesn't play very many hands. After the flop, tight players rarely bluff and generally only continue to play with strong hands or strong draws. A game is tight when there are not very many players who see the flop.

Tilt: A player who starts playing recklessly and wild because he is upset and angry.

Top Pair: A pair using one of your hole cards to match the highest card on the board.

Trap Hands: Hands that typically are dominated by other hands, such as KJ, KT, and QT. These hands rarely win large pots, unless you hit a straight, and can lose a lot of money to hands with better kickers.

Trips: Three of a kind when one of your pocket cards matches a pair on the board.

Turn: The fourth board card.

Under the Gun: The first player to act preflop in early position.

Weak: Term to describe poor poker players. They generally play too many hands preflop and will call too often after the flop.

About the Author

Matthew Hilger is from Atlanta, Georgia. He received his Bachelor's degree in Finance from the University of Georgia in 1989. He completed a Master's degree in Finance at Georgia State University in 1991 and also a Master's degree in International Business from Thunderbird in 1996.

In the last nine years Matthew has lived in Mexico, Venezuela, Costa Rica, Argentina, New Zealand, and is now residing in the United States with his wife, Diana, and son Joshua. He has worked in various accounting, finance, and consulting positions with Andersen Consulting (currently Accenture), Chiquita Brands International, and Bristol-Myers Squibb.

Matthew became an Internet poker professional in 2001 and has logged over 7000 hours on the Internet, playing at limits from $1-$2 up to $30-$60 and many online tournaments.

Matthew's live tournament accomplishments include winning the 2002 New Zealand Poker Championship and he finished 33rd out of 2576 entrants in the 2004 World Series Main Event taking home a prize of $80,000 in his first World Series.

Matthew now devotes a lot of his working time to his website and poker forum at www.InternetTexasHoldem.com where he answers questions about his book and general poker strategy. He also hosts online tournaments where players can win stakes to his live tournament earnings.

Matthew's other interests outside of poker include composing on the piano and traveling. His travels have taken him to over 25 countries throughout Europe, Latin America, the Caribbean, and "down under."